LEONARD COHEN
AN ILLUSTRATED RECORD

LEONARD COHEN
AN ILLUSTRATED RECORD

MIKE EVANS

Plexus, London

CONTENTS

1

A BEAUTIFUL LOSER

'Back then I was very self-confident. I had no doubts that my work would penetrate the world painlessly. I believed I was among the great.'

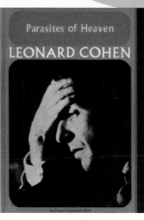

Leonard Cohen, at a party thrown by publishers McClelland and Stewart in honour of himself and Irving Layton, Toronto, March 1973.

Not many musicians with five decades of record-industry success behind them began writing songs because their poems and novels failed to find an audience. But – in art as in life – Leonard Cohen always displayed an admirable devotion to walking the road less travelled. When he signed with Columbia Records in 1967, having attracted the attention of the legendary producer John Hammond, many eyebrows were raised within the company at the prospects of success for a thirty-three-year-old Canadian poet who nobody seemed to have heard of.

Marianne Ihlen, followed by Leonard and others, on a mule ride in Hydra, 1960.

Montreal

Cohen had, in fact, already achieved a degree of literary recognition in Canada, where he had been born in Montreal, Quebec on 21 September 1934. Leonard had a privileged early life, growing up in the well-to-do district of Westmount. Although there were certainly wealthier families in the area, few could match his own in terms of status. The Cohens were one of the most prominent Orthodox Jewish families in Montreal. Leonard's father Nathan was a successful businessman, the owner of a high-end clothing store in Montreal, whose ancestors had built synagogues and founded several newspapers when settling in Canada. His mother Masha was a Rabbi's daughter of Russian descent, and only a recent immigrant from Lithuania when she married Nathan. Leonard would never deny that his was a fortunate childhood, with the family's staff including a nanny (who he and his sister Esther called 'Nursie'), an Irish maid named Mary, and an African-American gardener-cum-chauffeur called Kerry. It was a close-knit family: the Cohens and their relatives would gather together regularly – most often at the home of his paternal grandmother – for 'tea parties', as Cohen would later describe in his first novel, the semi-autobiographical *The Favourite Game*.

The security of this comfortable family life would be abruptly shattered when Leonard was just nine years old. In 1944, his father Nathan passed away following a long illness. Leonard would describe what happened in two unpublished short stories, 'Ceremonies' and 'My Sister's Birthday', written around fourteen years later. Nursie had broken the news to the Cohen children early in the morning. They should be quiet, she said, as their mother was still asleep. The funeral would take place the following day. But that couldn't be right, thought Leonard, for tomorrow was his sister's birthday. Significantly, at no point could Leonard remember crying. In fact, he would admit he wept more when his dog Tinkie died a few years later: 'I didn't feel a profound sense of loss . . . maybe because he was very ill throughout my entire childhood. It seemed natural that he died. He was weak and he died. Maybe my heart is cold.'

Whilst Cohen might have outwardly professed this, however, the very fact that he would continually return to his father's death in his writing calls his claims of emotional detachment into question. Years later, in *The Favourite Game*, Leonard would recall taking one of his father's bow-ties, slicing it open, and hiding a small piece of paper inside on which he'd written something, before burying it in the back garden. He said he had no recollection of what he had written and that he had been looking for his buried note for years. There can be little doubt that Nathan's death was integral in shaping the character of the young Leonard, leaving him with a self-confessed 'morbidly melancholy' outlook that would stay with him for the rest of his life.

An emotional catalyst of a very different kind occurred in Leonard's early teens, when his sudden adolescent obsession with girls coincided with the development of his interest in a rather more unusual field: hypnotism. His guide was the grandly titled *25 Lessons in Hypnotism: How to Become an Expert Operator* by M. Young, of which the first two lessons in particular might have been written as advice to the performer Cohen would become: 'Your features should be set, firm, and stern. Be quiet in all your actions . . . Let your voice grow lower, lower, until just above a whisper. Pause a moment or two. You will fail if you try to hurry.'

Undoubtedly nurturing pubescent fantasies about Mary, the family maid, Leonard embarked on a bizarre plan of seduction. Emboldened by what he had learnt from Young's handbook, he hypnotised her, and ordered her to undress. As he would recall in *The Favourite Game* via his alter-ego Lawrence Breavman, it was his first sight of a naked woman. Whether he had indeed mastered hypnotic powers, or the young maidservant was instead a fully conscious, compliant partner in the exercise, is open to conjecture. Regardless, after a time, Mary 'awoke', just as Leonard had begun to panic that his mother might return home, and find her employee *au naturel* with her teenage son. For the youthful Cohen, the whole episode was an early confirmation of the power of gentle persuasion – be it via the hocus-pocus repetition of the hypnotist, or the eloquence of the written word.

From the age of thirteen, Leonard would wander the streets of Montreal at night, getting a taste of the seedy nightlife of music, drink and casual sex that was still a grown-up world, out of his reach. These nocturnal ramblings were most often undertaken alone, although as he grew older he began to be regularly accompanied by his best friend, Mort Rosengarten. The two had first met back in 1944 at summer camp, just five months before the death of Leonard's father. By the time they attended junior high school together, at Westmount High, they were bosom buddies.

Cohen had attended Roslyn Elementary School until he was fourteen, followed by Westmount High. It was at the latter that he began to take a particular interest in the arts, literature and music, developing a fondness for the work of the Spanish poet and playwright, Federico Garcia Lorca. 'When I was a young man', Cohen recalled, 'I could not find a voice. It was only when I read, even in translation, the works of Lorca that I understood there was a voice. He gave me permission to find a voice, to locate a voice; that is, to locate a self, a self that is not fixed, a self that struggles for its own existence.'

Around the same time, Leonard began to teach himself the rudiments of playing a guitar on a second-hand Spanish acoustic he bought from a pawnshop for $12. He had met a young Spanish busker in Murray Hill Park, who gave him three lessons on the six chords found in all flamenco music. When Cohen returned for his fourth lesson, however, it was to discover that his teacher had tragically committed suicide. Leonard had never even learned his name. Cohen later expressed a great affinity for Spanish culture and remarked, 'It was that guitar pattern that has been the basis of all my songs and all my music.' Although it would be some years before the two disciplines came together in any meaningful way, the die was cast: words and music would be central to Leonard's evolution as a creative artist.

The notion of music as a vehicle for storytelling and the expression of ideas was brought home to Cohen in 1950, when he worked briefly as a voluntary counsellor at a community summer camp for underprivileged children. There, he came across a copy of *The People's Songbook*, a well-known collection of folk songs first published in 1948. This discovery sparked an interest in the music of Lead Belly, Woody Guthrie and Pete Seeger, which would inform his development as a self-accompanied singer. It also led to his first foray into making music on a semi-professional level: in 1952, he and two friends formed the Buckskin Boys, a country and folk trio. Cohen fondly remembered how the group would perform 'in church basements and high school auditoria', playing traditional country songs for barn-dancing socials.

Student

By that time, Cohen was a student at McGill University in Montreal. He had enrolled in September 1951, and during his first year there he studied general arts, followed by maths, commerce, political science and law. Academically, however, he was a distinct under-achiever. Like many a student before and since, Leonard entered the fray of university life enthusiastically, but more for the sense of freedom it offered than any desire for academic success. He admitted early on that his aim was for 'wine, women and song'.

The attractions of student bohemia far outweighed those of the lecture theatre: 'The disadvantage was that you had no way of knowing what you were going to be . . . I hardly went to any of the classes. Nobody really cared whether you turned up or not.'

Instead, he preferred the sleazy ambience of downtown Montreal, where he and Mort Rosengarten would tour the bars around rue Sainte-Catherine, checking out the latest sounds of rhythm and blues and country music emanating from dozens of jukebox dives.

In lieu of studying, Cohen chose to make his mark within the college precincts as a member of the drama group, and as president of the Debating Union. Then, during his third year at McGill, Cohen enrolled for a three-times-a-week literature course conducted by the eminent Polish-Canadian poet Louis Dudek. Studying the work of Tolstoy, Goethe, T.S. Eliot, Ezra Pound and James Joyce – among others – the course energised Leonard's interest in literature. By the end of the sessions, he was even said to have been 'knighted' by Dudek using a rolled-up copy of one of Leonard's poems. By that time, Cohen was convinced he was destined for literary greatness: 'Back then I was very self-confident. I had no doubts that my work would penetrate the world painlessly. I believed I was among the great.'

Hydra 1960, with other ex-pats including Charmian Clift (right).

In 1953, Leonard made his first trip across the border to America, where he spent a month at an experimental poetry course at Harvard University in Massachusetts. This first venture away from home was an essential coming-of-age experience, and when he returned to Montreal he moved out of the family home into an apartment on bustling Stanley Street, which he shared with his teenage accomplice Mort. According to Rosengarten, the two didn't live there permanently, but used it to hang out and entertain friends – including, inevitably, members of the opposite sex.

In the somewhat refined world of poets and poetry, it was the era of the 'little magazine'. In the absence of bookstores stocking the work of local poets – as was the case in most cities across North America and Europe – dozens of hand-printed magazines sprung up. One such publication was the mimeographed *CIV/n*, which was where Leonard Cohen's first published works – 'Le Vieux', 'Folk Song' and 'Satan in Westmount' – appeared in 1954. Indeed, that edition of *CIV/n* featured a cover picture of Leonard with his guitar entertaining a 'party of poets at Mort Rosengarten's house' – likely the flat in Stanley Street.

The same year, Cohen won first prize in the Chester Macnaghten Literary Competition at McGill for 'Sparrows' and a series of four poems under the title 'Thoughts of a Landsman'. The latter included 'For Wilf And His House', a surprisingly mature work for a twenty-year-old, one of the first of Cohen's poems to feature the allusions to religion that would be a characteristic of his writing for the rest of his career.

Poet

A year after his graduation, in 1956, Cohen's debut book of poetry *Let Us Compare Mythologies* – a collection of forty-four poems, written between the ages of fifteen and twenty – was published as the first book in the McGill Poetry Series. Edited by Louis Dudek, the book was designed by Leonard and included illustrations by his then-girlfriend, the artist Freda Guttman. With a modest first print run of 400 copies, the book was greeted with generally favourable reviews, and in retrospect stands as a monument of something that every artist inevitably loses: the innocence and uncompromising passion of youth. As Leonard would wryly comment some fifty years later: 'There are some really good poems in that little book; it's been downhill ever since.'

The book won the McGill Literary Award, elevating Cohen's name on the Canadian literary scene, and leading to his participation in a spoken-word album *Six Montreal Poets* – his first appearance on record – released in 1957 on the highly influential Folkways label. The other five poets represented were Dudek, Irving Layton, A. M. Klein, A. J. M. Smith and F. R. Scott, the leading members of the so-called 'Montreal Group' – prestigious company for a young writer. One member of this group in particular, Layton, would go on to be a lifelong friend of, and inspiration to, Cohen.

A professor at McGill who had befriended Cohen during his degree course, and an editorial board member on *CIV/n* magazine, Layton was a well-known Canadian poet twenty-two years Leonard's senior. In spite of their differences in age and background – Layton, in stark contrast to Cohen's upper class

Westmount upbringing, was raised in Saint-Urbain, Montreal's working class Jewish neighbourhood – the two were immediately drawn to one another. A flamboyant, outspoken character, Layton captured the imagination of the young Cohen as the personification of the larger-than-life bohemian writer, a definitive example of the creative nonconformist that he increasingly aspired to.

Layton would act as a quasi-mentor to Cohen, giving him advice that would shape his early artistic endeavours. 'I always think of something Irving Layton said about the requirements for a young poet', Cohen would recall. '"The two qualities most important for a young poet are arrogance and inexperience." It's only some very strong self-image that can keep you going in a world that really conspires to silence everyone.' Layton was an unapologetic enthusiast for Leonard's work, calling him 'a genius from the first moment I saw him'. The

> 'I always think of something Irving Layton said about the requirements for a young poet, and I think it goes for a young singer, too, or a beginning singer: "The two qualities most important for a young poet are arrogance and inexperience." It's only some very strong self-image that can keep you going in a world that really conspires to silence everyone.'

dynamic between the two poets was one of mutual admiration, as Layton would attest: 'I have nothing to teach him. I have doors to open, which I did . . . The doors of sexual expression, of freedom of expression and so on and so forth. Once the doors were opened, Leonard marched very confidently along a path somewhat different from my own.'

The small but dedicated circle of poets and writers that Layton represented in Montreal surfaced around the same time as the 'Beat Generation' movement, which was developing on opposite coasts of the United States. In San Francisco, Lawrence Ferlinghetti's City Lights Books published Allen Ginsberg's *Howl and Other Poems* in 1956, and the following year Jack Kerouac's beat odyssey *On the Road* appeared in print for the first time. One would have expected a would-be free spirit like the young Leonard Cohen to be inspired by the literary and social revolution the 'Beat' writers represented, but – stylistically, at least – the Montreal group were of the older order that the Beats were rebelling against. 'I was writing very rhymed, polished verses and they were in open revolt against that kind of form, which they associated with the oppressive literary establishment', Cohen recalled, conceding that he nevertheless felt an affinity with the Beats, albeit one that wasn't reciprocated. 'I felt close to those guys, and I later bumped into them here and there, although I can't describe myself remotely as part of their circle.'

Traveller

1956 also marked Cohen's first long-term move out of Montreal, when he

commenced post-graduate studies at Columbia University in New York City. Coincidentally, it was at Columbia that beat pioneers Allen Ginsberg and Jack Kerouac had first met and inspired each other in the late 1940s. But much as he threw himself into the bohemia of Manhattan, and the artistic milieu of Greenwich Village – meeting both Kerouac and Ginsberg in the process – the relatively unknown Canadian poet remained just that. He even made a brief attempt at starting a literary magazine, *The Phoenix*, in order to raise his profile among New York writers, but that was soon aborted due to lack of support.

It was in New York, however, that Leonard met Anne Sherman and began the first in what would become a series of all-consuming romances. Born Georgianna Sherman, she was a tall and beautiful upper-class American, working at Columbia University's International House where Leonard was lodging as a 'foreign' student. The two fell in love almost instantly, and Cohen soon moved to Sherman's smart apartment in Upper Manhattan. Anne was cool

Relaxing in Hydra, October 1960. From left to right are Marianne Ihlen, her son Axel Jensen Jr, LC, an unidentified friend, and married Australian authors George Johnston and Charmian Clift.

and cultured; she wrote poetry and played the piano, and knew everyone in the City.

But their relationship would prove short-lived, with Leonard bringing it to an end when things began to feel a little too serious for his liking. Nevertheless, Anne would be the muse for the poem 'For Anne' in his next collection, and the character Shell in his on-going novel *The Favourite Game*.

Returning to Montreal in 1957, he worked in various odd jobs to support his literary ambitions, which would eventually go one step nearer to being fulfilled with the publication of his next book of poems, *The Spice-Box of Earth*, in 1961. Before then, however, he had quit the routine of casual jobs, concentrating on his writing – including work on a never-to-be-published novel, titled *A Ballet of Lepers*, which

Cohen felt in hindsight was a better work than his debut *The Favourite Game*.

His closest ally Mort was now in London studying sculpture, so Leonard was spending even more time with Irving Layton, whilst at the same time applying for various scholarships to grant him enough money for some serious travelling. He proposed a trip that would take him to London, Athens, Jerusalem and Rome, based on which he would write a novel. In 1959, he received a grant of $2,000 from the Canada Council for the Arts, which saw him on his way to London at the end of the year.

After a few months in London where he continued to work on his first novel, *The Favourite Game*, Cohen began to tire of the persistently dreary weather. Although well-accustomed to the cold, having grown up in snowy Montreal, Leonard couldn't acclimatise to the dampness and lack of heating. In a now-famous string of events, Cohen walked into a Bank of Greece after a visit to the dentist. 'There was a young man, one of the tellers, and he had a suntan, he was smiling. And I said, "How did you get that expression? Everyone else is white and sad."' Upon hearing that the teller had returned from a sunny Grecian island, Leonard immediately bought a plane ticket that took him first to Israel, and on to Greece – not the capital Athens, as planned, but the small island of Hydra, which he instantly fell in love with. With its narrow streets, sun-bleached white houses and a semi-circular harbour full of fishing boats, it was the archetypal Aegean island paradise. More importantly, for a romantic like Leonard, it represented a retreat from the mechanised vulgarities of urban life; there were scarcely any cars, little electricity and few telephones. And television, ubiquitous in modern society, was non-existent.

Leonard soon discovered a thriving community of like-minded ex-pats – artists, writers and would-be intellectuals – eager, like himself, to pursue their dream of creative freedom in a simple, away-from-it-all environment. Among them were George Johnston and his wife Charmian Clift, both Australian ex-journalists who had lived on Hydra since 1954. They first met Leonard on the day of his arrival, gave him a place to stay the night, and fixed him up with somewhere to rent. The new arrival soon became a regular face in the waterfront bars and cafes, living the romantic idyll to the full.

In September 1960, with a modest inheritance from his grandmother of $1,500, he bought a house on the island, an ancient whitewashed three-storey building with five rooms that had no electricity or running water. Years later, he declared that it was the smartest decision he had ever made.

And it was on Hydra that he met Marianne Ihlen, the muse who would inspire the defining track on his debut album. She and her husband Axel Jensen, both Norwegian, had arrived on the island three years before Leonard. By the time Cohen first met her, the couple had broken up, reunited, got married, had a son and separated again. In later years, Marianne recalled how Leonard had 'enormous compassion' for both her and her child: 'I remember well that when my eyes met his eyes I felt it throughout my body'. Leonard was enraptured by the Norwegian beauty, describing her in a letter to Irving Layton as simply 'perfect'.

'There wasn't a man that wasn't interested in Marianne. There was no one that wasn't interested in approaching that beauty and that generosity, because it wasn't just that she was a traditional Nordic beauty – that was indisputable – but she was also very kind, and she was one of the most modest people about her beauty', Cohen recounted. 'And she had that other side too, where she drank wine and danced and became wild and beautiful, and threatening and dangerous if you were a man with her.'

Although Leonard and Marianne both felt an instant attraction to the other, their friendship would blossom slowly on Hydra.

It wasn't until Cohen's return to Montreal that each realised the depth of their feelings. Marianne received a telegram from Canada – 'Have house, all I need is my woman and her son. Love Leonard' – and emigrated, beginning a love affair that would last most of the decade. Cohen would go on to write several songs inspired by his 'muse', including 'Hey, That's No Way to Say Goodbye' and – of course – 'So Long, Marianne'.

In March 1961, inspired by both his favourite poet Garcia Lorca and the recent revolution that had ousted an American-backed dictatorship, Leonard flew from Montreal to Havana, Cuba. It was a visit that romantic idealists all over the world would have wished to make, and the impulsive twenty-six-year-old simply upped and went. Lorca had visited the Caribbean island before the 1959 uprising led by Fidel Castro, as had Leonard's sister Esther when she honeymooned there. But now there was a distinctly radical edge to any North American vacationing in Havana; indeed, an embargo on any United States citizens visiting had already been put in place by the Nixon administration, and even a Canadian making the trip was controversial to say the least.

Leonard wanted to experience things for himself, identifying with the new Cuba of Castro, Che Guevara and their compadres to such an extent that he roamed the streets and bars of the capital in the *de rigueur* uniform of beret, khaki fatigues and newly-grown beard. But on the diplomatic front, tensions were escalating between Cuba and their US neighbours. It was only weeks before the abortive Bay of Pigs invasion attempt, backed by the new US president John F. Kennedy. When the 'invasion' took place, on 17 April, officials of the Canadian embassy contacted Cohen – prompted, it turns out, by his anxious mother, via a cousin who was a Canadian senator – and arranged for him to join a flight home as soon as possible.

Leonard stuck it out in Havana until 26 April, by which times things were getting more chaotic for anyone wishing to leave the country. He joined a line of foreign nationals at the airport, awaiting a seat on a flight out, but just as he was about to board an aircraft his name was called, requesting he report to the security desk. Searching his bag, officials had found a photograph of Cohen posing with a couple of revolutionary soldiers, and – suspecting he might be a Cuban trying to escape the country – put him under an armed guard. Luckily, a scuffle broke out on the runway, and Leonard's guard rushed to see what was going on, omitting to lock the door first. Leonard casually walked out, went through the departure gate, and boarded the awaiting plane.

In hindsight, he would admit his political motives were naïve: 'I thought maybe this was my Spanish civil war, but it was a shabby kind of support. It was really mostly curiosity and a sense of adventure.' Nevertheless, the experience inspired at least one poem, written during his Havana sojourn, 'The Last Tourist in Havana Turns His Thoughts Homeward', which appeared in his 1964 collection of poetry, *Flowers for Hitler*.

The Spice Box of Earth

Leonard hardly had time to settle back into 'normal' life after his Cuban adventure when, at the end of May 1961, *The Spice-Box of Earth* was published.

Leonard working on a poem, August 1967.

1.

Catherine Tekakwitha, who are you? Are you (1656-1680)? Is that enough? Are you The Iroquois Virgin? Are you The Lily of the Shores of the Mohawk River? Can I love you in my own way? I am an old scholar, better looking now than when I was young. That's what sitting on your ass does to your face. I've come after you, Catherine Tekakwitha. I want to know what goes on under that rosy blanket. Do I have any right? I fell in love with a religious picture of you. You were standing among birch trees, my favourite trees. God knows how far up your mocassins were laced. There was a river behind you, no doubt the Mohawk River. Two birds in the left fore-ground would be delighted if you tickled their white throats or even if you used used them as an example of something or other in ... Do I have any right to come after you with my dusty mind ...

Typewritten pages from an early draft of Beautiful Losers

He had collated the poems in 1959, and, at Layton's recommendation, submitted it to the Canadian publishers McClelland & Stewart. Jack McClelland was so impressed with the book that he accepted it on the spot. The title of the eighty-eight-poem collection was taken from the decorative wooden box of spices used during the Jewish ceremony that marks the end of the Sabbath, but Leonard had concocted an earthly spice box, fluctuating between the sacred and the secular. As he put it himself in a radio interview at the time: 'I wanted to designate a kind of variety of experience. I wanted this book to be the kind of book that you could dig into and find many kinds of emotions and many kinds of encounters.'

These 'encounters' ranged from those with real-life individuals including Irving Layton and the painter Marc Chagall, to religious references citing biblical plagues, the wives of Solomon, Samson's destruction of the pagan temple ('Celebration') and even Cohen's Rabbi grandfather ('Lines From My Grandfather's Journal'). There were poems dedicated to his muses, including Marianne in 'Beneath My Hands', and his earlier love, Anne Sherman, in 'I Long To Hold Some Lady' and the critically lauded 'For Anne'.

The book was met with very favourable reviews, with the *Toronto Daily Star*'s Robert Weaver declaring that Leonard was 'probably the best young poet in English Canada right now'. Arnold Edinborough, writing in the *Canadian Churchman*, agreed, proclaiming that Layton had lost his crown to his younger friend. It was certainly the work of a seemingly mature writer, with an air of assurance that belied his comparative youth. And right from the opening poem in the book, 'A Kite Is A Victim', Cohen's own perspective was paramount as the ultimately lone voice of the poet. Selling out its first printing in three months, while not elevating Leonard Cohen to any kind of literary stardom, *The Spice-Box of Earth* certainly marked him as a writer of serious potential.

The Favourite Game
After much writing and re-writing over the previous few years – and having run through a variety of possible titles including 'The Mist Leaves No Scar', 'No Flesh So Perfect', 'Fields Of Hair' and 'The Perfect Jukebox' – Leonard's first novel finally appeared as *The Favourite Game*.

The book had been rejected back in 1960 by his publishers, McClelland & Stewart, with company executive Jack McClelland urging Cohen to stick to poetry. McClelland found the style humdrum and egotistical, with an uncomfortable preoccupation with sex. Major revisions would need to be made, he told Cohen, and even then, he couldn't guarantee that he would publish it. Foreign publishers were much more receptive. It would first be published by Secker and Warburg in England, in the fall of 1963, and then by Viking in the US the following year.

The Favourite Game is a *bildungsroman* of sexual and romantic experience, reading almost as a biography of Leonard, written by Leonard. Central to the text was the stand-in protagonist Lawrence Breavman, who had the same family and friends, love affairs and experiences as Cohen, with only the names of the characters changed. Most of the formative moments from Cohen's youth are featured, including Breavman's hypnotising and undressing of the family maid, the attempts of he and his friend Krantz (Mort Rosengarten) to pick up girls around Montreal, his father's death, and his romance with Shell (Anne Sherman). Structurally and stylistically, the unconventional form resembles that of a film more than a traditional novel. Each chapter is presented as a separate scene from a film, which the author films, directs and stars in, while at the same time he observes, as if from the back row of a cinema.

Much like his poetry, the novel was critically well-received, although this was not reflected in its sales figures. The US *Saturday Review* described it as 'interior-picaresque, extraordinarily rich in language, sensibility and humour', while in the UK, *The Guardian* declared it 'a song of a book, a lyrical and exploratory bit of semi autobiography'. It was even reviewed positively in the prestigious *Times Literary Supplement*, earning a short yet favourable critique in the 'Other New Novels'

round-up. *The Favourite Game* has continued to receive positive critical attention into the 21st century, even being referred to as Canada's *Catcher in the Rye*. Yet for years the book was only available in Canada as an import, until McClelland & Stewart finally published it in 1970, after Cohen had achieved international fame as a singer and performer.

Flowers for Hitler

Through the early 1960s, Leonard was commuting between Hydra and Montreal. Marianne still occupied the house on the Greek island while, in Canada, Cohen had rented a furnished duplex on the west side of Montreal. Though leading the life of the bohemian writer, the fruits of literary success were still to elude Leonard, and negotiating the next pay cheque or (mainly elusive) book deal necessitated him spending most of his time in Canada. So, once more, he was a regular denizen of the bars and literary cafes of his hometown, including Le Bistro, where most of the writer crowd congregated, and the 5th Dimension, a coffee house and folk music venue.

By this time, his relationship with Marianne was flexible to say the least. Even when she visited Montreal, there were other girlfriends, some of whom she would meet. As Erica Pomerance, a would-be folk singer with whom Leonard had a brief relationship, would recall: 'I think they must have had an understanding . . . Marianne was his common-law wife, his muse, the queen . . . but I think she probably put up with a lot to remain with him.'

As a follow-up to *The Spice Box of Earth*, McClelland & Stewart published Leonard's next collection of poetry, *Flowers for Hitler*, in 1964. Cohen had originally intended to call the book 'Opium and Hitler', but Jack McClelland objected to the title, and made it plain to Cohen that he wasn't entirely happy with the material within. Cohen's response was defiant: 'There has never been a book like this, prose or poetry, written in Canada.' In the

'There is no difference between a poem and a song. Some were songs first and some were poems first and some were situations. All of my writings has guitars behind it, even the novels.'

end, McClelland told Cohen he would publish it anyway – 'because you are Leonard Cohen'. After some fractious exchanges between the two, with Leonard conceding a little here and digging his heels in there, they agreed on a selection of fifty new poems.

The themes of the collection were broadly similar to those of his two previous poetry books: matters of the heart, mankind's cruelty to man, and the usual dedications to friends and lovers. But with their much looser, less rigid style, the poems had an intensity previously only hinted at, whether in reference to humanity's darkest hours or his own personal passions. To many, the poetry came across as being deliberately confrontational in its stark tastelessness, Cohen wilfully destroying the image of himself as a sweet romantic.

Reviews were mixed, with some controversy over accusations of exploitation of sensitive subject matter – specifically the Holocaust – but that didn't prevent the *Toronto Quarterly* critic Milton Wilson calling Cohen 'potentially the most important writer that Canadian poetry has produced since 1950 . . . not merely the most talented, but also I would guess, the most professionally committed to making the most of his talent'. Given that one of *Spice Box*'s poems, 'New Step', would later be staged as a theatrical ballet on CBC TV in 1972, and another, 'Queen

Victoria and Me', would become a song on his 1973 album *Live Songs*, this claim proved somewhat prophetic.

Beautiful Losers

Published in the spring of 1966, *Beautiful Losers* was very much a novel of its time, a literary indulgence involving a complex plot laced with mysticism and radical ideas. The ambitions of the author, for nothing less than a 'great' novel, were evident on every page, with language replete with rich imagery and graphic descriptions of sexual excess. Cohen wrote the book in two eight-month sessions on Hydra, in 1964 and 1965, in what can only be described as a self-conscious attempt at spontaneous creativity.

Perhaps hoping to emulate the famous account of Jack Kerouac writing *On the Road* as a three-week stream-of-consciousness aided by pills and bebop jazz, Leonard fasted and ingested amphetamines, to a background of his favourite Ray Charles album, *The Genius Sings the Blues*. It was an early instance of a long involvement with drugs, in which he recognised their dangers as much as their benefits: 'The recreational, the obsessional and the pharmaceutical – I've tried them all. I would be enthusiastically promoting any one of them if they worked.'

The novel, divided into three books, interweaves the story of 17th century Native Canadian Mohawk saint Kateri Tekakwitha with the love triangle between 'I', an unnamed Canadian folklorist, his Native wife Edith (who committed suicide by sitting at the bottom of an elevator shaft), and his friend 'F', a Member of Parliament and a leader in the Quebec separatist movement, who is in hospital dying from syphilis. So convoluted is the interrelationship between all three that, at times, they appear to be the same person. A sprawling, surreal narrative, *Beautiful Losers* has come to be seen as having introduced postmodernism into Canadian literature. It has since sold over three million copies, and is widely considered a part of the Canadian literary canon. The UK *Guardian* acknowledged this in 2008: 'Cohen's work as a novelist may be an acquired taste, but his experimental work *Beautiful Losers* is increasingly seen as a classic (and, as novels by musicians go, it's substantially more interesting than [Bob Dylan's] *Tarantula*)'.

However, at the time, sales were poor (although Lou Reed was one of the few who did pick up a copy). It sold better in the US than in Canada, but did not see significant sales until after Cohen achieved success as a singer-songwriter. The novel did, on the other hand, receive plenty of critical attention, and was met with much controversy. Robert Fulford of the *Toronto Daily Star* called *Beautiful Losers* 'the most revolting book ever written in Canada' while also stating it was 'an important failure. At the same time, it is probably the most interesting Canadian book of the year'. CBC concurred, describing *Beautiful Losers* as 'one of the most radical and extraordinary works of fiction ever published in Canada'. In the US, the *Boston Globe* declared: 'James Joyce is not dead. He is living in Montreal.'

Yet all of this praise meant little to Cohen, due to his by now traditional problem of this not being reflected in the financial rewards. Given how intense an experience writing the book had been, Cohen was truly disillusioned, engaging in a nasty spat with McClelland over who was to blame for the novel's poor sales figures. Ultimately, his disappointment in the novel's lack of commercial success proved the catalyst in his move into song writing: 'I couldn't make a living as an author. My books weren't selling, they were receiving very good reviews, but my second novel *Beautiful Losers* sold about 3000 copies worldwide. The only economic alternative was, I guess, going into teaching or university or getting a job in a bank, like the great Canadian poet Raymond Souster. But I always played the guitar and sang, so it was an economic solution to the problem of making a living and being a writer.'

For Cohen, going from writing to singing was no great leap, at least artistically. As he told the *New York Times* in 1969: 'There is no difference between a poem and a song. Some were songs first and some were poems first and some were situations. All of my writings has guitars behind it, even the novels.'

The truth of this statement was reflected in his next volume of poetry, *Parasites of Heaven* (1966). His last book before attaining musical fame, this volume was mainly notable for the first publication of poems that would later become well-known as songs, including 'Master Song', 'Teachers', 'Avalanche', 'Fingerprints', and, most significantly, 'Suzanne Takes You Down', which would go on to achieve international fame as 'Suzanne'. Overall, however, *Parasites* appears the work of a distracted Cohen, whose mind was seemingly elsewhere, and most critics would concur with Tim Footman's description of it as 'a half-hearted addition to the Cohen canon, lacking even the shock value of *Flowers for Hitler*'.

By this stage, Cohen was clearly more focused on his musical ambitions. Although he harboured no immediate ambitions to become an on-stage performer, as *Parasites of Heaven* illustrates, his portfolio was already beginning to include verses written specifically as songs.

2
SONGS OF LEONARD COHEN

'There was the economic pressure, I couldn't just live off literature. In retrospect, it seems madness that I believed I could go to Nashville and become a studio musician or a compositor in order to pay the bills and continue writing. It was not what happened'

All songs written by Leonard Cohen.

Side A
1. Suzanne
2. Master Song
3. Winter Lady
4. The Stranger Song
5. Sisters of Mercy
Side B
1. So Long, Marianne
2. Hey, That's No Way to Say Goodbye
3. Stories of the Street
4. Teachers
5. One of Us Cannot Be Wrong

Personnel
Leonard Cohen (vocals, acoustic guitar); Nancy Priddy (vocals); Willie Ruff (bass); Jimmy Lovelace (drums); Chester Crill, Chris Darrow, Solomon Feldthouse, David Lindley (flute, mandolin, Jew's harp, assorted Middle-Eastern instruments)

Recorded: October–November 1967, Columbia Records Studio B and E, New York City
Released: 27 December 1967
Label: Columbia
Producer: John Simon

Relaxing in a New York City diner, 1968.

Leonard Cohen would have been the first to admit that his transformation from struggling writer to internationally famous singer was hardly the result of years of careful planning. On the contrary, there was more than an element of Cohen simply falling into his new career due to the whims of chance. Prior to a planned trip to Nashville, where Leonard hoped to sell his songs to country music publishers, the somewhat disillusioned writer ended up staying in New York City, turning his hand to singer-songwriting almost by accident. 'I visited some agents and they'd say, "Turn around kid, let's have a look at you. Aren't you a little too old for this game?"' remembered Cohen. 'I was thirty-two at the time. I think I was eating very little. I was about 116 pounds, and going to all the clubs, and listening and playing and writing. Just the ordinary cliché of a young writer in New York.'

He had begun hanging out with the Andy Warhol 'Factory' crowd – artists, writers, musician and would-be actors all looking for Warhol's elusive 'fifteen minutes of fame' – but Leonard wanted rather more than that. The pop art pioneer always insisted that Cohen's eventual musical style was influenced by hearing his own protégé Nico, singing with the Velvet Underground in New York clubs at the

Joni Mitchell, playing acoustic guitar in a shoot for Vogue.

time – and Leonard was certainly impressed by the icy beauty and stark vocals of the German chanteuse.

Leonard first came across Warhol and his hip entourage in Max's Kansas City, a bar-cum-club that everybody who was anybody used at that time. He'd just seen Nico singing at the Dom club – 'the perfect Aryan ice queen' – and was so entranced he followed her to Max's. Still something of a stranger in town, he lingered at the bar, conscious of the fact he knew none of the important faces who hung out there but hoping for an 'in' of some kind – which came in the person of Lou Reed. The Velvet Underground front man approached Cohen, telling Leonard that he recognised him, and was a fan of his book *Beautiful Losers*.

Reed invited him to the table where Warhol and the rest were sitting, which was the first time Leonard met Nico. As with his first encounter with Marianne, the Canadian was struck immediately by the statuesque blonde and, soon, she by him.

Cohen immediately established himself part of the Warhol scene, but only as and when it suited him, and mainly in pursuit of Nico. 'I was only peripherally involved with the Andy Warhol/Velvet Underground scene. It was really Nico I was in love with.' He admitted to being besotted – 'paralysed by her beauty' as he once put it – and over the next weeks and months spent as much time as possible in her company. Nevertheless the relationship remained, as far as reliable accounts confirm, platonic. 'Nico eventually told me, "Look, I like young boys. You're just too old for me."'

Judy Collins

But it was his musical relationship with the folk singer Judy Collins that would prove the catalyst for Cohen's metamorphosis from poet to professional singer, when Collins successfully covered his song 'Suzanne' on her 1966 album, *In My Life*. The song, which had already been performed by the Stormy Clovers earlier that year, had originally appeared as a poem 'Suzanne Takes You Down' in *Parasites of Heaven*. 'I sang a few songs for Judy Collins and she liked them', Cohen explained. 'Then, I went back to Montreal, and I wrote a number of songs in that period. One of them was "Suzanne". I phoned Judy Collins, and kind of nestled the telephone between my ear and my shoulder, and I played her "Suzanne". She said, "I'm going to do that this week, in the studio".' Collins quickly became something of a champion of Leonard's material, which he provided prolifically. 'He was writing new songs all the time. By that time, I was in so over my head with his material that I was ready to record anything he sent me', Collins told Cohen biographer Sylvie Simmons. 'I think there was a Leonard song on practically every album after that.' Her next album, the 1967 hit *Wildflowers*, included three Cohen songs.

Now spending time in both New York – where he now had a room at 'bohemia central', the Chelsea Hotel – and Montreal, Cohen began playing gigs in both his home town and on the Greenwich Village folk scene. The latter was largely thanks to Mary Martin, a prominent Canadian-born New York-based artist-manager, through whom Leonard had first come to the attention of Judy Collins.

Leonard Cohen's first official live date was at a benefit concert in the Village Theatre on 22 February 1967. He (albeit nervously) appeared in front of 3,000 people in a line-up that included Pete Seeger and Tom Paxton as well as Collins, who introduced him to the crowd during her own performance. And it was through the enthusiastic, almost evangelical, support he was getting from Collins and Martin that his name came to the attention of Columbia Records producer John Hammond, whose impressive track record included jazz, blues and folk artists as diverse as Billie Holiday, Count Basie and Bob Dylan. Hammond took Leonard out for lunch, after which the pair returned to the soon-to-be-legendary Chelsea Hotel, where Cohen was staying, so that he could play the producer some of his material.

'I sang him six or seven songs', recalled Cohen. 'He didn't say anything between them. At the end of those six or seven songs, he said, "You got it, Leonard." I didn't quite know whether he meant a contract, or the "gift", but it certainly made me feel very good.'

'I thought he was enchanting', said Hammond. 'Because that's the only word you can use! He was not like anything I've ever heard before. I just feel that I always want a true original, if I can find one, because there are not many in the world; and the young man set his own rules, and he was a really first class poet, which is most important.'

It wasn't the first time that John Hammond had taken a chance on undiscovered talent, famously having launched Bob Dylan's career in the face of company ridicule. As unbelievable as it might seem today, the producer's signing of the young folk singer was once referred to in the studio as 'Hammond's Folly'. Now history was about to repeat itself: 'They all looked at me at Columbia and said, "What, are you . . .? A forty-year-old [sic] Canadian poet? How are we going to sell him?" I said, "Listen to him . . ." and, lo-and-behold, Columbia signed him.'

Columbia signed Cohen to a four-year contract in April 1967, with an advance of $2,000 on his first album. Preliminary studio sessions started in May, although the actual recording of Cohen's debut album would not begin in earnest until the fall of 1967, by which time Leonard Cohen had furthered his reputation as a live performer with three key appearances during the summer.

'I visited some agents and they'd say, "Turn around kid, let's have a look at you. Aren't you a little too old for this game?" I was thirty-two at the time. I think I was eating very little. I was about 116 pounds, and going to all the clubs, and listening and playing and writing. Just the ordinary cliché of a young writer in New York.'

Backstage with Joni Mitchell, Newport Folk Festival, 1967.

First there was the prestigious Newport Folk Festival, where Leonard headed a singer-songwriter workshop organised by Judy Collins. Another relative unknown, a Canadian singer by the name of Joni Mitchell, was also on the workshop line-up. The two young talents struck up an immediate relationship, beginning a love affair that – despite only lasting a few months – proved inspirational for both of them. Cohen's musical influence can be traced in the lyricism of Joni's track 'Chelsea Morning', which carries echoes of the iconic 'Suzanne'. A life-long admirer of her musical talent, Leonard would later draw comparisons between her and Beethoven. Although Mitchell would quickly tire of the comparisons drawn between her and Cohen's work, later dismissing him as a 'boudoir poet', the two would remain friendly over the years.

Mitchell was with Cohen for his sensational performance the following evening at the Rheingold Festival in New York's Central Park – again as an unbilled guest on Judy Collins' set. Later in the month he took Joni up to Montreal, where he would make another captivating appearance, at Expo '67, the Montreal World Fair.

The Album

The first preparatory sessions, overseen by John Hammond at Columbia Studios, with just Willie Ruff's bass and Leonard's acoustic guitar, seemed to suit Cohen better than those with the session players, who were later drafted in to augment the recordings. The singer would admit that the anonymous professionals put him ill at ease, compared to the intimate musical relationship achieved with just the double bass player. 'When I first went into the studio, John Hammond arranged for me to play with four or five, dynamite, New York studio musicians. Those takes were lively, but I kept listening to what the musicians were doing. It was the first time I had ever played with a really accomplished band, and I was somewhat intimidated by this.'

It was something of a baptism of fire, one that Leonard would acknowledge as part of a learning process, but equally, at the time, one he found disconcerting rather than helpful: 'I didn't really know how to sing with a band. I really didn't know how to sing with really good, professional musicians that were really cooking; and I would tend to listen to the musicians, rather than concentrate on what I was doing, because they were doing it so much more proficiently than I was.'

However, it was Hammond's 'no frills' approach that apparently put Cohen on edge, with the singer seemingly not having the confidence to carry an album without the support of some added arrangements and instrumentations. But by the time the sessions got under way in earnest in October 1967, Hammond had left the project – according to Cohen because of ill health (he had suffered a recent heart attack), though Hammond would deny that version – with a new producer, John Simon, being appointed.

Simon's style was equally at odds with Cohen's ambitions for the songs, and while the singer-songwriter favoured a sparse sound (not as sparse as Hammond's trademark production style, it has to be said), he took exception to the introduction of strings and horns – not to mention a drummer, which he had expressly stipulated he didn't want. Once added, the augmentations couldn't be deleted from

'I sang him six or seven songs. He didn't say anything between them. At the end of those six or seven songs, he said, "You got it, Leonard." I didn't quite know whether he meant a contract, or the "gift", but it certainly made me feel very good.'

the four-track master tape. So although Cohen was initially far from pleased with the finished product, short of re-recording the entire album, there was nothing he could do about it – and so this was what hit the stores on 27 December 1967.

The album contained what would become some of Cohen's most celebrated songs. The opener 'Suzanne', inspired by a friend's wife in Montreal, Suzanne Verdal, was already a commercial success via the Judy Collins album track, and a modest hit single by the English actor-singer Noel Harrison. The lyrics first appeared as the poem 'Suzanne Takes You Down' in Leonard's poetry collection *Parasites of Heaven*, inspired by his strictly platonic relationship with Verdal and the inspirational time they spent together in the summer of 1965. Verdal, who at the time was the girlfriend of the celebrated sculptor Armand Vallancourt, confirmed their friendship was non-sexual, as did Cohen in a 1994 BBC interview when he said that any sex with Suzanne was purely in his imagination – reflecting the song's chorus line.

Significantly, Leonard chose this track – the very first on his debut album – to reinforce the lyrical power of his songwriting via religious analogy, perhaps most notably when comparing Jesus to a sailor for walking on the water. Such references to both the Jewish and Christian faiths would be a constant device in his songwriting from thereon. Similarly, Cohen draws a contrast between mythical, religious imagery and the everyday and commonplace, with such comparisons going on to become a frequent motif in his work. Even tea and oranges are imbued with romance and a sense of otherworldliness, coming from faraway China. As one of Cohen's most popular compositions, 'Suzanne' would go on to be covered by many talented artists including Joan Baez, Neil Diamond, Roberta Flack, Peter Gabriel, Francoise Hardy, Pearls Before Swine, and Nina Simone.

'Sisters of Mercy', Cohen later revealed, was written during a storm in Edmonton, Canada, when he let two female backpackers with nowhere to stay, Barbara and Lorraine, shelter for the night in his hotel room. They crashed out in his bed while he sat in the armchair, writing as he watched them sleeping: 'By the time they woke up, I had finished the song and I played it to them.' The song would later be used in the celebrated western movie *McCabe & Mrs Miller*, as would the paean to lost love 'The Stranger Song', and 'Winter Lady'.

The subtly caustic 'Master Song' was likewise from his days in Canada, written, as Cohen would recall, sitting on a stone bench in Montreal. Here, Cohen uses a third party – in this case 'the Master' – to address the song to the listener.

Famously, the second side's opener 'So Long Marianne' was written for Marianne Ihlen, his long-standing lover since the early 1960s. With its upbeat, jaunty backing aided by some military-style drumming, it was an exaltation of the woman he described as the most beautiful he had ever met. By this time their relationship was coming to an end – hence the title as a goodbye eulogy.

From the start, it's clear the song is about the future – Cohen, in just the song's second line, expresses his wish to read Marianne's palm, admitting that he was once a kind of Gypsy boy, who should have settled down. Their future together, that he now realises should have happened, simply didn't; and now, after all they have been through, it's too late. Marianne, he admits to himself, would not wait for him forever.

In 'Stories of the Street' Cohen recalls the tough times of his early days in New York City, while 'One of Us Cannot Be Wrong' was written, according to Cohen, in 'a peeling room in the Chelsea Hotel'. Also written in a dreary New York hotel room, the gloomily-named Penn Terminal Hotel, 'Hey That's No Way To Say Goodbye' was, melodically and lyrically, a future template for the archetypal Leonard Cohen song. It's a celebration of the very image of love – tempered by the bitter-sweet reality that sometimes these things are best when of the moment, not meant to last.

Upon its release, *Songs of Leonard Cohen* met with mixed reviews. A less-than-flattering write-up by the *New York Times* drew a comparison between Cohen and 'two other prominent poets of pessimism', Schopenhauer and Bob Dylan. Nevertheless, the album became a cult classic almost immediately. In a pattern that would come to repeat itself over the coming years, the album garnered only a niche following in North America but successfully captured the imagination of the Europeans, becoming a Top Twenty hit in the UK. Cohen was now, slowly but surely, gaining an audience.

Cohen poses for a photoshoot in August 1967.

3
SONGS FROM A ROOM

'In hindsight, it seems like the height of folly to decide to solve your economic problems by becoming a singer. But I'd always played guitar, and I'd always sung.'

LEONARD COHEN

SONGS FROM A ROOM

All songs written by Leonard Cohen, except where stated.

Side 1
1. Bird on the Wire
2. Story of Isaac
3. A Bunch of Lonesome Heroes
4. The Partisan (Emmanuel d'Astier / Anna Marly)
5. Seems So Long Ago, Nancy
Side 2
1. The Old Revolution
2. The Butcher
3. You Know Who I Am
4. Lady Midnight
5. Tonight Will Be Fine

Personnel
Leonard Cohen (vocals, classical guitar); Ron Cornelius (acoustic and electric guitar); Elkin 'Bubba' Fowler (banjo, bass guitar, violin, acoustic guitar); Charlie Daniels (bass guitar, violin, acoustic guitar); Charlie McCoy (bass)

Recorded: October 1968, Columbia Records Studio A, Nashville
Released: 7 April 1969
Label: Columbia
Producer: Bob Johnston

Outside his house on Hydra, circa 1970.

Leonard onstage in 1970.

With his debut album attracting more attention – and certainly sales figures – in the UK and mainland Europe, Cohen had more coverage in the music press across the Atlantic in early 1968 than in North America. When promoting the release, both in the British and American media, he would shrug off the label of 'poet' that was already being attached to his 'literary' style of songwriting, insisting his aim was purely for musical success – much as Bob Dylan would deny his press-vaunted role as the 'spokesman of a generation'. The main difference was, of course, that Dylan was able to deny his media image after half a dozen hugely successful albums – and volumes of press coverage worldwide – while Leonard Cohen was still a relative unknown.

Rising Star

Talking to Karl Dallas, the folk music critic for the UK's leading music paper *Melody Maker*, Leonard insisted he wanted 'to write the kind of songs you hear on the car radio' while also declaring he was thinking of giving up his short-lived foray into the music business. How much of this apparent contradiction was pure Dylanesque perversity isn't clear, but whatever his inner inclination at the time, Cohen rode the promotional merry-go-round for all it was worth. And, being considered a 'serious' artist – in an era when rock and popular music was being taken more seriously in general – his media coverage tended to high-end 'quality' publications like the *New York Times*, the UK *Guardian*, and *Playboy* magazine.

Mindful of the publicity surrounding *Songs of Leonard Cohen*, his US publishers Viking released a second edition of *Beautiful Losers* before the publication of his first poetry collection, *Selected Poems 1956-1968*, in the US in June 1968. The latter, with its promotion taking every opportunity to mention the coverage of Cohen's work by other pop and rock artists, sold over 200,000 copies – an almost unprecedented scale for a volume of poetry.

What the uninitiated reader discovered in *Selected Poems* was a raw, passionate 'no frills' approach that owed a debt to the Beats, but that in many ways was even more accessible to the '60s generation, fresh from discovering the 'poetry of pop' in the lyrics of Lennon and McCartney, and, above all, Bob Dylan. And as with Dylan, a well-read intelligence allowed him to allude to classical and historical references without danger of being thought pretentious. Nevertheless it took the marriage of words and music, towards which Cohen was taking his first tentative steps, to add an extra emotional layer to his work.

After spending some time based at the dreary Henry Hudson hotel in New York, in the spring of 1968 Leonard was once more ensconced in the Chelsea Hotel on West 23rd Street. With its colourful history as a flophouse to the famous, from Mark Twain to Jackson Pollock, the Chelsea was a natural choice for Cohen. With his aspirations as a 'literary' writer still unfulfilled, and first venture as a recording artist hardly a roaring success, he could enjoy the sleazy grandeur of the Chelsea while retaining the bohemian credibility that he craved.

By the late 1960s the hotel counted the new rock aristocracy including Jimi Hendrix, Jefferson Airplane and Bob Dylan among its guests, but its 400-plus rooms still included the kind of fleapit accommodation that Leonard could afford. And it was during that period at the Chelsea that he famously had a brief affair with Janis Joplin – an encounter recorded for posterity in 'Chelsea Hotel #2' on his 1974 album *New Skin For The Old Ceremony*.

It was late one night, and Cohen had taken a walk from the hotel – first to the Bronco Burger diner for a cheeseburger, then the White Horse Tavern, where Dylan Thomas had famously drunk his last in 1953, while living at the Chelsea. 'I went to the White Horse Tavern looking for Dylan Thomas, but Dylan Thomas was dead', he would tell a concert audience years later.

Returning to the hotel and getting into the creaky elevator, he was joined by Joplin, who he had never met before. She and her band were in New York recording their second album *Cheap Thrills*, at the same Columbia studio Leonard had used for his debut disc. The Chelsea elevator was notoriously slow, and they had time to strike up a conversation. Joplin said she was looking for Kris Kristofferson, and although he bore no resemblance to the rugged country-rock songwriter, Leonard chanced his arm anyway, telling her he was Kristofferson. 'Those were generous times,' Cohen would recall, 'Even though she knew that I was somewhat shorter than Kris Kristofferson, she never let on.'

The two ended up in bed together, a genuine one-night stand that Leonard remembered with affection – 'She wasn't looking for me, she was looking for Kris Kristofferson; I wasn't looking for her, I was looking for Brigitte Bardot. But we fell into each other's arms through some process of elimination' – even though he would go on to regret revealing the identity of the doomed blues-rock diva, who died of a heroin overdose just a couple of years later.

But, characteristically, Cohen was continually on the move. He made a now-increasingly infrequent visit to his home on Hydra, where his relationship with Marianne Ihlen seemed to be slowly coming to an end. The long-standing love affair with the blonde Norwegian, whom Leonard had once described as the most beautiful woman he had ever seen, had begun idyllically in 1960 when she left her unfaithful husband and moved in with Cohen. She delighted in being his muse, but as his songwriting gradually progressed, things became more difficult. She tolerated his affairs with other women, confident in the belief that she was his ultimate love, but, as she put it, 'Everyone wanted a bit of my man.'

Fidelity never seemed to hold any great appeal for Cohen, a life-long womaniser. 'I had a great appetite for the company of women, and for the sexual expression of friendship, of communication', he mused. 'That seemed to be the obvious and simple and complicated version of the attraction between men and women that I came up with. I wasn't very good at the things that a woman wanted, which I don't know if many men are . . . I wanted that immediate affirmation of the, what can I call it, just the possibility of escaping from the loneliness, the sexual loneliness, just the pure loneliness of being, of living with that appetite. The pure loneliness of living with an appetite that you couldn't ever satisfy.'

The relationship seemed to draw to a natural close. 'Somehow we just moved and we just separated', Leonard recalled. 'The periods of separation became longer and longer, and then somehow it collapsed. Kind of weightlessly, like ashes falling.' Nevertheless, the bond remained strong enough for a photograph of Marianne, wrapped in a towel and sitting at a typewriter in the Hydra house, to feature on the back cover of Cohen's next album, *Songs from a Room*. She described the relationship as 'a gift' to her and Leonard both. They remained close friends for the rest of their lives.

After Hydra, Cohen made a short promotional visit to London, now something of a rock star in the UK with his debut album in the charts, appearing on a BBC radio show and a television special. Finally, after checking back in at the Chelsea, in September he made his long-intended trip to Nashville, Tennessee – but this time not as a would-be songwriter looking for publishers, but a recording artist about to make an album with one of the most influential producers of the era, Bob Johnston.

Nashville

Johnston already had a place in the pantheon of great record producers. His résumé by the fall of 1968 included such classics (all on the Columbia label) as Bob Dylan's *Highway 61 Revisited*, *Blonde on Blonde* and *John Wesley Harding*, Simon & Garfunkel's *Sounds of Silence* and *Parsley, Sage, Rosemary and Thyme,* and *Live at Fulsom Prison* by Johnny Cash.

As a staff producer at Columbia, while being able to produce sophisticated arrangements with strings, backing singers and session players, he could also

'She [Janis Joplin] wasn't looking for me, she was looking for Kris Kristofferson; I wasn't looking for her, I was looking for Brigitte Bardot. But we fell into each other's arms through some process of elimination'

With Marianne Ihlen and her son, Axel, on Hydra.

'There were no telephone wires. There were no telephones. There was no electricity. So at a certain point they put in these telephone poles, and you wouldn't notice them now, but when they first went up, it was about all I did – stare out the window at these telephone wires and think how civilisation had caught up with me and I wasn't going to be able to escape after all.'

(as most memorably on Dylan's landmark albums) 'capture the moment' of spontaneous magic in the studio. It would be a perfect combination for harnessing the best qualities of Leonard Cohen, both as songwriter and performer.

Johnston and Cohen had first met when the singer was signed to Columbia, and immediately hit it off. Johnston had been named as producer in Leonard's signing-on contract, but when the singer had turned up at the studio for his first sessions for *Songs of Leonard Cohen*, the label's top producer John Hammond was sitting in the control room in his place. Johnston had been taken off the project because he already had too many artists scheduled to work with: 'I told Leonard I wanted to do it so bad, and Leonard wanted me to do it, but they told me absolutely not because I had too many artists already'. When the two met up again in Los Angeles in May 1968, Johnston seized the opportunity that he'd missed first time round.

Cohen had been in LA for two days of sessions with the ex-Byrds singer David Crosby (who was about to form Crosby, Stills and Nash) as producer. Crosby had been involved in an abortive attempt to produce his new girlfriend Joni Mitchell; when the sessions came to nothing, Mitchell suggested he produce her friend Leonard Cohen's second album. The sessions with Cohen, which resulted in versions of 'Lady Midnight', 'Bird on the Wire' and 'Nothing to One', were similarly unsatisfactory, and the idea of a new Cohen album was put on hold. But when Bob Johnston spoke to Cohen, who initially was reluctant to pursue the project any further, the two soon agreed that they would work together on Leonard's second album in Columbia's Nashville studios.

Johnston rented a farm for Cohen near Franklin, Tennessee, and it was there Leonard would be based for the duration of their work on the new album, which began in Columbia Studio A on 16th Avenue, Nashville in October 1968.

Franklin

The farm that Bob Johnston had organised for Leonard to rent became a rural home-from-home, a new outpost in the middle of nowhere rivaling his beloved – but now increasingly urbanised – island of Hydra. Belonging to the legendary songwriting team of Boudleaux and Felice Bryant (who penned scores of country and pop hits including the Everly Brothers' 'Bye Bye Love', 'Wake Up Little Susie', 'All I Have to Do Is Dream' and many more), the 2,000 acre homestead was six miles of dusty side road from the city of Franklin, itself thirty miles from Nashville.

Like Hydra earlier in the decade, it was Cohen's version of the 1960s-hippie dream, an isolated spot where one could get back to nature, live off the land, and indulge in all the other clichés of the urban escapist. He had the tenancy for two years at $75 a month, and had the sole run of the place with its creeks, forest, cows and chickens.

Settling in for a prolonged stay after the album was completed, Leonard equipped himself with a gun, acquired a horse, and got to know the neighbours – the nearest of whom was a moonshine liquour merchant by the name of Willie York. But the prospect of living the simple life in the outback of rural Tennessee had to be put on hold once he started making daily trips into Nashville to work on his next album.

Recording

After what Leonard had regarded as the over-arrangement of much of *Songs of Leonard Cohen*, the plan this time was for an altogether more stripped-down spartan sound. It was one of the reasons Cohen had warmed to the idea of working with Johnston, who brought in a small group of local (but top of their game) session players comprising Charlie Daniels on bass, fiddle and guitar, Ron Cornelius on guitars, 'Bubba' Fowler on banjo, bass, fiddle and guitar, plus Johnston himself on keyboards.

Johnston created a relaxed atmosphere in the studio that was entirely sympathetic to Cohen's needs. The musicians were instructed to listen closely to the singer's solo performance of his songs before they began to provide a suitable, and non-intrusive, backing. On that first day, in a candlelit studio – which was how Cohen liked it – no fewer than ten songs were taped between six in the evening and one in the morning; five of which would end up on the new album.

For Johnston it was one of several projects he was working on at the same time, including Simon and Garfunkel in New York, and Bob Dylan and Johnny Cash (rehearsing *Nashville Skyline*) in the same Columbia studios as Cohen. The producer's ability to literally duck and dive between priorities, travelling some distance if necessary, was no better illustrated than when Leonard decided to include the only non-original song on the album, 'The Partisan'.

Cohen had first learned the song when he was fifteen, one of the *People's Songbook* politically-charged numbers he'd first learned at summer camp in 1950. Written during World War II by a member of the French Resistance, Emmanuel d'Astier, as 'La Complainte du Partisan', the English version would be recorded by several well-known artists including Joan Baez in 1972. Things weren't quite what he wanted with the recording, suggesting to Johnston that what the track needed were some French voices. The producer immediately organised to fly to Paris, where he recorded and overdubbed a trio of French female voices plus an appropriate-sounding accordion player.

The Album

Opening the album was what would become one of Cohen's most celebrated compositions, 'Bird on the Wire', inspired by his trip to Hydra earlier that year. The island had changed considerably since his previous visits, one noticeable element being the introduction of electricity across the landscape. 'There were no wires on the island where I was living to a certain moment,' Cohen would recall. 'There were no telephone wires. There were no telephones. There was no electricity. So at a certain point they put in these telephone poles, and you wouldn't notice them now, but when they first went up, it was about all I did – stare out the window at these telephone wires and think how

civilisation had caught up with me and I wasn't going to be able to escape after all.' Hence the bird sitting on the wire. Leonard wasn't happy with various takes and retakes of the song, until it was decided on a completely minimal instrumentation involving just himself and Charlie McCoy on bass, with Johnston adding keyboard effects and overdubs later. It was the last day of recording, 25 November 1968, and the result was magical.

Cohen would later describe 'Story of Isaac' as an anti-war song, which it clearly was, although the immediate reference was the traumatic Biblical story of Abraham binding his son Isaac to the sacrificial altar on God's command. He used the story as an allegory for sending young men off to war, but concluded that no man is blameless, even the man of peace is accountable, human sacrifice being made in all manner of ways, for all manner of causes. A similar analogy drawn from Bible sources was 'The Butcher', with the ancient Passover sacrifice a cipher for contemporary horrors and tribulations, including a reference to drug abuse, something Cohen himself would struggle with for years. A recurrent theme was beginning to emerge in Cohen's songwriting, where his lifelong adherence to the Jewish faith nevertheless raised as many doubts and questions as it answered.

The album was replete with images of death, sacrifice, infanticide and suicide, no more so powerfully than in 'Seems So Long Ago, Nancy'. Fans once speculated that it was written as a tribute to Marilyn Monroe, but as Cohen would confirm it was inspired by a woman he knew in Montreal through his old friend Mort Rosengarten. The disturbed young woman, just twenty-one at the time, shot herself in the bathroom of her father's

Leonard by his modest house on Hydra, October 1960. Cohen had bought the house on the island earlier in the year.

house, with her brother's shotgun, after her illegitimate baby had been taken from her. Talking on the Irish TV channel RTE, Leonard explained 'Another twenty years later she would have been just like you know, the hippest girl on the block. But twenty years before she was – there was no reference to her, so in a certain way she was doomed.'

The nearest the collection got to a regular country lilt was on the up-tempo 'Tonight Will Be Fine' and 'A Bunch of Lonesome Heroes', but despite the overall melancholy – which would characterise the music of the 'Bard of the Bedsit' for his many detractors – it far surpassed the commercial performance of Cohen's debut long player.

On its release in April 1969 it made it to #63 in the US charts, while hitting the #2 spot in the UK bestsellers – the latter quite an achievement when one considers the very mixed reviews it received on both sides of the Atlantic. One constant difficulty critics seemed to have was with Cohen's voice – like Dylan, his vocal manner was something of an acquired taste, for many balanced by the pure force of the lyrical imagery. In his review for *Rolling Stone* Alec Dubro declared 'Well, it looks like Leonard Cohen's second try won't have them dancing in the streets either. It doesn't take a great deal of listening to realise that Cohen can't sing, period. And yet, the record grows on you . . .' The English music press was more accommodating to Cohen's admittedly 'difficult' singing style, while likewise often hailing the lyrical content of the songs over their delivery.

In hindsight, of course, the album becomes more palatable as one grows accustomed to Leonard Cohen's particular vocal qualities and limitations. Nevertheless, on this second album, his delivery still sounds somewhat hesitant, and his timing a little shaky. But the sheer power of the language overshadows any shortcomings in its presentation; it was clear, from here on in, that lyrically his songwriting was a force to be reckoned with.

4
SONGS OF LOVE AND HATE

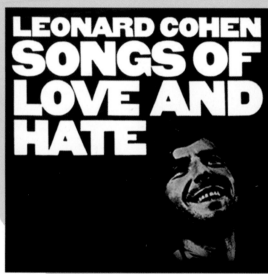

'When you walk on the stage and 5,000 people have paid good money to hear you, there's definitely a sense that you can blow it. The possibilities for disgrace are enormous.'

Personnel
Leonard Cohen (vocals, acoustic guitar); Ron Cornelius (acoustic and electric guitars); Elkin 'Bubba' Fowler (banjo, bass guitar, acoustic guitar); Charlie Daniels (bass guitar, violin, acoustic guitar); Bob Johnston (piano); Corlynn Hanney (vocals); Susan Musmanno (vocals); Corona Academy, London (children's voices)

All songs written by Leonard Cohen.

Side 1
1. Avalanche
2. Last Year's Man
3. Dress Rehearsal Rag
4. Diamonds in the Mine
Side 2
1. Love Calls You by Your Name
2. Famous Blue Raincoat
3. Sing Another Song, Boys [live recording]
4. Joan of Arc

Recorded: 22–26 September 1970, Columbia Records Studio A, Nashville
Trident Studios, London (overdubs)
'Sing Another Song, Boys' 30 August 1970, Isle of Wight Festival, UK

Released: 19 March 1971
Label: Columbia
Producer: Bob Johnston

At a London concert, 1976.

There would be a two-year gap between Leonard Cohen's second and third album release, during which time he embarked on his first serious touring schedules.

Given his greater popularity in the UK and Europe than in either the US or his native Canada, Columbia was anxious to for him to go on the road and capitalise on that success. There was also another album to be considered, but characteristic of Cohen's working dynamic, neither tour nor recording would transpire until 1970. His European trek wouldn't start until spring, a full year after the release of *Songs from a Room*. It was only after the tour that he went into the studio, once more under the production auspices of Bob Johnston, with *Songs of Love and Hate* appearing in March 1971.

Suzanne

As well as embracing the back-to-nature ethos personified by Leonard's lifestyle in both Hydra and the Tennessee farmstead, the hippie counterculture of the late 1960s –with the bleak reality of the Vietnam War a constant backdrop for young Americans in particular – was also characterised by a search for 'meaning' in life. This often involved esoteric religious and quasi-religious cults and groups, ranging from born-again Christianity to meditative Buddhism. In Leonard Cohen's case this first manifested itself with a brief dalliance with the Church of Scientology, which he had begun attending in 1968.

Scientology, founded by L. Ron Hubbard in 1954, involved a pseudo-psychotherapy process called 'Auditing', which relieved the individual of pain, trauma and psychological distress. The 'religion' also subscribed to a whole mythology created by Hubbard, involving contact with civilisations from outer space. Cohen would often visit the Scientology Centre when he was in New York City, and it was on one such occasion in the early spring of 1969 that he met nineteen-year-old Suzanne Elrod, a photographer and artist, in the elevator.

May 1970, performing at the Musikhalle in Hamburg, Germany on his first tour.

'He was going in, I was going out,' Suzanne would recall, and it was quite literally love at first sight. Within days, Elrod had left the man she was living with and moved in with Cohen in the Chelsea Hotel. This was quickly followed by trips to Italy and Hydra – and the farm in Tennessee: 'We admired the wild peacocks, listened to the stream in the morning, watched the sunset in the evening. I was devoted to him. As long as someone like him was in the universe, it was okay for me to be here. I was walking on tiptoe – anything for the poet. Our relationship was like a spider web. Very complicated.'

During those first whirlwind months together, Leonard and Suzanne also visited his mother Masha in Montreal (who Suzanne adored, apart from the fact that 'she always called me Marianne') where they bought a little house and set up home together. Never one to sit still for long, inevitably the Canadian address

became just one of several bases for Cohen, who flitted between there and New York (where he broke with the Scientologists after they began exploiting his name) and Nashville. But this time he would be accompanied by his beautiful dark-haired companion.

Touring

Early in 1970, Columbia Records were putting increasing pressure on Cohen to commit to a European tour. Personally, the singer didn't warm to the idea of full-blown touring, but realized if he was to play the role of successful singer-songwriter he would have to give in and agree to some dates. Meantime, Bob Johnston had now left Columbia as their currently most

'They woke us up and we got up there in this kind of daze and everyone was asleep in the audience, well, a lot were sleeping. I think our music fitted in well with the general mood of the wipeout that everybody felt'.

successful in-house producer, and set up as an independent. Cohen played his cards skilfully, saying he would only tour if Johnston was a member of the band, on keyboards. That way, depending on the other musicians' availability, he figured he could replicate on stage as near as possible what they had achieved in the studio.

'I ended up on the tour almost by accident', Johnston admitted. 'Getting ready I had said to Cohen "Man, I'll get you the best piano player in the world." "No, I want you." Leonard insisted. I had protested "I can't play piano. I can bang around, but I can't play, and you've got great musicians here, they're wonderful people." "Either you come and play, or I won't go", was Cohen's response. I thought, "Hell, I'm not gonna miss this." So we started off. I just played piano and guitar and organ, whatever. I couldn't play very well, but he couldn't sing very well.'

The band they put together for Europe, which became known as 'The Army', was almost identical to the line-up on the previous album, comprising Ron Cornelius, Charlie Daniels, 'Bubba' Fowler and Bob Johnston, plus Susan Musmanno and Corlynn Hanney, on backing vocals. Commencing in the Dutch city of Amsterdam in early May, Leonard Cohen and his Army performed in Germany (Hamburg, Frankfurt and Munich), the Austrian capital Vienna, before playing two dates in London, one at the Paris Olympia, then returning to the UK to finish at Leeds University.

Some of the scenes in Europe were frantic, more reminiscent of rock'n'roll crowd mania than that expected for as introspect a performer as Cohen. In Amsterdam and Paris the police had to be called to control the crowds, and in Hamburg there was a near riot when Cohen mimicked a Nazi salute on stage.

The latter gesture was a tongue-in-cheek response to the fatal Kent State shootings of four students by the National Guard in Ohio, which had taken place that same day. It was the start of the second half of the show, and Leonard's return to the stage was greeted by a standing ovation, which immediately turned to boos and catcalls when he clicked his heels and raised his arm. One man even rushed the stage with a gun, before being tackled by security guards. Many in the audience clearly didn't appreciate the ironic intention on the part of Cohen, with any casual or satirical reference to the Third Reich being strictly taboo in Germany. The crowd quietened down when he started playing, then erupted again as he broke into an old Yiddish folk song and danced around on one leg, seemingly caricaturing his own heritage. Only when Leonard returned to his regular repertoire did things calm down completely.

When the tour hit London, Leonard's popularity was at an unprecedented high in the UK. His first album had earned a gold record, and the second was a current hit. A certain mood of 'Cohenmania' was building up steam, and tickets for his concerts at the Royal Albert Hall sold out within an hour of going on sale.

Back on home territory, Cohen's next live date was in New York City, at the famous Forest Hills tennis stadium in the borough of Queens. It was a folk festival, headlined by Bob Dylan. Despite having the same producer in Bob Johnston, it was the first time the two

'Depression has often been the general background of my daily life. My feeling is that whatever I did was in spite of that, not because of it. It wasn't the depression that was the engine of my work . . . That was just the sea I swam in'.

singer-songwriters had actually met. Leonard was famously maudlin after his performance, convinced he had disappointed the audience, and didn't seem to care that Dylan had come backstage to meet him. Guitarist Ron Cornelius had worked with both musicians previously, and remembered a fraught introduction. 'It was like two cats with their hair up. It was like "What's going on?" The answer would be like, "Everybody's gotta be somewhere." "Oh yeah, well, where are you?"' There were whispers that Dylan had become jealous of the close working dynamic between Johnston and Cohen, and felt rivalled by the older Jewish poet who had stolen his producer away to Europe.

Two more dates had been earmarked in Europe that summer, both big rock festivals. The first was on 2 August, near the southern French city of Aix-en-Provence, the three-day event featuring many French and international names, including the US blues-rock star Johnny Winter. Then, at the end of the month, Cohen played the UK's biggest rock festival on the Isle of Wight.

The festival had gained almost legendary status the year before, when it hosted Bob Dylan's first big date since his three-year 'retirement', and was hyped as 'Britain's Woodstock' just two weeks after the landmark American gathering. This year the organisers were determined to go bigger and better, with a five-day event that included Jimi Hendrix, the Doors, Miles Davis and the Who. The climax of the last day was the appearance of the headliner, Jimi Hendrix. By way of complete contrast, the guitar superstar was followed by folksy Joan Baez, who introduced a dishevelled-looking Cohen – by this time it was two in the morning, and Leonard had to be woken from taking a nap in the trailer. He actually played the set in his pyjamas, covered with a raincoat.

As he would tell *Sounds* magazine in October 1971: 'The band and myself were sleeping in this sort of trailer, we were supposed to go on at midnight and the whole thing was delayed so we all flaked out in this trailer. They woke us up and we got up there in this kind of daze and everyone was asleep in the audience, well, a lot were sleeping. I think our music fitted in well with the general mood of the wipeout that everybody felt. I feel that the conditions of that festival were very unpleasant.'

Billed as Leonard Cohen and The Army, he played a relaxed though bleary-eyed set, to a crowd estimated to be as large as 600,000 – a performance enhanced, it has to be said, by his drug of choice at the time, Mandrax. Leonard had dabbled in drugs since his student days, and by the time of his long writing stints on Hydra had developed a working relationship (rather than dependency) on a variety of stimulants including hashish, LSD and 'speed' – as well as the hypnotic-sedative Mandrax.

This image from 1971 was later used on The Songs of Leonard Cohen Covered *(2012).*

It was raining, but nevertheless Cohen – in a gesture that had yet to become a clichéd ritual – urged everyone to light a match. The result was nothing short of magical. He admitted to being nervous about the event, as he later told *Melody Maker*: 'There are so many people on, and so many that I want to see. I'm not a top rank star you see, no, I'm not a top-ranker'.

In its review of the festival itself, the paper said of Cohen's set: 'Whether he's the kind of artist best heard in the company of half a million other people is another matter, though – he seems such a private singer, his music speaking to its listeners on such personal terms that it's best heard in comparative seclusion'.

Recording

Three weeks later, Cohen and Bob Johnston reconvened the Army in Columbia's Studio A in Nashville. But although there were no problems arising in the studio – with musicians of the calibre of the Nashville pros, that was unlikely

August 30, 1970, at the Isle of Wight Festival, UK.

– Leonard had slipped into a black mood as the sessions got underway.

Cohen had suffered from serious bouts of depression since his earliest days at Columbia, a condition that would colour his poetry and song-writing throughout his life. He was convinced he had inherited the tendency from his mother Masha, who had been admitted to a psychiatric ward with the condition in the late 1950s. 'Depression has often been the general background of my daily life', Leonard would later disclose. 'My feeling is that whatever I did was in spite of that, not because of it. It wasn't the depression that was the engine of my work . . . That was just the sea I swam in.'

Cohen had asked Columbia whether his next two contracted albums could be live recordings, as they'd recorded two of the shows on the recently-completed tour, and he felt unable to concentrate on a studio projects right then. But Johnston insisted that the company might tolerate one live album, but only if they delivered a studio album first. So Leonard took a room in a nearby hotel, and they set to work.

Much of the process was relatively painless, given the familiarity of the musicians with both each other and most of the material; almost all the eight songs that ended upon the album had either been tried in earlier sessions, or played on stage in the recent round of concerts that year. But reflecting Cohen's admittedly dark mood, the overall feel of the collection was gloomy to say the least.

To lift things a bit, and produce some added texture, after the five days of Nashville sessions Cohen and Johnston flew to London, where they overdubbed the children's choir on 'Last Year's Man', Cohen's spoken words on 'Joan of Arc', and some string arrangements by the cellist and rock bass player Paul Buckminster.

The Album

The opener 'Avalanche' would set the tone, based on an earlier poem, where Cohen sings from the perspective of a true social outcast, a hunchback who lusts over women despite his monstrous appearance. 'Last Year's Man', the only song that Cohen hadn't been playing on stage, had a chequered history to say the least, as he would reveal: 'I don't know why but I like this song. I used to play it on a Mexican twelve-string until I destroyed the instrument by jumping on it in a fit of impotent fury in 1967. The song had too many verses and it took about five years to sort out the right ones'. He would have similar problems with 'Dress Rehearsal Rag' – which Judy Collins had covered back in 1966 on her album *In My Life* – which he vowed he would never sing in public again, commenting 'I didn't write that song, I suffered it'. 'Diamonds in the Mine' closes the first side, with a lilting delivery that belies the dark negativity of the lyrics.

Opening the second side of the original vinyl release, 'Love Calls You by Your Name' was a rewrite of an unpublished 1967 song called 'Love Tries to Call You by Your Name', another plea for love lost. One of Cohen's most familiar songs, 'Famous Blue Raincoat' was written as a letter, describing a love triangle, but he would reveal that the raincoat referred to – a Burberry – actually belonged to him. It would be one of the best-received songs in his live repertoire.

The only track not recorded at the Nashville sessions, 'Sing Another Song, Boys' was a waltz-time lament replete with surreal imagery, recorded live at the Isle of Wight festival the previous month. And the album closes with 'Joan of Arc', in which the lyrics are a dialogue between the martyred 15th century French heroine, tied to the stake, and the flames that are engulfing her. Heavy stuff, which for many critics put a seal on the album's overall theme of darkness and hopelessness when it was released in March 1971.

Cohen himself was not pleased with the album, as confirmed in an interview in *New Musical Express* in March 1973: 'I suppose you could call it gimmicky if you were feeling uncharitable towards me. I have certainly felt uncharitable towards me from time to time over that record, and regretted many things. It was over-produced and over-elaborated . . . an experiment that failed'.

Like its predecessor, *Songs of Love and Hate* did far better in the rest of the world than it did in Canada or the United States. It hit #4 in the British album charts, #2 in the Netherlands and #8 in Australia, while only reaching the #63 position in both the US and Canada. And the release did, for good or bad, cement the idea of Leonard Cohen being a symbol of youthful angst and alienation. As he told biographer Sylvie Simmons in 2001: 'People were saying I was "depressing a generation", and "they should give away razor blades with Leonard Cohen albums because it's music to slit your wrists by" '. But, despite the less-than-flattering press coverage his music was receiving, Cohen's depressive state would eventually lift, allowing him to begin preparations for his next European tour.

5
LIVE SONGS

LEONARD COHEN: LIVE SONGS

'I rarely hear praise anymore,
I get the feeling that my songs have fallen out
of favor. One hears an echo, and the echo I have been
getting is not one of whole-hearted appreciation.
In England, my songs and person have been subject
to satire. My person has been satirised as being
suicidal, melancholy, and self-indulgent'.

All songs written by Leonard Cohen, except where indicated.

Side 1
1. Minute Prologue
2. Passing Through [Dick Blakeslee]
3. You Know Who I Am
4. Bird on the Wire
5. Nancy
6. Improvisation
Side 2
1. Story of Isaac
2. Please Don't Pass Me By (A Disgrace)
3. Tonight Will Be Fine
4. Queen Victoria

Personnel: Leonard Cohen (guitar, vocals), Ron Cornelius (guitar), Bob Johnston (guitar, keyboards), Peter Marshall (double bass), David O'Connor (guitar), Jennifer Warren [Warnes] (vocals), Donna Washburn (vocals)
1970: Leonard Cohen (guitar, vocals), 'Bubba' Fowler (banjo, bass), Charlie Daniels (fiddle), Ron Cornelius (guitar), Corlynn Hanney (vocals), Susan Musmanno (vocals)

Recorded: 1970: 'Please Don't Pass Me By' (A Disgrace) [London]; 'Tonight Will Be Fine' [Isle of Wight Festival]
1972: 'Minute Prologue', 'Passing Through', 'Nancy' [London]; 'You Know Who I Am' [Brussels]; 'Bird on the Wire', 'Improvisation' [Paris]; 'Story of Isaac' [Berlin]; 'Queen Victoria' [5435 Big East Fork Road, Franklin, Tennessee]

Released: 1 April 1973
Label: Columbia
Producer: Bob Johnston

Another long gap – over three years – between studio albums, would follow 1971's *Songs of Love and Hate*, during which time Columbia got increasingly frustrated at the lack of 'product' from Cohen. The record company decided he should go on the road again, if only to promote the previous album, which he did in the spring of 1972, taking in eighteen cities across ten countries in Europe, and two in Israel. And it was recordings from that trek that would constitute his next release, which eventually hit the stores in April 1973.

Writing
Following the release of *Songs of Love and Hate* in March 1971, Leonard and Suzanne spent the next few months in Montreal, in the little cottage in the Parc du Portugal that he'd bought in 1969. There he settled once more into writing, not just songs, but a new collection of poetry, and a long-worked on novel.

Cohen had consciously decided, some time before, that writing was more of an end in itself – rather than later singing what he had written on stage. That would explain the apparent 'scarcity' of his material, be it on record or in live performances, as he told Billy Walker for the UK music paper *Sounds* in October 1971: 'That's why I don't want to get into performing too much because I've always seen song and poetry as the evidence of the life rather than the life itself, the picture of life is straight and if you really are experiencing things then this work is the evidence of that experience. If your experience only becomes putting out for the public, and we are all whores in a certain level because we're out there every night like the entertainer, but for me I couldn't live that life totally because I know it would dry things up. I already feel that I am spending more time by myself, I did get into it for a little while.'

The poetry book he had been working on, along with several poems dating back as far as 1956, appeared via a Montreal publisher in 1971, then worldwide in 1972, as *The Energy of Slaves*. The poems, like many of his recordings, were sparse, brutal even, but struck a chord with his (predominantly) young audience; it was a style of verse more akin to the 'anti-poetic' hard-hitting works of many of the 1950s 'beat' poets, than more traditional writers.

In June 1971, the motion picture *McCabe & Mrs Miller* went on release. Directed by Robert Altman, the movie soundtrack featured three songs by Leonard Cohen, all from his debut album *Songs of Leonard Cohen*, of which the director was a big fan. The revisionist Western, starring Warren Beatty and Julie Christie, was a Warner Bros. film, so a deal had to be done with Columbia to use the songs – 'The Stranger Song', 'Sisters of Mercy', and 'Winter Lady'.

'I was in the studio and received a call from Hollywood. It was from Bob Altman saying he would like to use my music in a film. Quite honestly, I said, "I don't know your work, could you tell me some of the films you've done?" He said *Mash*, and I said that's fine, I understand that's quite popular, but I'm really not familiar with it. Then he said there was a film I've probably never seen called *Brewster McCloud*. I told him I just came out of the movie and thought it was an extraordinary film, use any music of mine.'

In an unprecedented move, Cohen arranged for the company to license the music cheaply, even putting in the contract that on any sales of *Songs of Leonard Cohen* after the movie's release, some of the royalties would go to Altman.

Apart from a one-off gig in Montreal in early December, Leonard didn't appear on stage until Columbia's pleas for another tour finally came to fruition. He had been beginning to feel increasingly disenchanted with the reception his music had been receiving, both live and in record form. But on the insistence that he concentrate on his biggest record-buying audience – his European fan base – a new band was assembled in the early spring of 1972.

The Tour

Bill Donovan, tour manager from the previous outing, was once again recruited, alongside Bob Johnston and Ron Cornelius. Neither Bubba Fowler nor Charlie Daniels would make this trip, as would neither of the backing singers: Susan

Posing in a fashionable trench coat, 1972.

Musmanno had eloped with the already-married Fowler, and Corlynn Hanney moved on to a solo career singing gospel material. The instrumentalists were replaced by guitarist David O'Connor, and a jazz double bass player, Peter Marshall. The two female vocal back-ups comprised Donna Washburn, a time-served professional from Los Angeles who'd worked with, among others, Joe Cocker, and a twenty-two-year-old singer from Seattle, Washington: Jennifer Warnes. Although young, Warnes' musical talent had already made itself known. Having rejected an opera scholarship in LA, she had launched herself onto the folk club circuit in the late 1960s, opening for various bill-toppers including Randy Newman, Jackson Browne and Jose Feliciano. Soon after the production of her third solo studio album, *Jennifer*, by ex-Velvet Underground member John Cale, she would be introduced to Cohen.

The two first met in the lobby of a hotel before beginning the tour and, like countless women before and since, she fell in love with him almost instantly. But Warnes was very aware of Cohen's dalliances with a string of other women. 'I made a decision to become an artistic friend, a creative friend, rather than a romantic friend', she recalled, 'Because there was no way I could be his only girl.' And so she did. Leonard and Jennifer connected deeply on a musical level and began to collaborate extensively, eventually working together on six of his albums. She later described how Cohen was always sending her new material for approval: 'Sometimes I'd return home to find he'd recited a new song into my answer machine and I'd marvel at how fortunate I was.' The two would remain life-long friends.

Prior to the tour, negotiations had been underway for a film to be made on the road. The deal was negotiated by Bob Johnston's business manager Marty Machat, who was now also acting on behalf of Cohen. Machat had extensive experience in rock 'n' roll management, having been an assistant to Allan Klein, who had managed both the Beatles and the Rolling Stones. The film was to be made by a young British director, Tony Palmer, who had already made something of a name for himself with films about Frank Zappa and the UK band Cream.

In early March, a couple of weeks before the tour was due to start, Leonard stopped off in London on his way back from Hydra to the United States. There he talked to Billy Walker for *Sounds*, enthusing about the new challenge that the film represented.

'We hope it will emerge out of the performances, I think it's going to surprise me. I would like it to be a kind of essay and I would like the character, who'll be me, to emerge as a surprise. I don't think it will really be anything I am.'

Walker went on ask whether the filming might open up new possibilities, directing even, but Cohen gracefully demurred: 'I would love to be a great film-maker, it's a wonderful notion. I would also like to be a great mason, but I would like to find areas in which I can summon energy. If it's films it would be wonderful but I myself don't think it will be, I don't think I have the talent for it.'

The tour itself kicked off with two concerts in the Irish capital Dublin, both at the National Stadium on the day after St Patrick's Day. During the Dublin appearance, Cohen was asked to recite some of his poetry, which he did, with a short three-line verse written to a girl some years earlier. Talking to the *New Musical Express* the next day, he explained why this would not be a regular feature of his shows: 'I never really enjoyed myself doing poetry from the stage, but I'm sorry I didn't have a book of poems with me because people were so hospitable and interested and I did feel so relaxed. I might just have said "Well here are some poems I've written, if you want to hear them."'

After Dublin, the entourage travelled to the UK, where dates in Glasgow, Manchester, Leeds and Newcastle preceded a concert at London's Royal Albert Hall. Then a few days off in the

British capital were followed by a whirlwind fortnight of one-nighters taking in Sweden, Denmark, Germany, Austria, Switzerland, Belgium and France. By Leonard Cohen's laid-back standards this was hectic to say the least, the frantic energy of the schedule was matched only by the sheer dynamism of the events themselves, all captured in Palmer's filming. There were ecstatic audiences, backstage traumas, technical hitches, groupies, even an instance in Frankfurt when Cohen invited the crowd onto the stage, resulting in him being pulled to the floor and physically smothered by fans: 'There were people all over him, writhing like a pile of worms' Ron Cornelius would recall.

'That's why I don't want to get into performing too much because I've always seen song and poetry as the evidence of the life rather than the life itself'.

All the madness and mayhem of that trip, as well as the musical highs and lows, would feature on Palmer's completed documentary *Bird on the Wire*. Released in 1974, from forty hours of raw footage edited down to 106 minutes, it chronicled what Cohen would later describe as a 'confused and directionless' time in his life. Before the tour began, Cohen and Palmer had agreed that only one in five concerts would be filmed, as the set list would essentially be the same every night.

But it was the off-stage material that most graphically revealed the tensions on the tour. On a purely professional level, instances when the audio equipment was malfunctioning were met with stifled anger by a visibly frustrated Cohen. Likewise encounters with his bandmates and others backstage saw him trying to maintain a stable, mild persona despite potential mayhem. And he was seen often struggling to deal with 'outsiders' – from would-be groupies to intrusive journalists – with the same desire to preserve an air of calm amid madness. But despite Leonard's attempts at steadying the ship, the tensions were often compounded by the captain himself, revealed in Palmer's fly-on-the-wall revelations of Cohen sharing LSD with the band and crew directly before going on to perform.

Cohen had mixed feelings about the film: 'A film crew followed me around twenty-three cities, and spent an enormous amount of money. It was my money. I was paying for the film. Well, the film was shot, and when all the concerts were finished I was happy. I wanted to get out of the scene, and just forget it. But, a couple of months later we get a call saying that the film's ready. So we fly to London, and see the film, and well, it's totally unacceptable – so like that was 125,000 dollars on something that was totally unacceptable. That's a lot of money, and I don't really have all that much money.'

The tour wound up with two concerts in Israel, in Tel Aviv and Jerusalem. Both were incident-packed, to say the least. At the first show, a near-riot ensued when – on Leonard's encouragement – the crowd, who had been restricted to the edges of the stadium, surged forward to the front of the stage. Security guards began to attack the audience, who responded with chairs, bottles, anything they could get their hands on. Eventually, after retreating backstage, Cohen and the band managed to calm things down and resumed their set.

'We were supposed to be playing a small hall – 2 to 3,000 people' Cohen would recall, 'Well, when we got off the plane they drove us into this sports arena! It was huge – there were about 10,000 people there . . . nobody was allowed to be seated on the floor – so the audience was about a quarter of a mile away. They had huge speakers – about six feet tall. So I asked the people to come down, and sit closer to me, and they started to come, and the usher wouldn't let them. It wasn't a serious riot, but one or two people got it. It made me sad.'

Jerusalem was equally tense, this time after an adoring audience was treated to a freak-out by Cohen who left the stage mid-set. Pandemonium broke out when the star suddenly exited in tears, saying he couldn't go back on and the audience should be given their money back. There had been mounting emotional pressure for Leonard, contemplating the last night of the tour being in the holy city; that and the undoubted influence of drugs triggered the melt-down, with a distraught Cohen refusing to return to the stage despite the pleas of the musicians and his manager.

Responding to an announcement that the concert was over, the audience began singing the Hebrew song 'Zim Shalom' ('We Bring You Peace'). Hearing it, Leonard suddenly decided he needed to shave, after which he handed out LSD to the rest of the band and returned to the stage, tears running down his face as he sang 'So Long, Marianne'.

The tears were as much from relief as the passion evoked by his rapport with the audience; it was the final date of the tour, and the next day the company was winging its way westward. Leonard was soon back in the comfort of his domestic life with Suzanne, who was now pregnant. Although their relationship was fractured to say the least – Leonard made no secret of his liaisons, both on the road and elsewhere – they were still partners when he did return home. Early on in their on-off romance, Cohen had gone so far as to give her a delicately filigreed Jewish wedding ring, but the union was never formalised further. Workwise, there was nothing in Cohen's schedule for the next few months; any absences from Suzanne – of which there were plenty – were purely of his own making. Nevertheless, he was elated when they became the proud parents of a son, Adam, born in Montreal on 18 September 1972.

The Album

The live album earmarked as Leonard Cohen's next release eventually appeared on 1 April 1973. All but two of the tracks were recorded during the 1972 tour, with most of the performances chosen being of songs from his second album, *Songs From a Room*. Side 1 of the vinyl release opened with 'Minute Prologue' before a version of the old folk standard 'Passing Through', the only non-original on the collection. 'You Know Who I Am' appears twice, under its own title and as a guitar trio reworking of the backing melody from the song in 'Improvisation'. On 'Bird on the Wire', recorded in Paris, Cohen recites part of a French translation of the lyric.

'Seems So Long Ago, Nancy' was reworked with the simple title 'Nancy', and 'Story of Isaac', recorded in Berlin, was performed much as the original. Three tracks were culled from other recordings than those of the tour: 'Tonight Will

Posing with pigeons, Amsterdam, April 1972.

On stage, Royal Albert Hall, London, March 1972.

'We used to play music for fun. Much more than now. Now nobody picks up a guitar unless they're paid for it.'

Be Fine' came from tapes made at the Isle of Wight performance in 1970, while 'Please Don't Pass Me By' was recorded in London the same year. 'Queen Victoria' – an adaptation of a poem from his collection *Flowers for Hitler* – was recorded solo just before the 1972 tour, on Bob Johnston's tape recorder in Cohen's cabin in Tennessee.

Live Songs was greeted with muted praise from reviewers, and a disappointing response from the buying public. It failed to chart in the UK, where Cohen's first three albums had all made the Top Twenty album list. Talking to Roy Hollingsworth of the *Melody Maker*, two months before the album's release, Cohen expressed a positive (although somewhat begrudging) view of the upcoming release: 'I taped some stuff off the tour – which "they" wanted me to do, and which I wanted to do, because the treatment of some of the songs was very different. It really does show the band.'

But no reviews, good or bad, could surpass the sheer enthusiasm of Jaan Uhelszki in *Creem* magazine: 'In *Live Songs* Leonard sings about real life – hunchbacks, whores, and sandwich signs. Lennie's no apathetic armpit. He's got a mission, looking out for the little guy . . . On that dismal Wednesday night when you're keeping company with a mute phone, there's your friend Len, with an antidote for your loneliness. When you get sick of leaning on Jagger, try Lennie's shoulder.'

In retrospect, the album stands as a unique entry in the Cohen back catalogue, with some live versions sounding better than the (mainly from *Songs from a Room*) studio originals. Some have new lyrics, like the two extra verses in 'Tonight Will Be Fine', while the sublime version of 'Bird on the Wire' counts as a classic take on a classic number. And if only for the twelve-minute epic 'Please Don't Pass Me By', with its naked outrage referencing a horrific army of Holocaust victims, the collection must be counted among Leonard Cohen essentials.

6

NEW SKIN FOR THE OLD CEREMONY

'My songs are strangely romantic, but so are the kids. I somehow feel that I have always waited for this generation.'

Personnel: Leonard Cohen (guitar, vocals); John Lissauer (woodwinds, keyboards, backing vocals); Gerald Chamberlain (trombone); Lewis Furey (viola); Ralph Gibson (guitar); Jeff Layton (banjo, mandolin, guitar, trumpet); Armen Halburian (percussion); Barry Lazarowitz (drums, percussion); Roy Markowitz (drums); John Miller (bass); Don Payne (bass); Emily Bindiger (backing vocals); Erin Dickins (backing vocals); Janis Ian (backing vocals); Gail Kantor (backing vocals)

All songs written by Leonard Cohen.

Side 1
1. Is This What You Wanted
2. Chelsea Hotel #2
3. Lover, Lover, Lover
4. Field Commander Cohen
5. Why Don't You Try
Side 2
1. There Is a War
2. A Singer Must Die
3. I Tried to Leave You
4. Who By Fire
5. Take This Longing
6. Leaving Green Sleeves

Recorded: February 1974, Sound Idea Studio, New York
Released: 11 August 1974
Label: Columbia
Producer: Leonard Cohen, John Lissauer

Posing with a cigarette, London, June 1974

The birth of Adam should have signalled a new era of domesticity for Leonard Cohen, and for a while that certainly seemed to have been the case. He moved his things out of the Tennessee cabin, and settled back in the Montreal house where Suzanne spent most of her time. Cohen was in one of his periodic downsides ('were there any other sides?' the cynics might ask) as regards to the music business, ruminating on whether he would indeed make another album. Nevertheless, he was back in the studio early in 1974, ten months after the release of *Live Songs*.

The seemingly idyllic months in Montreal, a time when Leonard concentrated once more on 'pure' writing unhindered by the demands of his record company, would inevitably be interrupted. In the early fall of 1973, rehearsals began for an adaptation of some of his songs in an off-Broadway musical in New York, *Sisters of Mercy*. Initially Cohen had resisted the idea of his songs being strung together in a theatrical montage, but warmed to the project, attending some of the rehearsals of what he hoped would be 'a pleasant evening'. As he explained to a *New York Times* journalist, he was often a poor judge of such things, because 'I get inordinately happy when I hear my words or music on someone else's lips'.

Soon after the opening of *Sisters of Mercy* at

the Theatre de Lys, Leonard travelled to Hydra, where Suzanne had already moved into his house with new-born baby Adam. Marianne, Cohen's ex-partner, was still living in the little white building on the hill when Suzanne arrived, and although Cohen graciously offered to buy her another house – or even a new one for Suzanne – she decided it was time to move back to her native Norway.

Yom Kippur

Leonard hadn't been on Hydra long when, on 6 October, what became known as the Yom Kippur War broke out, between Israel and the combined forces of Syria and Egypt. He immediately decided to go to the aid of the Jewish homeland in whatever way he could, and boarded a flight to Tel Aviv. 'I will go and stop Egypt's bullet' he would write in one of his poems. His plan was to volunteer for work on a kibbutz, the Israeli collective farms that were severely undermanned because most able-bodied men had been conscripted to fight.

Almost as soon as he arrived, Cohen was introduced to Oshik Levi, a well-known Israeli singer, who told the Canadian star that he could put his talents to better use than working on a kibbutz. Levi was assembling a group of performers (satirically calling themselves The Geneva Conference) to entertain the troops, and suggested Cohen join them. Leonard was a little reluctant at first, saying he didn't think his gloomy songs would do much to raise the troops' morale, but when Levi assured him everything would be alright, Cohen joined them that same day.

The band, which included one of Israel's finest guitarists, Matti Caspi, headed for the Sinai Desert where the front line troops were defending their country. They headed for the Hatzor military base in Levi's 1961 Ford Falcon, with Cohen in particular having no idea where they were going, and what dangers lay ahead. They all tried to put on a brave face, but none of them knew what they might be getting themselves into.

For their first performance, conditions were primitive to say the least, and a foretaste of things to come. With Caspi accompanying him on guitar, Leonard sang into a single microphone that a soldier volunteered to hold for him. The musicians camped out with the soldiers, and after their first performance Leonard scribbled down the words to what would be one of his best-known songs, 'Lover Come Back to Me', also known as 'Lover, Lover, Lover'. Cohen would later say he wrote the song for soldiers on both sides of the battle lines, Israeli and Egyptian, but he later told a Tel Aviv audience that it was inspired 'by the grace and the bravery of many Israeli soldiers at the front'.

The song would appear on Cohen's next album, as would 'Who By Fire?', which

'War is wonderful. They'll never stamp it out. It's one of the few times people can act their best… There are opportunities to feel things that you simply cannot feel in modern city life.'

Backstage at the Musikhalle, Hamburg, 1974.

is also believed to have been inspired by his experience in the Yom Kippur conflict. (The words of the latter song were based on the Hebrew prayer 'U'netanneh Tokef', recited on the Jewish High Holy Days at noontime). The improvised tour of the conflict zone lasted over three months, during which time the group would sometimes make as many as seven or eight appearances a day. They were under frequent shellfire, and played for soldiers about to go into battle – and for others, in the field hospitals, who had returned injured. Some of the sights he experienced were hard for Cohen, who had never been exposed to war before. Nevertheless, he refused any preferential treatment on account of his celebrity status, like the rest of the band sleeping on the floor in sleeping bags on many nights.

When he returned to the United States, Cohen would declare in an interview for *Zig Zag* magazine: 'War is wonderful. They'll never stamp it out. It's one of the few times people can act their best… There are opportunities to feel things that you simply cannot feel in modern city life.'

From Israel Cohen flew to another war zone, Ethiopia, for reasons that remain unclear, other than the fact that he went 'looking for a suntan'. He spent most of the time in the Ethiopian city of Asmara in his hotel room, as he had in a hundred hotel rooms over the previous few years, writing new songs and re-writing old songs. 'It rained, including in the Sinai desert, but through this whole period I had my little guitar with me, and it was then I felt the songs emerging – at least, the conclusions that I had been carrying in manuscript form for the last four or five years, from hotel room to hotel room.'

Finally, at the end of the year, he went home to Montreal, where Suzanne and their son Adam had returned from Hydra. But again, any domestic tranquillity was short-lived. Although Suzanne became pregnant once more, and Leonard had yet again dismissed the music business in favour of home-grown literary pursuits, by the opening months of 1974 he was preparing for his next album with Columbia.

'I have to fight too many people on too many levels to have to fight about money as well. There is much to regret in the system of placing songs at the disposal of others. Now the record companies pressure me to force my songs because the stores want them to sell. I will not force my songs for them.'

Lissauer

An unlikely successor to Bob Johnston as Cohen's next producer, John Lissauer had not been out of music school long when he met Cohen for the first time. It was a chance encounter at a gig in Montreal's Nelson hotel, where Lissauer was playing keyboards in a band with violinist Lewis Furey, who Leonard had known since the mid-1960s. After the show Furey introduced the two, who immediately hit it off. Leonard liked what Lissauer was doing, and asked him if he would be interested in recording.

When Leonard was next in New York City, he rang Lissauer and arranged to visit him in his 18th Street loft apartment to talk things over. Cohen went though some new songs on his guitar, and the pair agreed to cut some demos and take it from there. Having studied classical music and jazz at Yale, Lissauer's approach from the start was radically different to the musical direction Leonard had experienced with Johnston and the Nashville musicians. Three demos were cut in an afternoon session at Columbia's Studio E (where Cohen had recorded his debut album back in 1967) – 'Lover, Lover, Lover', 'There Is a War', and 'Why Don't You Try' – before they moved to the Sound Ideas studio in February 1974.

Lissauer assembled an impressive line-up of musicians for the recordings, with violas, mandolins, banjos, guitars, woodwinds and other instruments giving the recordings a more orchestrated sound than on Leonard's previous albums. There was also an increased emphasis on percussion and drums (a rarity for Cohen), achieving what the producer would describe as

Relaxing in London, June 1974.

'an Ethiopian, Middle Eastern kind of thing'. The musicians included a much-respected bass player, John Miller, and Cohen and Lissauer's mutual friend Lewis Furay on viola. As well as a total of eleven instrumentalists, there was also a four-strong ensemble of backing vocalists that included the well-known singer-songwriter Janis Ian.

The Album

New Skin For The Old Ceremony opened with the aggressive 'Is This What You Wanted'. One UK reviewer would refer to the album as opening with a hangover, although the strident feel was not typical of most of the album. Equalling the

opener in its confrontational stance was the closing song, 'Leaving Greensleeves' which was a re-working of the 16th century English folk song. But contrasting with these stentorian bookends was an almost conversational style on many tracks, with Cohen's voice sounding almost strained, but certainly with a marked passion.

'Chelsea Hotel #2' described a sexual encounter Cohen had with Janis Joplin several years previously. When introducing the song in concert, he would explain to the audience who his partner in question was, although he

Deep in thought, Toronto, January 21, 1975.

'I get inordinately happy when I hear my words or music on someone else's lips'.

would later regret his lack of sensitivity in revealing her identity, later telling the BBC that it was 'an indiscretion for which I'm very sorry, and if there is some way of apologising to the ghost, I want to apologise now, for having committed that indiscretion'.

Next came two songs inspired by his time on the battlefront of Sinai in the Yom Kippur war, the almost singalong 'Lover, Lover, Lover' (which he had written while actually encamped with Israeli soldiers), and 'Field Commander Cohen', which uses the battlefield as an analogy for relationships of the heart. It was a metaphor he would draw again in the first track on side two of the original vinyl release, 'There Is A War', a brooding, dark lyric carried by an effective use of the percussion section.

The spectre of death is never far away, no more so than in the doom-laden 'A Singer Must Die', where again love relationships are called into question with an almost inevitable pessimism. Interviewed on Irish television in 1988, Cohen expanded on the motives behind the song: 'There's something I listen for in a singer's voice and that's some kind of truth. It may even be truth of deception, it may even be the truth of the scam, the truth of the hustle in the singer's own presentation, but something is coming across that is true, and if that isn't there the song dies. And the singer deserves to die too, and will, in time, die.'

One of the best-received songs of the collection, the stark enumeration of suicide and death 'Who By Fire', was chillingly enhanced by the contrast between the darkness of the lyrics and the warm voice of Janis Ian in duet mode with Cohen.

Although it didn't break any album sales records – it failed to make the Top 200 in the United States, and only scraped into the Top Thirty in the UK – *New Skin For The Old Ceremony* met with a mixed reception from the critics.

Rolling Stone, while deciding the album was 'not one of his best', conceded that 'there are songs on it which will not easily be forgotten by his admirers'. In the *New Musical Express*, Bob Woffinden was more positive, but in measured tones: 'It's not a great album by any means. It lacks any attempted tours-de-force like 'Joan of Arc', and also the sheer weightiness of the first albums (Maybe that's a good thing). But it will certainly do. Nice one, Leonard.' And Michael Watts in the *Melody Maker*, describing Leonard as 'a romantic, and an incorrigible one', concluded that 'the album would appear to imply that Cohen has not fundamentally changed since he announced his retirement last year, only that he's combed his hair and brushed his teeth for the return'.

7

DEATH OF A LADIES' MAN

'There are some
people who come
to me for some
illumination on their
problems, I guess they
feel I'm writing about
some of the things
they themselves are
going through. But
I don't usually have
much help to give –
there isn't much you
can say to someone in
the midst of their
own crises.'

All songs written by Leonard Cohen (words) and Phil Spector (music).

Side 1
1. True Love Leaves No Traces
2. Iodine
3. Paper Thin Hotel
4. Memories
Side 2
1. I Left a Woman Waiting
2. Don't Go Home with Your Hard-On
3. Fingerprints
4. Death of a Ladies' Man

Cohen in the recording studio, c1979.

Personnel: Leonard Cohen (vocals); Art Blaine (guitar); Hal Blaine (drums); Bobby Bruce (fiddle, violin); Conte Condoli (trumpet); Jesse Ed Davis (guitar); Steve Douglas (flute, saxophone, wind instruments); Gene Estes (percussion); Terry Gibbs (percussion, vibraphone); Barry Goldberg (keyboards); Tom Hensley (keyboards); David Isaac (guitar); Pete Jolly (keyboards); Jim Keltner (drums); Dan Kessel (organ, synthesizer, guitar, keyboards, backing vocals); David Kessel (guitar, backing vocals); Sneaky Pete Kleinow (guitar, pedal steel, slide guitar); Michael Lang (keyboards); Charles Loper (trombone); Bill Mays (keyboards); Don Menza (flute, saxophone, wind instruments); Jay Migliori (saxophone); Art Munson (guitar); Ray Neapolitan (electric bass, double bass); Al Perkins (pedal steel, slide guitar); Ray Pohlman (bass, guitar); Emil Radocchia (percussion); Don Randi (keyboards); Jack Redmond (trombone); Bob Robitaille (synthesizer); Devra Robitaille (synthesizer); Phil Spector (guitar, keyboards, backing vocals); Robert Zimmitti (percussion); Ronee Blakley (backing vocals); Brenda Bryant (backing vocals); Billy Diez (backing vocals); Oma Drake (backing vocals); Bob Dylan (backing vocals); Venetta Fields (backing vocals); Gerald Garrett (backing vocals); Allen Ginsberg (backing vocals); Clydie King (backing vocals); Sherlie Matthews (backing vocals); Bill Thedford (backing vocals); Julia Tillman Waters (backing vocals); Oren Waters (backing vocals); Lorna Willard (backing vocals)

Recorded: 24 January – February 1977, June 1977, Gold Star Studios, Los Angeles; Whitney Studios, Glendale, Los Angeles; Devonshire Sound Studios, San Fernando Valley, Los Angeles
Released: 13 November 1977
Label: Warner Bros
Producer: Phil Spector

Not unlike Cohen, the legendary – and notoriously volatile – rock producer Phil Spector was experiencing something of a slump commercially by the late 1970s. Matching the singer's sparse delivery with Spector's 'Wall of Sound' approach was, to many ears, a recipe for disaster. It would, however, be over three years after the release of *New Skin For The Old Ceremony* before the unlikely collaboration saw the light of day in *Death of a Ladies' Man.*

New Skin Tour

Barely a month after his latest album release, September 1974 would be a landmark stage in Leonard Cohen's life. In the same month his son Adam turned two, Suzanne gave birth to their daughter Lorca, named after the Spanish poet Leonard had tried to emulate since his teenage years. Although always reticent to discuss his young children, Leonard would later talk about the profound impact fatherhood had on him. 'Having children takes the edge off that fundamental loneliness that people who don't have children might feel. I'm probably a lousy dad, but I'm sure that everyone concerned knows I did the best I could.' But even fatherhood couldn't tie him down. By the time Cohen would get round to celebrating his own birthday on the 21st, he would already be back on the road for his next tour.

Although the album wasn't showing well in the charts, Leonard's biggest tour yet had been organised to take in Europe and, for the first time, North America. Beginning in the Belgian capital of Brussels on 1 September, the first leg wound up in Paris in October, before resuming in New York at the end of November.

For the tour, Leonard's producer on *New Skin For The Old Ceremony* John Lissauer put together a small outfit consisting of musicians and singers who had played on the album: multi-instrumentalist Jeff Layton, bass player John Miller, Lissauer himself on keyboards, plus backing singers Emily Bindiger and Erin Dickins.

Although the tour was largely without incident, one of the most memorable dates was in Paris, when they played at a huge *Fête de l'humanité* at the Parc de la Courneuve, in front of hundreds of thousands of left-wing political activists. According to Lissauer, they deliberately 'dressed down' for the occasion, given the sensitivities of the gathering, arriving in a fleet of beat-up cars rather than ostentatious limousines. The memory of the performance would linger with Cohen: 'When you're singing for that many people, it becomes private again . . . the stage was high, like the side of a building, and the audience was way, way, way down there, so you're really only dealing with the microphone. They're at an event, they're outside, the wind is howling, it's an event on a different order and you take your place in the moment.'

The European leg of the tour wound up in the Paris Olympia hall on 19 October, followed by concerts in New York and Los Angeles in late November and early December. The latter booking was a week's residency at the prestigious Troubadour folk club, doing two shows a night. The performances were sold out, with visiting celebrities that included Bob Dylan – who would cite Cohen as one of his favourite poets – and the man who, to many people's surprise, would be at the production desk for Leonard's next album: Phil Spector.

The Best Of Tours

Following the holiday break, there would be more North American dates across the United States and Canada, after which Cohen planned to begin work on his new studio album with John Lissauer. Provisionally called *Songs for Rebecca*, the two had worked on some new songs while touring, including 'Came So Far for Beauty', 'I Guess It's Time' and 'Traitor Song'. They worked on the new material in New York, Leonard usually just supplying the lyrics and leaving the melodies and chord structures to his more musically sophisticated collaborator. Things seemed to be going well, with Lissauer making demos of some of the songs earmarked for the new album, when Cohen upped and took off for his island retreat in Greece.

'Working with Phil, I've found that some of his musical treatments are very… foreign to me. I mean, I've rarely worked in a live room that contains twenty-five musicians – including two drummers, three bassists, and six guitars.'

His summer sojourn on Hydra at an end – during which time he had written no new music, instead working on the (unpublished) novel *My Life in Art* – Leonard met up once again with Lissauer in the fall and resumed work on the new album. There were also some US concert dates in the offing, this time to promote a compilation album *The Best Of Leonard Cohen*, released in Europe as *Greatest Hits*.

Cohen was keen to reach a new generation of fans with the album, over which he had complete artistic control: he designed the cover, wrote the liner notes, picked the songs, and insisted that the lyrics were included in the package. Although *Greatest Hits* seemed something of an exaggeration, it was certainly the best of Cohen's concert repertoire, with all the crowd-pleasing favourites and critically acclaimed classics including 'Suzanne', 'So Long Marianne', 'Sisters of Mercy', 'Bird on the Wire', and 'Famous Blue Raincoat' – adding up to a dozen songs, from all four of his studio albums.

For the tour Cohen and Lissauer put a new line-up together, and tried out some of the new material alongside Leonard's regular set. Then, in the December, just as the pair prepared to start recording *Songs for Rebecca* in earnest, Cohen did his disappearing act once again, hightailing it home to Montreal, without so much as a by-your-leave.

While he was in Montreal, Bob Dylan also hit town with his Rolling Thunder Revue, a travelling rock caravan featuring an all-star line-up of guests that included such disparate talents as Joan Baez, Joni Mitchell, Ramblin' Jack Elliott and the poet Allen Ginsberg. Dylan's mother Beatty Zimmerman even made an appearance on stage during the fifty-seven-date trek, which ran from the fall of 1975 through spring 1976. Dylan tried to persuade the Canadian, on home territory, to sing a number during his show, but Cohen declined.

Larry 'Ratso' Sloman, a journalist who accompanied the Revue, recalled the incident in his memoir of the tour *On the Road with Bob Dylan*: "'Let it be known that I alone disdain the obvious support', Cohen chuckles. "I'm going to sit out there and watch". "Why not sing?" Joni begs. "No, no, it's too obvious", Leonard brushes off the request.' But despite Cohen refusing his invitation to take part, Dylan dedicated a number to him – 'Isis' from his up-coming album *Desire* – announcing 'This is for Leonard, if he is still here'.

By early 1976, due to the distinct lack of enthusiasm – or indeed activity – on the part of Cohen, any plans that John Lissauer still entertained for *Songs for Rebecca* were finally abandoned once and for all. Nevertheless, Leonard acknowledged his musical debt to Lissauer while making it clear he was about to move on: 'Lissauer has the deepest understanding of my music. I had finished most of the songs that previous summer, got the group together and toured the US for the last year. Now I've entered into another phase, which is very new for me.'

On 22 April Leonard commenced a fifty-five-date European tour – including his first appearance at the famous Montreux Jazz Festival – by July ending up in London. Again in support of the *Greatest Hits* compilation, he assembled a new band under the musical direction of bass player John Miller, who had appeared on *New Skin For The Old Ceremony* and the subsequent tour. The other musicians were Sid McGinnis on guitar, Fred Thaylor on keyboards, and drummer Luther Rix, with backing vocals Cheryl Barnes and the soon-to-be-famous Laura Branigan.

It was generally acknowledged that the band, allowing for the melancholic and often bleak nature of most of the material, were surprisingly upbeat given the chance, as the music paper *Sounds* reported from their final dates in London when they played a new unreleased song 'Do I Have To Dance All Night': 'It's unusually lively for a Cohen song, but it fits the mood of his backing band, who seem to relish the opportunity to rock out – a guitar and pedal-steel player, drums, bass, a keyboards-player with a taste for synthesiser swirls and two strong girl singers who sound mournfully ethereal in all the right places.' The *Melody Maker* went so far to say that Leonard actually appeared cheerful on stage 'Gone is the doom and gloom . . . at his funkiest and wittiest'.

Spector

As soon as the tour was over, Cohen repaired once again to Hydra, where he joined Suzanne and the children. It was time once again to contemplate what to do next. His collaboration with John Lissauer was now definitely at an end, and it was only when he returned to America, renting a house in Los Angeles, that it gradually became apparent who his next producer would be – none other than the one-time wunderkind of 1960s teen pop, Phil Spector.

Spector had forged a name for himself in the early 1960s with his innovative 'Wall of Sound', using multi-layers of instrumentalists recorded simultaneously to achieve an echo-driven background to his classic 'two minute symphonies'. Archetypal girl groups – over whom Spector seemed to have a Svengali-like hold – included the Crystals and the Ronettes, with classic hits such as 'Da Doo Ron

Being Interviewed at Stouffer's Hotel, Atlanta, Georgia,
while on tour in November 1975.

Ron' and 'Be My Baby'. The Righteous Brothers hit the top of the charts for Spector in 1963 with 'You've Lost That Lovin' Feeling', and he would regard his 1966 recording of 'River Deep – Mountain High' by Ike and Tina Turner his greatest achievement.

After disappearing off the map somewhat in the later 1960s, Spector once again hit the headlines with his involvement in the final phases of the Beatles' recording career, when his controversial 'doctoring' of the *Let It Be* sessions was an element in the group's subsequent break-up. Nevertheless, George Harrison and John Lennon were both happy with his work, and the album topped the charts around the world. He went on to produce further works by the two ex-Beatles, including Harrison's *All Things Must Pass* in 1970, and Lennon's *Imagine* in 1971.

From his earlier hit-making days as 'the first tycoon of teen', as the writer Tom Wolfe eloquently put it, Spector had become increasingly reclusive. Barbed wire fences and armed bodyguards fortified his Hollywood mansion, in which his first wife Ronnie Bennett (lead singer with the Ronettes) was kept a virtual prisoner. According to Ronnie, he would spend days watching his favourite movie, Orson Welles' parable of wealth and ambition *Citizen Kane*, over and over again. By the end of the decade, a genuine paranoia had cast its shadow over Spector's frame of mind, with him often referred to as the Howard Hughes of rock 'n' roll.

Into the 1970s, Spector's emotional state became more unpredictable, and stories abounded of drinking bouts, violent scenes in restaurants, and a disturbing predilection for guns. He wore a shoulder holster around his home, and rarely went out without one. Likewise, his behaviour in the recording studio became more and more chaotic. One famous incident involved the producer firing off a pistol during a Lennon recording session in a portent of things to come – as Leonard Cohen would soon find out.

Cohen had first met the legendary producer during his season at the Los Angeles Troubadour in 1975. His lawyer and manager, Marty Machat – who also represented Spector – had introduced the two backstage. Whether the meeting was circumstantial or not is open to conjecture. According to John Lissauer, Spector was in debt to his recording company, Warner Bros, who he owed a new album. They had paid him a $2 million advance – a good portion of which had been pocketed by Machat – but Spector's increasingly unstable behaviour was now beginning to threaten the wisdom of the investment. In a cunning move to pacify the recording company, who were threatening to recoup the advance, the Spector-Cohen meeting was engineered to strike up a working relationship.

Whatever subterfuge was involved, it worked. Spector invited Cohen and Suzanne to dinner at his Beverly Hills mansion shortly after and, after the other guests had left, the Cohens found themselves locked in. Whether Cohen was aware or not isn't clear, but there were various accounts circulating of Spector refusing to allow visitors to leave his mansion, locking the doors and warning that his guard dogs would attack them should they try to 'escape'. This would be just one of the many Spector eccentricities that Leonard would come to experience. Having drunk a little too much anyway, Cohen just shrugged his shoulders and gave in to Spector's insistence that they start writing songs together.

It was the beginning of a series of get-togethers in the early part of 1977, when the two worked for a solid month writing new material. The arrangement, involving long drink-fuelled sessions through the night, seemed to suit Cohen at the time, despite various warnings from several music business friends – including Joni Mitchell – about Spector's erratic behaviour.

Recording
The two honed a dozen or so songs together

– including re-workings of some of the pieces Cohen had already fashioned with John Lissauer for the abandoned *Songs for Rebecca* project – and were ready to go into the studio. Spector booked time at the Gold Star Studios complex in Hollywood, and brought in some of the top LA session players including drummers Jim Keltner and Hal Blaine, trumpeter Conte Condoli, guitarist Jesse Ed Davis, vibraphone player Terry Gibbs, and the guitarist brothers Dan and David Kessel. The Kessels had already been involved in some of the preliminary songwriting sessions at the Spector mansion, as Dan Kessel would recall: 'Leonard was notoriously slow and deliberate, Phil got straight on it and got it done.'

> 'I had the option of hiring my own private army and fighting it out with him [Phil Spector] on Sunset Boulevard or letting it go… I let it go.'

Including over a dozen backing vocalists at various times (this was, after all, a Phil Spector project), more than forty people played or sang on the album. That could have been a recipe for chaos in itself, people coming and going session to session. But as the studio 'audience' grew, Spector's difficult side began to show. The producer's well-documented megalomania, and paranoia about being in total control, meant that Cohen began to feel increasingly disenchanted with the project almost as soon as recording started in earnest.

The first thing that struck Leonard about the Spector set-up was what he would describe as a dangerous atmosphere, created by a potentially lethal combination of hard liquor and loaded guns. The producer had armed bodyguards wherever he went, and his own .45 revolver would be lying on the production desk throughout the sessions. In one well-documented incident, reminiscent of his gunplay while recording John Lennon, Spector pressed the loaded pistol on Cohen's throat; 'I love you, Leonard' he intoned drunkenly, Leonard replying: 'I *hope* you love me, Phil'.

On the second night in the studio, poet Allen Ginsberg turned up with Bob Dylan. An old friend of Dylan, Ginsberg had been intrigued by the rock music scene since the mid-1960s, and was never shy of making an impromptu contribution – live or recorded – when prompted. Of the former 'beat generation' writers, by the 1970s he was certainly the most active in his collaboration with musicians, both in his own projects and those of others. As was his way, Spector immediately dragooned the pair into joining the vocal chorus of the raucous 'Don't Go Home With Your Hard-on', conducting proceedings with a typically maniacal flair.

Leonard would later confess to be 'too ashamed' about all that happened during those sessions, admitting: 'Guns were all over the place. It wasn't safe. It was mayhem, but it was part of the times. It was rather drug-driven.' One of the session musicians, fiddle player Bobby Bruce, had Spector pull a gun on him during the recording of 'Fingerprints'. It was only when the engineer Larry Levine stepped in that Spector backed down, but it was enough for Bruce, who packed up his instrument and quit there and then.

Bit by bit, Cohen felt he was losing control of the entire project. Spector would spend hours in take after take, getting the instrumental backing right, as was his regular *modus operandi*. By the time it came for his vocal contribution, Leonard was either exhausted or just plain out of it. 'I'd lost control of my family, of my work, and my life, and it was a very, very dark period', he would later remember. 'I was flipped out at the time and he certainly was flipped out.'

For Cohen the crunch came when one day Spector simply didn't turn up at the studio. It was normal practice for him to take tapes home (under armed bodyguard), as he was paranoid that the studio might damage them or worse. But this time Spector wasn't coming back; he had decided to mix them at home, alone. Leonard was furious. He didn't consider the recordings finished in any way, and had treated some of the vocal tracks as rough guides for the musicians. Now Phil Spector was determined to put his own imprint on the whole album at the expense of Cohen's musical integrity.

And, of course, that was exactly what happened. Short of physically wrestling the tapes from Spector's possession, which would have involved burglary and armed robbery at the very least, there wasn't much Cohen felt he could do. Leonard would later look back on the conflict with wry amusement: 'I had the option of hiring my own private army and fighting it out with him on Sunset Boulevard or letting it go . . . I let it go.' He wasn't up for a legal battle: his relationship with Suzanne was growing increasingly fragile as tensions between the pair grew, and his slow spiral into a state of depression was showing no signs of improvement. At the time of its release in November 1977, it was all Cohen could do to simply declare the album 'a catastrophe'.

The Album

From the opening bars of 'True Love Leaves No Traces' – based on Cohen's earlier poem 'As the Mist Leaves No Scar' – listeners were treated to the epic grandeur of a Phil Spector production, voices and orchestra dominant, the voice of Leonard Cohen (in duet with Ronee Blakely) almost sounding like another person in such an unfamiliar setting. Likewise, 'Iodine' was an adaptation of 'Guerrero' – a song earmarked for *Songs for Rebecca*, as was 'Beauty Salon', which was transformed via the Spector treatment to become the good-time sing-along 'Don't Go Home With Your Hard-on'.

Most of the songs, like 'Paper Thin Hotel' with its blatant voyeurism, were classic Cohen given their dark subject matter, but to many fans sounded trivialised in such a mainstream musical environment. And at least one track – the semi-autobiographical 'Memories' – was redolent of the late-1950s pop sound that Phil Spector was a product of. The nearest the album got to Cohen's normal delivery was in the semi-spoken introduction to the melancholy 'I Left a Woman Waiting', while the influence of Nashville and its music on Cohen is very evident in the hand-clapping hoe-down 'Fingerprints'. The album closed with the monumental title track, which took nearly nine hours to record in short instrumental bursts before Leonard even sang a note. Again, it was an archetypal Cohen lyric of love gained and love lost, and the loneliness of the aftermath. More than on any other part of the album, the swirling audio landscape created by Spector seemed to work perfectly – although many would undoubtedly disagree on the album's release.

Not unexpectedly, *Death of a Ladies' Man* met with a mixed reception. Many die-hard fans were confused as to Cohen's motives in teaming up with the former 'tycoon of teen', while press reviews varied widely. *The Toronto Star* declared it was for 'musical sadists', and *Rolling Stone* called it 'Cohen's doo-wop nightmare'. The *Los Angeles Times* reviewer, on the other hand, was 'convinced it's *the* album of '77', while in the UK *Sounds* declared: 'Cohen's dirge-like pessimism would hardly appear to be the perfect fodder for Spector's Wall-of-Sound cum Richard Wagner ecstatic street noise, but amazingly enough it works.'

Predictably, *Death of a Ladies' Man* fared miserably sales-wise in the United States, where it failed to make the charts at all, performing better in the UK where it reached the #35 slot. But over the years, critical opinion – and that of life-long Cohen followers – has warmed somewhat to the album, seeing it as a one-off with its virtues as well as vices.

As many had already experienced when working with Phil Spector, out of chaos come order, and the end result was not nearly as disastrous as Leonard and those working with him might have feared. At the time of the album's release, Paul Nelson accurately predicted in *Rolling Stone*, 'It's either greatly flawed or great *and* flawed, and I'm betting on the latter.'

8
RECENT SONGS

'I probably am working somewhat out of what appears to be the mainstream. But I know secretly that I'm in the mainstream, and a lot of the other stuff in it is just fashion. And that older and stronger traditions that are just below the surface sustain the culture.'

All songs written by Leonard Cohen, except where indicated.

Side 1
1. The Guests
2. Humbled in Love
3. The Window
4. Came So Far for Beauty [Cohen, Lissauer]
5. The Lost Canadian (Un Canadien errant) [Traditional, Antoine Gérin-Lajole]
Side 2
1. The Traitor
2. Our Lady of Solitude
3. The Gypsy's Wife
4. The Smokey Life
5. Ballad of the Absent Mare

Personnel: Leonard Cohen (vocals, acoustic guitar); Mitch Watkins (guitar); Ricardo Gonzalez (guitar); Filipe Perez (guitar); Everado Sandoval (guitarrón); Abraham Laboriel (bass); Charles Roscoe Beck (bass); John Miller (bass); John Lissauer (piano); Garth Hudson (Yamaha piano, accordion); Bill Ginn (electric piano); Randy Waldman (organ); Steve Meador (drums); John Bilezikjian (oud); Raffi Hakopian (violin); Agostin Cervantes (violin); Armando Quintero (violin); Luiz Briseño (violin); Miguel Sandoval (violin); Paul Ostermayer (saxophone); Edgar Lustgarten (cello); Jose Perez (trumpet); Pablo Sandoval (trumpet); Earl Dumler (oboe); Jennifer Warnes (backing vocals); Jim Gilstrap (backing vocals); Julia Tillman Waters (backing vocals); Maxine Willard Waters (backing vocals); Roger St. Kenerly (backing vocals); Stephanie Spruill (backing vocals)

On stage in Germany, 1979, during the Recent Songs *tour.*

Recorded: April - May, 1979, A&M Studios, Los Angeles
Released: 27 September 1979
Label: Columbia
Producer: Leonard Cohen, Henry Lewy

After the mixed reception that had greeted his previous release, Leonard's 1979 album *Recent Songs* was universally welcomed as a sign that he was back on form, marking a return to his more traditional, simpler style. And, significantly, it was also the first album Cohen would co-produce.

Although he would reflect on the album more favourably in retrospect, as 1977 came to a close Leonard was still smarting from the whole experience surrounding *Death of a Ladies' Man*. He felt he had been cheated by Phil Spector in the way the producer took over the entire project, and was aggrieved that this contributed to the negative response the album received in many quarters. Cohen fans were the first to notice that, contrary to usual practice, he didn't put a band together to promote the album. Instead, not for the first time, he turned his back on the music business to concentrate on matters closer to home.

'I think any artist – writer, singer, or painter – has only one or two paintings that he does over and over'.

Death of a Lady's Man

Through the latter half of 1977 he and Suzanne had been drifting apart, with Cohen spending most of the time in the house he'd rented in the affluent Los Angeles suburb of Brentwood. Theirs had always been an on-off relationship, but now it seemed as though this really was the end. Meanwhile, Leonard's inner turmoil was exacerbated when his seventy-three-year-old mother Masha became seriously ill with leukaemia. As her condition worsened, he vacated the Brentwood house and moved back to Montreal to be near her. In the constantly shiftng landscape of his romantic life, Cohen's relationship with his mother was the one consistent beacon that had always been there, and now that too was fading fast.

Setting aside their differences, Suzanne and Leonard still regarded themselves and the children as a family. When Cohen rang her to report that Masha was nearing her end, Suzanne immediately travelled back to their Montreal home with Adam and Lorca. Masha died in February 1978. Not long after, Suzanne and Leonard moved once again, this time back to LA and a rented house in the Hollywood Hills. But any renewed stability in their relationship was short lived. Within a few weeks Suzanne had upped and gone, leaving Leonard to look after the children. As Suzanne would later put it: 'I loved him one day and said goodbye that evening.'

Cohen spent most of the following months putting the finishing touches to his new book of poems and prose, *Death of a Lady's Man*. Although they shared a title, this work had little in common with the album released the previous November. The material, comprising poetry and prose, lyrics, discursive passages and diary

On stage, 1979.

extracts, had been written over a period of ten years. Like much of Leonard Cohen's music, it dealt frankly with love and all its dilemmas from an essentially autobiographical standpoint. Published by Leonard's regular Canadian publishing house, McClelland and Stewart, on 7 October 1978, the book would be dedicated 'to Masha Cohen, the memory of my mother'.

After leaving Cohen in Montreal with the children, in the spring of 1978, Suzanne had moved to Hydra with a new man. A summer would pass when Leonard was in sole charge of Adam and Lorca, an opportunity for him to bond with them as never before. But the doting father idyll was short-lived. On her return in the fall, Suzanne collected the children and moved to the small town of Roussillon in south-east France, much to Leonard's dismay. With nothing to keep him in Canada he moved back to Los Angeles, where he would begin thinking about a new album once again.

Recording
It was Spring 1979. After the fraught working relationship that he'd experienced with Phil Spector – not to mention the results, which he still felt were far from satisfactory – Cohen decided that for his next album, he would get formally involved in the production himself. To that end he asked the advice of his old friend Joni Mitchell, whose judgement he had come to respect: she had, after all, warned him from getting involved with Spector in the first place.

Mitchell suggested Leonard should approach her own long-time recording engineer and producer Henry Lewy, which he did, and very soon the two were working together on his new album, provisionally titled 'The Smokey Life'. Lewy, a German by birth, sensed from the start that the songs of Leonard Cohen required a subtle approach – not always totally laid-back, but certainly requiring backings that were sympathetic to the 'folk music' texture of the material.

Initially they made some demos together,

mainly on new songs that Leonard had been working on in Montreal. On Lewy's suggestion they used a small eight-track LA studio called Kitchen Sync, and from there things developed to the point where they felt ready to hire some more musicians.

First in was Roscoe Beck, whom Lewy had worked with before, a jazz-rock bass player with a band called Passenger based in Austin, Texas. Passenger had been earmarked for a tour backing Joni Mitchell that never happened, and now they were at something of a loose end in LA. Enjoying running through numbers with the bass player, Leonard told Beck to bring the whole band in for the next session.

For the recordings proper, the prestigious A&M studios in Hollywood were booked. In contrast to the mayhem that ensued during the recording of *Death of a Ladies' Man*, the sessions for *Recent Songs* (as the album had been retitled) were structured and professional. 'Sessions started in the afternoon and we'd go into the evenings. No drinking, that I saw, no visitors. Finished at a reasonable time, no early hours stuff,' one of the session musicians would recall.

As well as Passenger, who played on four songs, instrumentalists hired for various tracks included a Gypsy violin player, an Armenian oud player, and even a Mexican mariachi band, giving the album a distinctive Mediterranean, Eastern European and Mid-Eastern flavour. Backing vocals were led by Cohen's friend and previous collaborator Jennifer Warnes. Garth Hudson of The Band would also appear on one track, playing electric piano and accordion. The recording at A&M took place through April and May 1979, and the album was released at the end of September.

The Album
In his album credits, Leonard thanked his mother for reminding him, 'shortly before

In Germany, 1980.

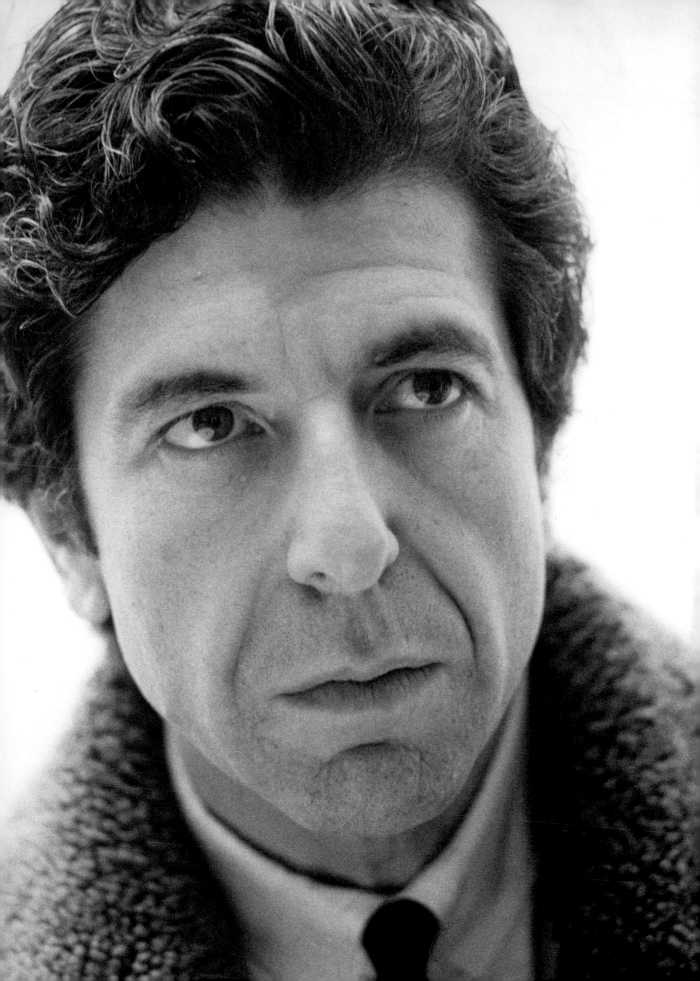

she died, of the kind of music she liked'. Upon hearing his last album, *Death of a Lady's Man*, she had asked her son why he never made songs like the ones they used to sing together around the house, many of these being old Russian and Jewish songs, whose sentimental melodies were often played on the violin. And so, when recording *Recent Songs*, Cohen did just that.

The opening track, 'The Guests', based on a 13th century Persian poem, set the scene for much of the collection. Its Middle Eastern-sounding accompaniment of oud and violin would also feature on 'The Window', 'The Traitor', 'and 'The Gypsy's Wife' – the latter directly alluding to Suzanne's recent departure from Cohen's life. Likewise the Mexican mariachi band added their own blend of the exotic on 'The Guests', 'The Ballad of the Absent Mare', and on Cohen's interpretation of 'Un Canadien errant', a French-Canadian song written in 1842 that had been renamed 'The Lost Canadian'. Another track with an equally obscure origin was 'Ballad of the Absent Mare'. As Cohen would describe in the liner notes to the album, the lyric was based on a 12th century Chinese Zen text *Ten Bulls (or Ten Ox-Herding Pictures)*. The song went on to be covered by various artists, including Emmylou Harris (as 'Ballad of a Runaway Horse') on her 1993 album *Cowgirl's Prayer*.

Three of the tracks had originated on the *Songs for Rebecca* project of 1975 – which Cohen had walked out on after developing an albums-worth of material with John Lissauer – 'Came So Far for Beauty', 'The Traitor' and the jazz-tinged 'The Smokey Life'. Leonard had planned to co-produce *Songs for Rebecca*, and now, with Henry Lewy as his creative partner, he was billed in that role on *Recent Songs*.

Although the album was generally well received by the reviewers, their enthusiasm wasn't reflected in actual sales. It didn't even make the charts in either the USA or Canada, and only scraped into the #53 position in the UK. Indeed, the only country where *Recent Songs* made the Top Thirty was Austria, where it hit the #24 spot and earned a gold record.

But the press notices were, by and large, very encouraging in their praise – especially after the mixed reaction to *Death of a Ladies' Man*. The *New York Times* would list it among its top ten records of 1979, saying it represented for Cohen 'an ideal musical idiom for his idiosyncrasies', while in February 1980 *Rolling Stone*'s Debra Rae Cohen enthused 'at least four or five tunes are full-fledged masterpieces'.

It was certainly a return to form in terms of lyrical consistency, with the inevitable sexual imagery and religious reference generally evocative rather than biting, and any bitter allusion to his own isolation (as in 'Came So Far for Beauty') balanced with warm helpings of Cohen's characteristically wry humour.

The Tour

Having avoided – or indeed never addressed – the possibility of touring in support of *Death of a Ladies Man*, when the *Recent Songs* tour took off in Sweden on 13 October 1979, it had been a full three years since Leonard Cohen had last been on the road. For the European trek, which wound up in Brighton, England, on 15 December, he took the five-piece Passenger as his backing group. They were augmented by oud player John Bilezikjian and Raffi Hakopian on violin, both key session men on the album, and the vocal duo of Jennifer Warnes and a singer new to Cohen line-ups, Sharon Robinson.

Warnes had recommended Robinson, who at the time was working as a back-up and dancer behind the singer Ann-Margret in Las Vegas. After auditioning for Cohen, she was given the job on the spot: 'I knew immediately I would get the gig' she would remember, 'right away there was a connection, a sort of mutual understanding'.

At the beginning of December, for the final UK-based dates, Henry Lewy joined the entourage to record the shows with a view to releasing a live album. The concerts recorded

'I never think of myself as a solitary poet. I don't feel any conflicts in what I do. There are economic pressures, and there's a desire too, to keep singing and keep playing, just because that's the thing you know how to do.'

were at London's Hammersmith Odeon from the 4th to 6th of December, and the closing date at the Brighton Dome a week later. These recordings would eventually provide the material for a live album – *Field Commander Cohen* – albeit one that would not be released for another twenty years.

After a two-month furlough that welcomed in the 1980s, the tour resumed in March with a week in Australia, taking in Melbourne, Adelaide and Sydney. A gushing review of one of the two Sydney concerts appeared in the Australian music paper *Rock Australia Magazine*, enthusing over just about every aspect of the performance, including the band: 'They are breathtaking. A combination of electric and carefully mic'd acoustic instruments, the hardest concert sound in the world to balance. But these guys are crème de professional and there are sheerly wonderful times when, say, the guitar player is holding a fuzz tone, the oud player is sprinkling triplets, the violin soars and ol' Len overlays everything with a lugubrious coating of honey-thick vocals.'

Contrary to common practice, when artists would tour specifically to promote their most recent album release, there was little hype of *Recent Songs* in Leonard's set lists. The majority of his nightly stage repertoire was still being drawn from his first two 'classic' albums, *Songs Of Leonard Cohen* from 1967, and 1969's *Songs From A Room*. Those were the songs – 'Suzanne', 'Sisters of Mercy', 'So Long, Marianne', 'Bird on the Wire' and so on – that audiences clearly wanted to hear as much as any new, unfamiliar material.

By the time the tour ended, new personal relationships had been forged. Specifically, Jennifer Warnes had become involved with bass player Roscoe Beck, as would Leonard – albeit more professionally – with the newcomer Sharon Robinson.

The latter friendship would develop later in the year, when the same personnel would play another five weeks of European concerts, followed by a couple of dates in Tel Aviv, Israel. This time Jennifer Warnes was absent from the line-up, Sharon Robinson fulfilling the back-up duties on her own. She and Leonard began writing songs together – 'It just happened, like falling off a ladder', she would remark years later – creating a songwriting and performing bond that would last throughout Leonard Cohen's career.

9

VARIOUS POSITIONS

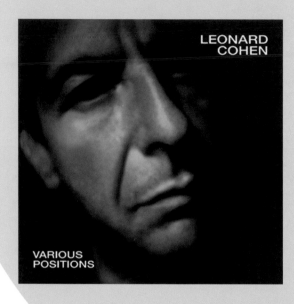

'After a long period of barrenness, it all just seemed to click. Suddenly, I knew these weren't discrete songs I was writing . . . I could see – I could sense a unity. *Various Positions* had its own life, its own narrative.'

All songs written by Leonard Cohen.

Side 1
1. Dance Me to the End of Love
2. Coming Back to You
3. The Law
4. Night Comes On
Side 2
1. Hallelujah
2. The Captain
3. Hunter's Lullaby
4. Heart with No Companion
5. If It Be Your Will

Personnel: Leonard Cohen (vocals, guitar); Jennifer Warnes (vocals); John Lissauer (piano, keyboard, backing vocals); John Crowder (bass guitar, backing vocals); Sid McGinnis (guitar); Ron Getman (harmonica, backing vocals); Richard Crooks (drums); Anjani Thomas (backing vocals); Crissie Faith (backing vocals); Erin Dickins (backing vocals); Lani Groves (backing vocals); Merle Miller (backing vocals); Yvonne Lewis (backing vocals)

Recorded: June 1984, Quadrasonic Sound, New York
Released: 11 December 1984 (Canada), February 1985 (US, Europe)
Label: Columbia / Passport
Producer: John Lissauer

An interview with the Toronto Star, *20 May 1983*

After *Recent Songs* there would be a five-year gap before Cohen produced any further records. He would explain that this time was largely taken up by attending to his children, who were living with Suzanne in the south of France. Released at the end of 1984, *Various Positions* would open either side with two of his best-known anthems, 'Hallelujah' and 'Dance Me to the End of Love'. Leonard would enlist the talents of the new love in his life, French photographer Dominique Issermann, to capture the music video for the latter track.

Following the end of the *Recent Songs* tour, which finished in Tel Aviv on 24 November 1980, Leonard very much distanced himself from the music industry. For the next four years, he would spend most of his time between Montreal, Hydra, and the house where Suzanne was now living in the south of France.

Despite their often fractious relationship, the pair conducted their domestic responsibilities – that is, their duty towards the children – with an admirably 'civilised' attitude. Unlike most separations, Leonard and Suzanne managed to make arrangements almost as if they were still together, to the point where Suzanne chose a suitable house for herself and the children, which Leonard dutifully paid for.

It was in the quaint medieval town of Bonnieux, just south of the ochre-coloured village of Roussillon where Suzanne had been staying since leaving Cohen in 1978. Now that they had a permanent 'family home' there, Leonard was able to spend a lot more time with the children in France – which he did, usually staying in a trailer parked near the entrance to the house. He successfully avoided what in many post-separation relationships would have been the 'absentee father' syndrome, making as much time as possible for his children between working on a new book and other 'non-music-biz' projects.

I Am a Hotel

On one of his frequent trips to Hydra, in the early months of 1982, Leonard became involved once again with his old friend Lewis Furey, who he had known since the mid-1960s and worked with on *New Skin For The Old Ceremony* in 1974. Furey was working on an idea for a musical – a 'rock opera' as he would describe it in the fashionable parlance of the time – and asked Leonard if he would like to be involved in writing the song lyrics.

At first Cohen declined the offer, saying he was more interested in finishing his next book, provisionally called 'The Name'. But over bottles of wine and late-night conversation, Furey was persuasive, and Leonard finally agreed to try out some lyrics to match the plotlines that Furey had already been working on. Over the next few weeks the two bounced lyrics and music back and forth. The Faust-like plot, concerning a down-on-his-luck musician who meets an angel who will realise his fantasies, seemed to be coming together, and after Furey returned home to Paris the two continued developing the project for the next eighteen months or so.

When Furey had arrived in Hydra with his wife, the singer Carole Laure, the couple had been accompanied by their friend Dominique Issermann, a

A recording session in Lower Manhattan, New York, c1985.

'The word Hallelujah is so rich; it's so abundant in resonances. It is a wonderful word to sing and people have been singing that word for thousands of years. It seems to call down some kind of beneficial energy just when you declare in the face of the kind of catastrophes that are manifesting everywhere just to say hallelujah. To praise the energy that manifests both as good and evil just to affirm our little journey here. It is very invigorating to sing that word.'

photographer. It wasn't long before Leonard became romantically involved with the beautiful and talented Dominique, a relationship that would develop during his frequent visits to Paris to work with Furey on the musical. In what was becoming the typical Cohen fashion, there was an instant spark when the two were first introduced on Hydra. Leonard was completely smitten, declaring that he had never fallen in love before meeting the enigmatic Frenchwoman. The feeling was mutual: Dominique described the connection as 'a thunderbolt on both sides'. The relationship would fuel the creative imaginations of both artists as they each worked on their separate projects. 'Art brought us closer together', Dominique remembered years later.

Meanwhile, Cohen had another project in development, a short TV film based on his life and experiences called *I Am a Hotel*. In it, he drew on the lyrics of his song 'The Guests', and his own observations in the King Edward Hotel, Toronto (where the piece was filmed), to create a sequence of five imaginary events each accompanied by one of his songs.

Leonard appeared himself as a curious bystander ('the Resident'), looking on the five scenes. First there was 'The Guests' in which the characters enter the lobby and are taken to their rooms; the bellboy and chambermaid meet in the corridor; and the manager and his wife apparently have angry words in the lobby after which she strides off. Then came 'Memories' where the bellboy pursues the chambermaid, set at a dance where Cohen is up on stage leading the band. The third scene was 'The Gypsy Wife', which sees the manager's wife dancing wildly on a table top. 'Chelsea Hotel #2' has the two lovers trying in vain to make love, while 'the diva' takes the fancy of a guest, an admiral. In the conclusion, 'Suzanne' sees the two couples dancing together, while the manager drowns his sorrows at the bar.

The whole thing was played out against the background of Cohen's songs, with no dialogue and extensive dance sequences. It aired on the Canadian CBC television network on 7 May 1983. The twenty-seven-minute film went on to win the prestigious Rose d'Or (Golden Rose) award at the 1984 Montreux International Television Festival in Switzerland. Although critically well-received, Cohen later expressed disappointment with his work: 'I don't think it's very good. I think it's respectable television but it was the first time I've gone into it, and I didn't really know what I was doing and I kind of lost the handle on the thing.'

Book of Mercy

April 1984 saw the publication of the tenth book by Leonard Cohen, *Book of Mercy*. A collection of fifty prose-poems that Cohen would refer to as 'prayers', it was influenced by both the Hebrew Bible and Zen Buddhist writings. Coming at a time of personal reassessment without the immediate pressure of the record business treadmill, it remains Cohen's most deeply meditative work.

It was his one, definitive, effort to create a book of psalms, and the book allows the reader to see into a soul struggling with what Cohen called 'a sacred kind of conversation'. *Book of Mercy* is now widely rated as one of the most significant confessionals of its kind in modern literature. For the dedicated Leonard Cohen fan, it's a key work in understanding his later commitment to a period of monastic retreat. Soon after its publication, the Canadian Authors Association gave the book its much coveted Literary Award for Poetry.

Recording

By the time *Book of Mercy* was published, Leonard had finally decided it was time to begin recording another album. And his choice as potential producer was, perhaps surprisingly, John Lissauer. The two hadn't met, or even spoken, since the aborted *Songs for Rebecca* project had been brought to a sudden halt through the machinations of Leonard's manager Marty Machat that allowed the 1977 Phil Spector album to go ahead. But that was now all in the past, and when Lissauer was invited by Cohen to meet at the Royalton Hotel in New York and listen to some new songs, he came without hesitation.

The producer – who since last seeing Leonard had been working with the likes of Barbra Streisand and Manhattan Transfer – was struck by one thing immediately: 'Instead of presenting me with the new songs exclusively on a Spanish guitar as usual, he had this dinky little Casio keyboard with him.' The cheap mini-synthesizer, which allowed you to press one button and get a primitive instrumental or rhythm effect, was Cohen's new toy, and surprisingly it worked – one of the first songs he created on the gadget and played over to Lissauer was 'Dance Me to the End of Love', among the most successful numbers he would ever write.

Lissauer also noticed there had been a marked change in Cohen's singing voice, which sounded significantly deeper, as Cohen himself would wryly observe: 'I thought it was because of 50,000 cigarettes and several swimming pools of whiskey that my voice has gotten low.'

A creative team once again, Leonard and John Lissauer went into the Quadrasonic Sound studio in New York with a small group of musicians – mainly from a group called Slow Train – in June 1983, with Leanne Ungar engineering. Ungar, at the time one of the few female recording engineers in the business, had worked with Cohen as assistant engineer on *New Skin For The Old Ceremony* in 1974, and would go on to be involved on many more projects with him over nearly thirty years.

Leonard was so enamoured of his little Casio machine that it featured throughout the recordings, with the only 'drum' track on 'Dance Me to the End of Love' being the same one he had played to Lissauer at their first run-throughs. As the producer would recall: 'We tried to do that song with real drums and percussion but he liked the simplicity of the Casio and had become accustomed to it.'

The recordings at Quadrasonic also marked a fuller involvement by backing vocalist Jennifer Warnes, who would be credited equally to Leonard Cohen as vocalist on all of the tracks on *Various Positions*.

The Album

Released initially in Canada on 11 December 1984, *Various Positions* opened with 'Dance Me to the End of Love'. Described variously as 'Serge Gainsbourg-esue pop' and 'like a Greek dance mixed with a French street song', the song was paradoxically inspired by the Holocaust, as Cohen would reveal. '[It] came from just hearing or reading or knowing that in the death camps beside the crematoria . . . a string quartet was pressed into performance while this horror was going on . . . And they would be playing classical music while their fellow prisoners were being killed and burnt.'

A number of the songs had a marked country flavour, including the 'The Captain', 'Coming Back to You' and 'Heart with No Companion' – the *Rolling Stone* noting that the latter 'wouldn't sound out of place on a Johnny Cash record'. And tracks like the equivocal-sounding 'The Law', the atmospheric 'If It Be Your Will', and the meditative 'Night Comes On' were pure classic Cohen in their multi-layered messages.

Along with 'Dance Me to the End of Love', the opener on Side 2 of the vinyl release, 'Hallelujah', would turn out to be an all-time favourite with Cohen fans, and many more music lovers besides. As in many of Leonard's songs, biblical references abounded, including the story of Samson betrayed by the *femme fatale* Delilah, and the illicit affair between King David and the beautiful Bathsheba. Prior to the recording sessions, Cohen wrote no fewer than eighty draft versions of the song,

which would go on to be voted 'the greatest Leonard Cohen song of all time' in a *Rolling Stone* readers' poll, and be covered by over two hundred artists worldwide.

Cohen himself was more than pleased with the album, describing it in 2000 as something of a breakthrough: 'After a long period of barrenness, it all just seemed to click. Suddenly, I knew these weren't discrete songs I was writing . . . I could see – I could sense a unity. *Various Positions* had its own life, its own narrative.'

It therefore came as even more of a blow when Columbia decided not to release the album. Cohen was furious. He and John Lissauer were convinced that this was the album that would facilitate a genuine breakthrough in America, while the company (amazingly, given the more 'contemporary' feel of the instrumentation and recording) felt it wasn't good enough a commercial proposition.

Initially the album was released in Canada alone, on 11 December 1984. Then in February 1985 it was picked up by the small independent Passport label, and released in the US and Europe. Historically, it was not one of Leonard Cohen's most successful releases, not even making the Top 100 in the US and just hitting #60 and #52 in Canada and the UK respectively. It fared better in Scandinavia, climbing to #12 in Sweden and a heady #3 spot in Norway.

When it appeared, the record wasn't met with universal acclaim. In Britain, the *NME*'s Richard Cook wrote of 'Dance Me to the End of Love': 'Like much else here, it resembles a fragment from a French movie soundtrack, or even (an underhand suggestion) Scott Walker in his Brel period.' The lacklustre sales of the album – not helped by the record company's decision-making at the time of its release – seem all the more ironic in hindsight, given the subsequent popularity of the two key songs, 'Dance Me to the End of Love' and 'Hallelujah'.

'Dance Me . . . ', when released as a single, was supported by a video made by Leonard's French girlfriend, photographer Dominique

On the road, 1985.

Issermann, and went on to be covered by, among others, the French jazz singer Madelaine Peyroux. 'Hallelujah', which became regarded as *the* Leonard Cohen anthem, would be covered successfully by John Cale, Jeff Buckley, k.d.lang, and many others, Bob Dylan and Willie Nelson among them. The song's burgeoning popularity received a further boost in 2001 when it was featured in the animated children's film *Shrek*, and again after Cohen's death in 2016 when it entered the *Billboard* singles chart for the first time.

The Tour

Cohen would go on to support the album with his biggest tour to date, and the first that would include Canada and the United States since 1975. John Lissauer was unavailable as his wife was expecting their first child, but he put a small group together for Leonard, consisting of bass player John Crowder, Ron Getman on harmonica and vocals, and drummer Richard Crooks (all three having played on the album), plus guitarist Mitch Watkins, who'd played on the 1979-80 *Recent Songs* tour. Another addition to the line-up was a new voice performing backing vocals: Anjani Thomas, a Hawaiian singer and pianist who had recently moved to New York. She was the only back-up singer on this trip, doubling on keyboards and sharing the vocals with Crowder, Getman and Watkins.

Relaxing on a park bench in Toronto, April 22, 1985.

'I thought it was because of 50,000 cigarettes and several swimming pools of whiskey that my voice has gotten low.'

The first date on the road was in Mannheim, Germany, on the last day in January 1985. The initial leg of the tour, lasting until 24 March, also took in Norway, Finland, Sweden, Denmark, Holland, France, Spain, the UK, Ireland, Belgium, Austria, Poland and Italy. Everywhere, audiences were ecstatic, and by and large so were the reviews. 'This was a performance of taste and discretion', wrote the UK *Guardian* newspaper covering his concert at London's Hammersmith Odeon. 'The sound of Cohen's five-piece band is rich and meticulous; plangent guitars and keyboards woven together like a hushed symphony of tweeds and worsteds.'

Of particular significance to Leonard were the four dates in communist-run Poland, where a translated version of his song 'The Partisan' had been adopted as the unofficial anthem of the Solidarity movement for democracy. Poland had been in a state of crisis since 1981, the same year the government had banned Solidarity, and many were fearing an invasion by the Soviet Union as had occurred in Czechoslovakia in 1968. The concerts, which were politically sensitive to say the least, were complete sell-outs from the moment the tickets went on sale.

With his own ancestry rooted in Eastern Europe, Leonard was concerned by what was happening in the country, but admitted to being unprepared for the response to his appearances: 'They had cassettes of my songs and Xeroxes of my books. Tickets were scalped for a month's wages. It was almost embarrassing.' The Polish translation of 'The Partisan' had become, according to Cohen, 'a kind of anthem in the detention camps after Solidarity was outlawed and there was a large roundup of people'. The track had a profound political importance, acknowledged by Solidarity leader Lech Walesa, who would send Leonard greetings as a mark of gratitude.

The second part of the seventy-seven-day tour commenced in Philadelphia at the end of April. This was soon followed by dates in the USA and Canada, Australia and Israel, as well as more European concerts. The latter included two prestigious open-air festivals; the Roskilde music festival in Denmark in June, and the famous Jazz Festival at Montreux, Switzerland in July. The marathon trek finally wound up in the Atlantic fishing town of St Jean De Luz, in south-west France on 21 July.

Returning home to LA, Leonard was back in the driving seat where his life was concerned. Again unbound by tour schedules, he was able to pursue interests – not least some uninterrupted writing – other than those dictated by record companies and concert promoters. While he had been away, one such project had already been premiered in Europe – the film of the 'rock opera' he had been developing with Lewis Furey since early 1982.

10

I'M YOUR MAN

'On *I'm Your Man*, my voice
had settled and I didn't
feel ambiguous about it.
I could at last deliver the
songs with the authority
and intensity required.'

Personnel: Leonard Cohen (vocals, keyboards); Jennifer Warnes (vocals); Jude Johnstone (vocals); Anjani Thomas (vocals); Jeff Fisher (keyboards); Bob Stanley (guitar); Sneaky Pete Kleinow (pedal steel guitar); Pete Kisilenko (bass); Tom Brechtlein (drums); Vinnie Colaiuta (drums); Lenny Castro (percussion); Michel Robidoux (drums, keyboards); John Biezokjian (oud); Richard Beaudet (saxophone); Raffi Hakopian (violin); Mayel Assouly (backing vocals); Evelyine Hebey (backing vocals); Elisabeth Valletti (backing vocals)

Recorded: August-November, 1987, Studio Tempo, Montreal; Rock Steady, Los Angeles
Released: 2 February 1988
Label: Columbia
Producer: Leonard Cohen, Roscoe Beck, Jean-Michel Reusser, Michel Robidoux

All songs written by Leonard Cohen, except where indicated.

Side 1
1. First We Take Manhattan
2. Ain't No Cure for Love
3. Everybody Knows (Cohen, Sharon Robinson)
4. I'm Your Man
Side 2
1. Take This Waltz (Federico Garcia Lorca, Cohen)
2. Jazz Police (Cohen, Jeff Fisher)
3. I Can't Forget
4. Tower of Song

Leonard relaxes at his Paris hotel, February 1988.

I t would be more than two years after the *Various Positions* tour before Leonard's next album saw the light of day. But when it did, *I'm Your Man* became Cohen's most successful album since the early 1970s – despite a move to the unlikely musical textures of synthesised 80s pop – and would be hailed as a return to form by critics.

Night Magic

The 1985 tour was still in full swing, with Leonard flying between dates in Vancouver, Canada and Brisbane, Australia, when the long-anticipated project with Lewis Furey was finally revealed to the world via its May premiere at the Cannes Film Festival. Originally planned to be released as *Angel Eyes*, the musical fantasy had reverted to its first working title, *Night Magic*, before finally hitting the big screen.

The film was, according to Furey, 'very much a Faust story, only the Mephistopheles character is three teenage angels who appear at the window, and the price you have to pay is

'I always considered myself a minor writer. My province is small and I try to explore it very, very thoroughly. It isn't like I chose this. This is what I am.'

suffering, joy, redemption and decay.' At the centre of the plot was Michael, an out-of-work musician and music hall artist (played by Nick Mancuso) who meets an angel, Judy (who was played by Furey's wife, Carole Laure), the epitome of all his dreams. Written by Cohen and Furey (who also directed the movie), the film went on to show how the hero's fantasies might be realised, but only at a price, be it in love, music, or wealth. With a supporting cast that featured some well-known names in French cinema, including Stéphane Audran and Jean Carmet, *Night Magic* was in the official selection at Cannes, where it had its first public showing.

The film also gained four nominations in the 1986 Genie Awards – Canada's answer to the 'Oscars' – for Best Art Direction, Best Original Score, Best Original Song for 'Angel Eyes' and Best Original Song for 'Fire'. At the awards ceremony on 20 March, it went on to win the Best Original Song award for 'Angel Eyes'. A double album of the movie soundtrack was also released in France in 1985.

Famous Blue Raincoat

In 1987, Leonard's less than consistent recognition in both the United States and his native Canada would be given an unexpected boost by his old friend and erstwhile vocal collaborator Jennifer Warnes. Having worked with Cohen off and on since his European tour of 1972, appearing on most of his albums, Warnes had developed a deep love and understanding for his songs, while also carving out a name for herself.

Her solo breakthrough had come in 1976 with the album *Jennifer Warnes*, which contained the hit single 'Right Time of the Night', #1 on *Billboard*'s Easy Listening chart in April 1977, and #6 on the regular Hot 100 a few weeks later. Then, in 1979, 'It Goes Where It Goes' won an Academy Award for Best Original Song as the soundtrack for the film *Norma Rae*. The same year, her single, 'I Know a Heartache When I See One', hit the Top Twenty on both the Pop and Adult Contemporary charts.

Warnes would enjoy even bigger success in 1982, with her duet with Joe Cocker 'Up Where We Belong', which was recorded for the smash hit film, *An Officer and a Gentleman*. As well as an Academy Award for Best Original Song, and a Golden Globe Award, the song won Warnes and Cocker a Grammy Award for Best Pop Performance by a Duo or Group. It went on to top the *Billboard* singles chart for three weeks running, and was certified for a platinum disc for sales of over two million in the United States alone. Then in 1987, she collaborated with vocalist Bill Medley for '(I've Had) The Time of My Life', used in the film *Dirty Dancing* and earning her another Academy Award, a Golden Globe Award, a Grammy Award and another #1 in the singles chart.

*January 1988, filming a music video with
Dominique Issermann.*

It was on Cohen's *Recent Songs* tour, in 1979, that Warnes first had the idea for recording an album of Leonard's songs. She had begun a relationship with bass player Roscoe Beck on the tour, and the two came up with the proposition of an album celebrating the work of Leonard Cohen, performed by Warnes and produced by Beck. The original notion came to Warnes during the '79 tour, when Leonard had helped her with the lyrics of a song she was writing, 'Song of Bernadette'. Over the next few years, she and Beck tried in vain to get a record company interested.

After being rejected by Cohen's label Columbia, Arista (who had released her previous albums) and the giant MCA, eventually Warnes and Beck concluded a deal with the small independent Cypress Records. During 1986, a total of two dozen instrumentalists, as well as Warnes and another dozen backing vocalists, laid down the nine tracks that would become *Famous Blue Raincoat*. Major names among the plethora of top studio musicians at the sessions included the multi-instrumentalist David Lindley, keyboard player Van Dyke Parks, and the blues guitar supremo Stevie Ray Vaughan.

Listening to some of the early takes, Leonard was enthusiastic about the project, and agreed to sing a duet with Warnes on her version of 'Joan of Arc'. He would tell Steve Turner in *Q* magazine: 'I was writing for my new record and Jennifer, who is an old friend and musical collaborator, said she wanted to do an album of my songs. She'd been saying this for a long time and I always thought it was just an expression of friendship. I never thought she'd actually do it.' He also gave her two new, unrecorded numbers to include on the collection, 'Ain't No Cure for Love' and 'First We Take Manhattan'.

When it was released, in January 1987, the album immediately did better than most of Cohen's own output in home territory, selling 750,000 copies in the US and earning a gold record in Canada. Importantly, it set the songs of Leonard Cohen in a more accessible musical environment for many listeners, taking into account the smoother quality of Warnes' voice. As a review in the *New Musical Express* bluntly put it: 'Cohen's problem all these years has clearly been that, while he qualifies as one of the most sensitive lyrical poets, he's always sung like a beaver with toothache . . . So Warnes has done us all a big favour.'

The liner notes of the album included a rough sketch of a torch being passed on, with the inscription 'Jenny Sings Lenny'. Jennifer Warnes would later attest that this was originally intended to have been the title and cover art for the release. She explained that the pair had been having dinner in Mario's Italian restaurant in Hollywood, when Cohen drew the cartoon on a paper napkin: 'Leonard . . . has never forgiven me for not using it on the cover.'

There was also a single of 'Ain't No Cure for Love', which hit both the Adult Contemporary and Country charts in *Billboard*. The song, along with 'First We Take Manhattan', wouldn't be recorded by Cohen until the fall of 1987, as he began putting together tracks for his next album, *I'm Your Man*.

Recording

As always, for Leonard Cohen, writing songs for a new album was a long, drawn-out process, a labour of love where there often wasn't a lot of love involved. It was something he felt he had to do, a creative vocation as much as his poetry and books. It wasn't as if he had the record company snapping at his heels for new 'product' – they knew better than that by now – and his modest sales in North America and elsewhere were sufficient to keep the Columbia accountants happy, so long as his ongoing balance stayed in the black.

So through 1986 to the summer of '87, Leonard commuted between the south of France to see his children, to Paris, where he still saw Dominique (although the glow of their romance was beginning to fade), to Montreal, where he still had his house, and to Los

Angeles. He was writing as he went, recording demos (and sometimes more developed tracks) at home, or in local studios. It was very much a solo affair.

Even when he went into a studio proper, as at Studio Tempo in Montreal, he was relying on full-sounding backing tracks created alone, via synthesised keyboards –rather than the sparse guitar self-accompaniment he had relied on previously, which always required some added instrumentation to give it body.

Nonetheless, there came a stage where Leonard felt he needed some extra texture, and another presence at the production end of things. He'd been suitably impressed by Roscoe Beck's work on *Famous Blue Raincoat*, despite it being the bass player's first ever production job, and hired him to take on his new project.

> 'My songs last about 30 years – that's about the lifespan of a Volvo. But they're designed to last as long as possible. My own critical examination of the songs is very severe: if it can survive examination by the heart, the mind and the gut, then I think the song can last a little while.'

Much of the 'instrumentation' was still a combination of electronic effects like sequencers, synthesised string sections, drum machines and so on. A few handpicked studio players would be brought in to give some added musical atmosphere – mainly names who had appeared on previous Cohen productions, such as violin player Raffi Hakopian, Armenian oud maestro John Biezokjian, and Sneaky Pete Kleinow on pedal steel.

With studio sessions shared between Montreal and Los Angeles, four producers were involved in the recording – Beck, Jean-Michel Reusser, Michel Robidoux and Leonard himself. Cohen felt that his deeper voice improved things, as he would explain some years later in *Uncut* magazine: 'On *I'm Your Man*, my voice had settled and I didn't feel ambiguous about it. I could at last deliver the songs with the authority and intensity required.'

The Album

Opening the album, 'First We Take Manhattan' (originally titled 'In Old Berlin') addressed the stark issue of global terrorism, which Coen would explain in a backstage interview, paraphrasing a poem by his friend Irving Layton: '"Well, you guys blow up an occasional airline and kill a few children here and there", he says. But our terrorists, Jesus, Freud, Marx, Einstein. The whole world is still quaking . . .'

On tour, Leonard would introduce the song with a preamble mentioning cities he would be visiting, as at a London concert in 1988: 'But I want to tell you that even though your hospitality is profound it will not detour me from my appointed task which is to take Manhattan, then Berlin and several other cities . . .' In hindsight, of course, the title itself would represent an eerie prediction of the events that took place on 11 September 2001. 'First We Take Manhattan' had already appeared on Jennifer Warnes' *Famous Blue Raincoat* album, as had the love song 'Ain't No Cure for Love' (its title inspired by the AIDS crisis) in a slightly shorter version than Cohen's.

'Everybody Knows' was written in collaboration with vocalist Sharon Robinson, a sometime backing singer with Cohen, and a gifted composer in her own right. With its Dylanesque repetition of the title throughout, the song presents a stark vision of a dystopian future, described by Stephen Holden as a 'bleak prophecy about the end of the world as we know it.' Cohen himself said of the song that 'it embodies all my darkest thoughts', and its lyrics certainly support this claim; the dice are loaded, the good guys lost, the boat is leaking, the captain lied, the poor stay poor, the rich get rich, the plague is coming and moving fast – and everybody knows it. Yet as comprehensive as the song is in its overview of the threats facing humanity, the constant repetition of the title phrase suggests that Cohen has not been blessed with some unique power of perception, but that these truths should be self-evident.

The title track, which closed the first side of the vinyl release, has since become a firm favourite at Leonard Cohen concerts, and has been described by *Rolling Stone* as 'A profoundly horny song of pure lust'. Or is it love? Here, the two are interchangeable, and arguably inseparable. A paean to the focus of all he desires, Leonard offers himself in any guise or situation. The song is a selfless surrender to the woman he loves, on whatever terms she might demand, whether that is acting as a father for her child, or simply accompanying her on a walk along the beach.

A song with a highly literate history, 'Take This Waltz' was a loose translation of a Spanish poem, 'Pequeño vals vienés' ('Little Viennese Waltz'), by one of Leonard's favourite writers, Federico Garcia Lorca. A previous version by Cohen had been recorded in Montmartre Studios, Paris, in September 1986, as part of the Lorca tribute album *Poets in New York (Poetas en Nueva York,)* released by CBS in celebration of the fiftieth anniversary of Lorca's death. It was also released as a single, which topped the charts in Spain. The version on *I'm Your Man* had an added violin part, plus the duet vocals of Jennifer Warnes.

The song was Cohen's way of paying homage to his literary hero: 'With the Lorca poem, the translation took 150 hours, just to get it into English that resembled – I would never presume to say duplicated – the greatness of Lorca's poem. It was a long, drawn-out affair, and the only reason I would even attempt it is my love for Lorca.' Of course, he had already paid an even greater tribute to the Spanish poet, over a decade before: 'I named my daughter Lorca, so you can see this is not a casual figure in my life. She wears the same name beautifully.'

The experimental 'Jazz Police' was, as described by biographer Anthony Reynolds, Leonard's tongue-in-cheek response to the tendency of his backing musicians to add tricky jazz phrasing to their live performances. Cohen would often have to take on the role of the 'policeman' during rehearsals to ensure that such indulgences didn't get out of hand.

Like 'I'm Your Man', 'I Can't Forget' – despite originally being a song about the Jews' exodus from Egypt – was a deliberate attempt to 'lighten up' on Cohen's part, evidenced by snatches of ironic humour and a less complicated approach. He would explain to a BBC interviewer on the album's release: 'I had to go back to the beginning and determine where I was in regard to my own song and I realised that I'd have to find another kind of language that was much flatter, which I think this record has'. In the song he's chasing a half-recalled memory; it's a reminder that even important

In the Netherlands, during the I'm Your Man tour, February 15, 1988.

On tour in Germany, April 1988.

events are soon reduced to fleeting recollections: 'I can't forget but I don't remember who'.

Closing the album, 'Tower of Song' is often regarded as the crucial number of the collection, dealing with the very essence of what it means to be a songwriter. Cohen first recorded the song in one take on his little Casio synth, and in it ruminates on the often solitary existence of the lone musical wordsmith. Leonard would recite the lyrics in full when he was inducted into the Rock & Roll Hall of Fame in 2008.

Success

In many ways, *I'm Your Man* would be Leonard Cohen's most successful album to date. It certainly did better in the United States than previous releases, and earned gold and silver discs across Europe and Canada – plus platinum in Norway, where it occupied the #1 spot for sixteen weeks. With its synth-pop backings, it was accessible to a younger than usual audience, as well as his army of faithful followers, and the critics were almost unanimous in hailing it a welcome return to form.

In the UK, a *Guardian* journalist said it was a clue to the hidden humour and warmth in many of Cohen's earlier, often derided, works: 'Not only does it display such drollery and self-parody as to confound expectations of the man and the genre, but it forces one to exhume the Cohen back-catalogue and discover that, yes indeed, he had been quite an ironist all along.' *Q* magazine called it his best LP since the mid-70s, while the *New Musical Express* declared 'The atmosphere he creates is one of awe. His symmetry, insight and consequential home truths make the throat gulp.' And in *Rolling Stone*, David Browne called it 'the first Cohen album that can be listened to during the daylight hours.' The *New York Times* went one better, simply calling it 'a masterpiece'.

Touring

Although he was often reluctant to follow up an album with a tour, used to following record company dictates as much as anything else, Leonard was keen to get on the road this time with a band that Roscoe Beck was putting together. Just five days after the release of *I'm Your Man*, on 7 February he was off to Europe for a series of promotional interviews, in anticipation of a concert trek starting in the April.

Beck himself wasn't part of the line-up due to prior commitments in the studio, but assembled a tight outfit consisting of John Biezokjian on oud and drummer Steve Meador, who had both played on *Recent Songs*, Bob Metzger on guitars, keyboard players Tom McMorran and Bob Furgo, and Steve Zirkel on bass. There were also two new backing vocalists, Perla Batalla and Julie Christensen.

The European tour, taking in fifty-nine concerts, began on 5 April 1988 in Mainz, Germany. Leonard was feted, and even mobbed on occasion, like a true star. In the UK, he was invited to take part in the Princes Trust charity event, Prince Charles apparently being a fan. 'He's a remarkable man and he has this incredibly laid-back gravelly voice', the prince later said of Cohen in an ITV interview. His profile in Great Britain was sufficiently high for the BBC to make a documentary about him, while in Iceland he was received by the country's President. Cohen's main audience had always been in Europe, but now he was a genuine superstar there.

Yet perhaps even more remarkably, given that his last album had not even been released in the US, Cohen's popularity extended to his native continent for the first time in his career. He commenced his North American tour with a 5 July concert at the Ritz, New York, followed by Carnegie Hall the next evening. A few dates in California followed, before a welcome break until October, when the tour resumed through the US and Canada until mid-November. Reviews everywhere were ecstatic, with the *New York Times* citing *I'm Your Man* as its Album of the Year. On his home continent, Leonard Cohen had finally arrived.

11

THE FUTURE

LEONARD COHEN

THE FUTURE

'I had wonderful love, but I did not give back wonderful love. I was unable to reply to their love. Because I was obsessed with some fictional sense of separation, I couldn't touch the thing that was offered me, and it was offered me everywhere.'

All songs written by Leonard Cohen, except where indicated.

Side 1
1. The Future
2. Waiting for the Miracle (Cohen, Sharon Robinson)
3. Be For Real (Frederick Knight)
4. Closing Time
5. Anthem
Side 2
1. Democracy
2. Light as the Breeze
3. Always (Irving Berlin)
4. Tacoma Trailer

Personnel: Leonard Cohen (vocals, keyboards, saxophone, violin); Bob Metzger (guitar); Paul Jackson Jr. (guitar); Dean Parks (guitar); Dennis Herring (guitar); Freddie Washington (bass); Bob Glaub (bass); Lee Sklar (bass); Steve Lindsey (keyboards); Greg Phillinganes (keyboards); Jeff Fisher (keyboards); Randy Kerber (keyboards); John Barnes (keyboards); James Cox (keyboards); Mike Finnigan (keyboards); Stephen Croes (keyboards); Steve Meador (drums); James Gadson (drums); Vinnie Colaiuta (drums); Ed Greene (drums); Lenny Castro (percussion, tambourine); Brandon Fields (tenor saxophone); Lon Price (tenor saxophone); Greg Smith (baritone saxophone); Lee Thornburg (trumpet, trombone); Bob Furgo (violin); Anjani Thomas (backing vocals); Jacquelyn Gouche-Farris (backing vocals); Tony Warren (backing vocals); Valerie

August 1988, at home in Canada.

Pinkston-Mayo (backing vocals); Julie Christensen (backing vocals); Perla Batalia (backing vocals); Jennifer Warnes (backing vocals); Edna Wright (backing vocals); Jean Johnson (backing vocals); Peggi Blu (backing vocals); the LA Mass Choir (choir)

Recorded: January – June 1992: including Image Recording Studio, Los Angeles; Cherokee Recording Studio, Los Angeles; Capitol Recording Studio, Los Angeles; The Complex, Los Angeles; House Of Soul, Vallejo, California; Village Recorder, Los Angeles; Studio II, Los Angeles; Ocean Way Recording Studio, Los Angeles; Studio Tempo, Montreal; Studio 56, Los Angeles; Sunset Sound, Los Angeles; Mad Hatter Studios, Los Angeles
Released: 24 November 1992
Label: Columbia
Producer: Leonard Cohen, Steve Lindsey, Bill Ginn, Leanne Ungar, Rebecca De Mornay, Yoav Goren

September 1992, at a music business party with his girlfriend Rebecca De Mornay.

*T*he *Future* would be Cohen's most politically pessimistic work, with song references to World War II, Joseph Stalin, Hiroshima, the Los Angeles riots, and the Tiananmen Square massacre. Before working on the album in the studio, Cohen had taken a year off to help his son Adam convalesce from a serious car accident, and struck up a relationship with the glamourous Hollywood actress Rebecca De Mornay.

Adam

Following the success of *I'm Your Man*, Leonard – for once – didn't let the grass grow. As soon as the tour wound up in November 1988, he began working on songs for his next album. Nevertheless, Cohen being Cohen, it was a long process, and one that would be seriously interrupted in 1990 when his son Adam suffered a serious road accident.

Adam, just seventeen at the time, had been working as a roadie for a calypso band in the West Indies, when he was involved in a terrible car crash on the Caribbean island of Guadeloupe. He broke his neck, nine ribs and his hip, and suffered a punctured lung among other injuries: 'I have a metal hip right now' he would recall, 'I broke my knee, my ankle. One of my lungs was collapsed. My abdominals were crushed. I was out, man.'

Immediately following the accident, the unconscious teenager was flown by air-ambulance to Toronto, Canada, where he was taken into intensive care. Leonard was in Los Angeles when he was notified, and flew straight to the hospital to be near his son. Adam was in a coma for four months, during which time his father kept up an almost non-stop vigil at his bedside.

Leonard spent the next year or so with his son, who was gradually recovering. The process was a slow one – Adam had to learn how to walk again – and the two bonded as never before. Although he would eventually enjoy a full recovery, the incident had been physically and mentally traumatic for Adam, who decided to quit any musical ambitions and go to college. But, his father's son, he soon found himself inexorably drawn back to music.

The accident had resonated similarly deeply with Leonard. 'You find out something about the human body and about frailty, and you find out something about courage. Not just of the love between you and that other person, but what human beings are capable of', Cohen recalled. 'There was a very strong psychic element in his recovery – both involved with my love and his understanding of my unconditional love, and my understanding of his incredible courage and his incredible effort. There were very deep and mysterious human mechanics of love and the heart going on that I couldn't even presume to describe.'

Rebecca

Talking to Cohen biographer Sylvie Simmons, actress Rebecca De Mornay said Cohen claimed to have first seen her when she was just five or six-years-old, when he was playing a concert at her school in England. He would have been in his early thirties at the time. For her own part, De Mornay remembered first hearing Cohen when she was ten: 'My mother was going out on a date and wanted me to go to sleep, so she lit a candle – for a child alone in a house – and said, "I'll put a record on that'll put you right to sleep". And that's when I first heard Leonard. And I remember it did put me to sleep. But it was comforting.'

Their paths would next cross in the late 1980s, by which time De Mornay was an up-and-coming Hollywood actress with several film credits to her name. She lived just a couple of miles from Cohen in Los Angeles, and what was initially a strictly platonic friendship slowly transformed into a genuine love affair by the early 1990s. 'When I first met Rebecca all kinds of thoughts came into my mind', Leonard would recall. 'How could they not when faced with a woman of such beauty? And they got crisscrossed in my mind. But she didn't let it go further than that: my mind. Except it did.' Cohen was completely enraptured by his young lover, describing her as 'the light of my life'. There was even an engagement – Leonard gave her 'a very beautiful ring' – and the two seemed perfectly matched, each finding inspiration in the other's success. Rebecca had just landed the lead role in the 1992 psychological thriller *The Hand That Rocks the Cradle*, and Leonard, having returned from caring for Adam, was once more busily entrenched in preparations for his next album.

I'm Your Fan

I'm Your Man had certainly appealed to a younger audience than previous Cohen releases, a process that continued when a track from the album, 'Everybody Knows', was used in the 1990 film *Pump Up the Volume* alongside *Various Positions'* 'If It Be Your Will'.

Confirmation of the broadening scope of the Cohen repertoire came in November 1991 with the release of *I'm Your Fan*, a Leonard Cohen tribute album put together by Christian Fevret, editor of the French rock magazine *Les Inrockuptibles*.

Leonard was made aware of the project from the start, with Fevret running through some of the names involved: 'I didn't know all of them, but I knew Ian McCulloch whom I've met on several occasions, and R.E.M., and The Pixies and Lloyd Cole and John Cale. It seemed like a really nice thing but I said, "Yeah, seems like a great idea. Goodbye and good luck". I never thought I'd hear from him again.'

Over eighteen tracks, some of the biggest rock names of the period were featured playing covers of Leonard's songs. They included R.E.M with 'First We Take Manhattan', 'Hey That's No Way to Say Goodbye' by Echo & the Bunnymen

'You find out something about the human body and about frailty, and you find out something about courage. Not just of the love between you and that other person, but what human beings are capable of.'

front man Ian McCulloch, Lloyd Cole's 'Chelsea Hotel', 'Tower of Song' by Nick Cave and the Bad Seeds, and John Cale's memorable version of 'Hallelujah'.

Upon listening to the completed tribute Leonard was suitably touched, describing the record as 'a very pleasant surprise'. He later cited it as a source of inspiration and, when interviewed about the album, said that it had helped to spark new ideas for the arrangement and production of his older tracks.

The Album

The studio recording of Leonard's new album began in January 1992, but the project would involve no fewer than a dozen studios in both California and Montreal. The production team, which included Cohen, engineer Leanne Ungar and Rebecca De Mornay, likewise altered between various tracks. In fact the whole project, with its huge cast of players, was, as writer Anthony Reynolds described in his Leonard Cohen biography, 'more akin to a movie production and included both a choir and an orchestra.'

Some of the songs had been long in preparation. The title track, 'The Future', had originally been called 'If You Could See What's Coming Next' and had been rewritten countless times, with its various iterations stretching over fifty pages of Leonard's notebook. The writing process for 'Closing Time' had been similarly laborious, with Cohen taking over two years to be satisfied.

Opening the album, 'The Future' set the political tone of much to follow, with its overt references to times of upheaval, from the bombing of Hiroshima to the raising of the Berlin Wall, and also to radical figures from history, ranging from Stalin to St Paul. The track laid bare Leonard Cohen's vision of the apocalypse, seen through the prism of both the sacred and the profane, a theme that persisted throughout the rest of the album. With its rocking lilt and gospel-tinged backing vocals, the title track was reminiscent of some of Bob Dylan's bleak chronicles of a doomed future, a socially engaged Cohen at his most concerned and pessimistic.

Starting with a militaristic drum roll heralding an up-tempo march, 'Democracy', which opened Side 2, was, by Cohen's reckoning, originally sixty verses long. Inspired by the falling of the Berlin Wall and the government-led massacre of civilians in Beijing's Tianamen Square, the terse lyrics serve as a reminder to the listener that the USA was also enduring social tensions.

There have been various interpretations of the song. For instance, the 'heart' of Chevrolet could be taken refer to the essence of America, the automobile, or – conversely – to the decaying 'Motor City' of Detroit, which had seen its share of racial trouble since the 1960s onwards. The latter reading seems most likely,

At the Beacon Theater, New York City, November 16, 1988.

'When I first met Rebecca all kinds of thoughts came into my mind. How could they not when faced with a woman of such beauty? And they got crisscrossed in my mind. But she didn't let it go further than that: my mind. Except it did.'

especially in the light of the 1992 LA riots, which had erupted in the April as recording was taking place, with the optimism of the Civil Rights era having given way to new domestic confrontations.

Cohen would affirm that the song was as much about the challenges facing America as the apparent triumph of democracy elsewhere: 'I think the irony of America is transcendent in the song. It's not an ironic song. It's a song of deep intimacy and affirmation of the experiment of democracy in this country. That this is really where the experiment is unfolding. This is really where the races confront one another, where the classes, where the genders, where even the sexual orientations confront one another. This is the real laboratory of democracy.'

Rebecca De Mornay would be credited as a co-producer on 'Anthem', which she had enthused about when they were rehearsing it at home, helping Cohen with it when he seemed to be getting stuck. She would describe it as 'the pinnacle of his deep understanding of human defeat', and it was on De Mornay's suggestion that a gospel choir was used, to stunning effect. In many ways the song was the centrepiece of the album, the conclusion of years of development on Cohen's part, which started life as 'Ring the Bells' a decade earlier. The gentle rhythm belies

the stature of the song's message, addressing the contradiction in death and rebirth.

In 'Waiting for the Miracle' a loping tempo and haunting background melody evoked images of a 1960s Western movie, with Cohen deep in melancholy, awaiting the eponymous miracle. Written with vocalist Sharon Robinson, the song actually included Leonard's marriage proposal to Rebecca. Unfortunately, the romantic overture came to nothing; the couple would separate a short time after the album's release. Cohen was sanguine about the song and its promise: 'The miracle is to move to the other side of the miracle, where you cop to the fact that you're waiting for it and that it may or may not come'.

There was a nod to a country barn dance hoe-down in 'Closing Time', but as always even some good-time music could serve as background to disillusion. Initially, it appears little more than a euphoric song about the end of a particularly wild party, but as the song goes on, the drinks are laced with acid, and what looked like freedom, starts to feel like death.

'Light as the Breeze', in Cohen terms at least, was a more conventional piece of confessional than most of the songs on the album, the slow waltz-time ballad reminding listeners that this was the man who had come to personify personal angst.

The Future would also include two non-original covers. R&B singer Frederick Knight's 'Be For Real', and a bluesy rendition of the old Irving Berlin standard 'Always', the latter with an arrangement featuring brass section and sassy vocal group straight out of the Ray Charles songbook. Plus the album featured the first instrumental ever to appear on a Leonard Cohen studio release, 'Tacoma Trailer', written while he accompanied Rebecca on her location shoot for *The Hand That Rocks the Cradle* in the Seattle suburb of Tacoma.

Overall, the album marked a significant change in Cohen's songwriting, from his characteristic stance of personal introspection to making a more directly political comment about the contemporary world and current events. At times nearer to a collection of oral poetry than a conventional album of songs, it acts almost as a personal manifesto in drawing attention to the conceits and hypocrisies of modern society.

Released on 24 November 1992, *The Future* would be Leonard Cohen's most celebrated album to date, going gold, platinum, and finally double-platinum in Canada. It sold over a quarter of a million records in the USA, and hit the Top Forty in the UK. Leonard also won the Canadian Juno Award for Best Male Vocalist for the album in 1993.

Cohen's immediate comment on the album was one of relief: '[*The Future*] involved a four-year struggle; the songs, some of them, are eight, ten years in the works. The record is there for keeps. There's flesh and blood attached to it. I did what was necessary, and I sit here kind of wrecked.'

The captivatingly alluring music video for the song 'Closing Time' would also win the Juno Award for Best Music Video. When the shooting for 'Closing Time' began, director Curtis Wehrfritz struggled to get Leonard to inject the right spirit into the video. Rebecca had accompanied Cohen to the set that day and, in a flash of inspiration, set about performing a mock-striptease directly beside the camera. As journalist Ian Pearson would later describe: 'The singer responded with an intensely erotic gaze. He sang every word to De Mornay and came up with a true performance under the most artificial of circumstances. The song ended, and De Mornay turned to Wehrfritz and laughed, "We really put a sparkle in his eye."'

The critics were almost unanimous in their praise for *The Future*, with *Rolling Stone* declaring that the album 'might as easily have been a book: A more troubling, more vexing image of human failure has not been written'. Cliff Jones of *Rock CD* called it 'Little short of a bloody marvel'. And for *Q* magazine, Andy Gill wrote 'Though the album doesn't quite achieve the rarefied success of *I'm Your Man* . . . It's as worthy a successor as could be hoped for, and compared to his contemporaries' recent efforts, blooming genius.'

Three songs from the album – 'Anthem', 'The Future', and 'Waiting for the Miracle' would appear prominently on the soundtrack of the 1994 Oliver Stone movie *Natural Born Killers*. A provocatively cynical satire on the state of mass-media obsessed America, the film was highly controversial but a box office hit nonetheless, in no small part due to the success of its soundtrack. Writing two decades later, the AV Club would continue to praise the inclusion of Leonard Cohen's tracks. 'They bookend the film in a thematic triptych, with Cohen's cracked ballads of cruelty, regret and moral decay making many of Stone's points with just a mordant turn of phrase.'

The Tour

A tour promoting the album was scheduled to begin on 22 April 1993 in Holstebro, Denmark. The eight-piece band would include drummer Steve Meador, guitarist Bob Metzger, Bob Furgo on bass, and vocalists Perla Batalla and Julie Christensen – all from the previous touring line-up – plus Bill Ginn on synths, saxophonist Paul Ostermayer and guitarist Jorge Calderon. The reception on the European leg, and on the subsequent North American dates, was rapturous. In the UK, there were women screaming like teenage pop fans at the Royal Albert Hall. 'The screams don't belong to teenyboppers', noted Andy Gill in *The Independent*, 'but to mature women, utterly beguiled by this gentle existential serenader.'

A number of Leonard's shows were recorded by Leanne Unger, who was accompanying her husband Bob Metzger on tour, and would form part of the next album release, *Cohen Live*, in 1994. This was just as well: Leonard Cohen wouldn't release another studio album for the next nine years.

12

COHEN LIVE

'Seriousness, rather than depression is, I think, the characteristic of my work… I like a good laugh, but I think there's enjoyment that comes through seriousness. We all know when we close the door and come into your room and you're left with your heart and your emotions, it isn't all that funny.'

All songs written by Leonard Cohen, except where indicated.

1. Dance Me to the End of Love
2. Bird on the Wire
3. Everybody Knows
4. Joan of Arc
5. There Is a War
6. Sisters of Mercy
7. Hallelujah
8. I'm Your Man
9. Who by Fire
10. One of Us Cannot Be Wrong
11. If It Be Your Will
12. Heart with No Companion
13. Suzanne

Personnel: Leonard Cohen (vocals, guitar, keyboards); Bob Metzger (guitar, pedal steel); Bill Ginn (keyboards); Tom McMorran (keyboards); Paul Ostermayer (keyboards, saxophone); Bob Furgo (violin, keyboards); Stephen Zirkel (bass, trumpet, keyboards); John Bilezikjian (mandolin); Jorge Calderon (bass, backing vocals); Steve Meador (drums); Perla Batalla (backing vocals); Julie Christensen (backing vocals)

Recorded: 19 April 1988, Amsterdam, Netherlands; 20 May 1988, San Sebastian, Spain; 31 October 1988, Austin, Texas; 17–18 June 1993, Toronto, Ontario; 29 June 1993, Vancouver, British Columbia
Released: 28 June 1994
Label: Sony
Producer: Leanne Ungar, Bob Metzger

The singer's first live release in over twenty years, *Cohen Live* was the product of performances recorded during the 1988 *I'm Your Man* tour and 1993's *The Future* world tour. Many reviewers saw it as a stopgap between studio releases – which was probably more accurate than they knew, in light of the fact that it would be another seven years before Cohen's next original album.

Stranger Music

Almost as soon as he had finished recording *The Future* in the summer of 1992, Leonard threw himself into the long-awaited project of his next book of poems. He'd been working on material on and off since the mid-1980s for a proposed anthology of poetry and song lyrics, and now – with his profile higher than it had ever been – his publishers felt the timing couldn't have been better. All he had to do was get it organised.

The layman would assume that a straightforward collection of already written works shouldn't be too hard to put together, but with Leonard, nothing could ever be that simple. He chopped and changed things right until the last minute, even faxing in eleventh hour amendments to his publishers. The collection eventually appeared in March 1993.

Titled *Stranger Music: Selected Poems and Songs*, the anthology included some of Cohen's best known lyrics – such as 'Suzanne', 'Sisters of Mercy', 'Bird on a Wire' and 'Famous Blue Raincoat' – plus selections from most of his books (including *Flowers for Hitler*, *Beautiful Losers*, and *Death of a Lady's Man)*, and eleven previously unpublished poems. As a cross-section of Cohen's work, the 400-page volume covered every period chronologically, and provided an ideal introduction for a younger generation of fans who had only cottoned on to Leonard Cohen in later years via his recent successes. This was reflected in the anthology's reviews, with the *Ottawa Citizen* describing *Stranger Music* as 'a godsend for Cohen fans . . . A remarkable body of work that takes us back to the earliest days'.

Indeed, the book sold so well that inevitably the old question resurfaced as to why Cohen had chosen to pursue a career in songwriting rather than poetry. Talking in 1994, Cohen acknowledged that it had largely been a financial decision: 'There was the economic pressure, I couldn't just live off literature. In retrospection, it seems madness that I believed I could go to Nashville and become a studio musician or a compositor in order to pay the bills and continue writing. It was not what happened.'

As the influential *Publishers Weekly* would point out, the essential immediacy of Leonard's song lyrics was a double-edged sword, with his words not always having the same power on the printed page: 'In reading through this generous selection, one often hears the ghost of musical accompaniment, and sometimes its actual presence is missed. The writing alone, forthright in its rhythms, plain of speech, often rhymed, and almost immediately accessible, seems well suited to the ears of a live audience.'

When Bob Dylan was awarded the Nobel Prize for Literature in 2016, it highlighted once again the distinction between poet and songwriter. The vast

'If I had been given this attention when I was 26, it would have turned my head. At 36 it might have confirmed my flight on a rather morbid spiritual path. At 46 it would have rubbed my nose in my failing powers and have prompted a plotting of a getaway and an alibi. But at 56 – hell, I'm just hitting my stride and it doesn't hurt at all'

majority of Dylan's lyrical output had been presented in a musical context, yet the words were often potent enough to qualify as significant in themselves. With Cohen's songs, the music may have aided and abetted the impact of lyrics, but in many instances the writing works equally effectively on its own.

With or without music, Cohen was a masterful poet, and in *Stranger Music* he would prove this to his audience yet again. The anthology was, as the *Toronto Star* would put it: 'A massive record of the poet's imaginative journey, through beauty, through horror, through the extremes of love and despair, from the deepest abyss of self-abnegation to the rare and necessary moments of ecstasy. The language ranges from the exquisitely beautiful to the darkly obscene, from the romantically inspired to the ironically banal . . . A poetic record like no other.'

Honours List

In 1992, the year before the publication of *Stranger Music*, Leonard had been awarded an honorary degree by his old Montreal seat of learning, McGill University. Although it may have seemed exceptional for an ex-student who was now something of a rock 'n' roll star to be granted such prestigious recognition, it was just one of several honours bestowed on Cohen in the early 1990s.

The previous year, he had been made an Officer of the Order of Canada, inducted into the Canadian Music Hall of Fame and then nominated by the same body for the Juno Award for Songwriter of the Year. In his acceptance speech for the Hall of Fame honour, he drew attention to the timing in terms of his own career: 'If I had been given this attention when I was twenty-six, it would have turned my head. At thirty-six it might have confirmed my flight on a rather morbid spiritual path. At forty-six it would have rubbed my nose in my failing powers and have prompted a plotting of a getaway and an alibi. But at fifty-six – hell, I'm just hitting my stride and it doesn't hurt at all.'

Following the success of his 1992 album *The Future*, Cohen won the Juno Award for Male Vocalist of the Year in 1993, with the music video for the song 'Closing Time', directed by Curtis Wehrfritz, winning the Juno Award for Best Video. He was also nominated for the Juno Award as Producer of the Year (with co-producer Leanne Ungar), for 'Closing Time'.

May 1993, at the Concertgebouw, in the Hague, Netherlands, as part of his tour promoting The Future.

But the most prestigious accolade came at the end of 1993, when he won the Governor General's Performing Arts Award for Lifetime Artistic Achievement. Back in 1968 he had already turned down the Governor General's Award for Literary Merit. *The Globe and Mail* memorably reported that Cohen had declined the award on the grounds that 'the world is a callous place and he would take no gift from it'. Cohen was also claimed to have written in a telegram: 'Much in me strives for this honour, but the poems themselves forbid it absolutely.' In a much later interview with the *LA Times*, Cohen was said to have acknowledged that 'he was just being a smart-ass', and that his reasons for rejecting the award were 'no more clear to him now than it was then'. His acceptance

Performing at the Paramount Theater, New York City, June 14, 1993, on the next leg of his The Future *tour.*

in person at the ceremony in Ottawa's Rideau Hall may therefore have been an indication of a more secure Cohen, both personally and professionally. At the event, his backing singers Perla Batalla and Julie Christensen sang 'Anthem' with a full orchestra and gospel choir, and Leonard accepted the honour with characteristic modesty, saying much of what he was being decorated for was probably 'just in the line of duty'.

While his record company, in the absence of any forthcoming studio material, decided to put out a live album from his two previous tours, 1994 saw Leonard being feted with yet more appreciations, this time winning the Juno Songwriter of the Year Award. Juno nominations that year were also on the cards for *The Future* as Album of the Year, and Curtis Wehrfritz's video for 'The Future' title track as Video of the Year.

> 'I never had any musical standard to tyrannise me. If you told the story, that's what the song was about.'

Cohen Live

Released on 28 June 1994, *Cohen Live* featured eight songs from the 1993 *The Future* tour, and five from the 1988 tour promoting *I'm Your Man*. While many fans were delighted with the surprisingly high quality of the sound, given the track record of live albums in general, it met with a mixed reception from the critics. Obsessive Cohen collectors, of course, were treated to the fact that several of the songs had different lyrics to the originals, which were printed on the liner notes as sung.

Many reviewers felt it was not much better than a 'Greatest Hits' collection, though they did concede that Cohen's voice benefitted from the lower pitch he had developed since making most of the originals of the songs featured. While *Time* magazine dismissed it with the bleak recommendation that 'this glum, melancholy collection should be dispensed only with large doses of Prozac', others recognized that the live backing singers and carefully orchestrated instrumental arrangements enhanced, rather than devalued, some of the tried and tested classics. Although regretting 'the absence of the droll between-songs patter which framed these songs in live performance', *Mojo,* for instance, called it 'a decent enough summation of the singer's mature style'.

The main attraction of the recording to most committed fans was hearing Cohen's songs in a different setting than the studio version, with the strength of the musicianship from the live band enhancing his delivery of familiar material. On songs like 'Bird on the Wire' and 'Sisters of Mercy' the tempo is more restrained, the instrumental accompaniment more intense, and the backing vocals simply sexier. From the short keyboard intro preluding the vocal riff of the opening 'Dance Me to the End of Love', to the sparsely effective arrangement of 'Suzanne' that closed the album, these alternative (and sometimes lyrically altered) renditions of classics were worthy of any Cohen devotee's attention.

Nevertheless, despite Leonard Cohen's burgeoning popularity in North America since *I'm Your Man* in 1988 and 1992's *The Future*, *Cohen Live* failed abjectly to make the charts in either Canada or the United States. It didn't do remotely as well as his studio albums in continental Europe, although it managed to secure a comfortable position in the UK albums chart at #35.

Leonard Cohen's next releases, which included both live and studio albums, would not be until 2001, another seven years away. A star already famous for his reclusive nature, Cohen would once again withdraw from the public eye over this period. But this time, his seclusion from the outside world would be almost total, as he embraced a philosophy that he had been interested in for decades – Buddhism.

13
FIELD COMMANDER COHEN: TOUR OF 1979

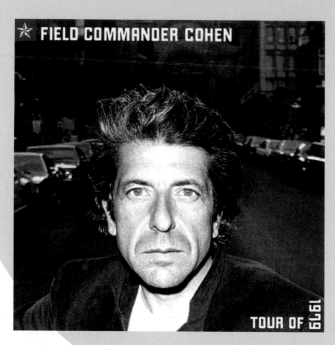

'I wasn't looking for a religion, I already had a perfectly good one. And I certainly wasn't looking for a new series of rituals. But I had a great sense of disorder in my life, of chaos and depression, of distress. And I had no idea where this came from. The prevailing psychoanalytic explanations of the time didn't seem to address the things I felt.'

All songs written by Leonard Cohen, except where indicated.

1. Field Commander Cohen
2. The Window
3. The Smokey Life
4. The Gypsy's Wife
5. Lover Lover Lover
6. Hey, That's No Way to Say Goodbye
7. The Stranger Song
8. The Guests
9. Memories (Cohen, Phil Spector)
10. Why Don't You Try
11. Bird on the Wire
12. So Long Marianne

Personnel: Leonard Cohen (vocals, guitar); Mitch Watkins (guitar); Bill Ginn (keyboards); Paul Ostermayer (saxophone, flute); Roscoe Beck (bass); Steve Meador (drums); Raffi Hakopian (violin); John Bilezikjian (oud, mandolin); Jennifer Warnes (vocals); Sharon Robinson (backing vocals)

Recorded: 4–6 December 1979, Hammersmith Odeon, London; 15 December 1979, Dome Theatre, Brighton
Released: 20 February 2001
Label: Columbia
Producer: Leanne Ungar, Bob Metzger, Sharon Robinson

Cohen in London, January 2001.

After five years of seclusion at the Mount Baldy Zen Centre near Los Angeles, during which time he was ordained as a Buddhist monk, Cohen returned to the city in 1999 and began overseeing the revival of his career. First came the 2001 release of *Field Commander Cohen,* live recordings from his 1979 UK visit, which the singer had referred to as his best tour ever.

Zen

Leonard Cohen was first introduced to Zen Buddhism via his friend Steve Sanfield, as he recalled in an interview in the 1990s: 'Twenty-five years ago, when I was living in Hydra, I made the acquaintance of a friend, Steve Stanfield. He was part of a small group of people who were studying Buddhist texts in a very interesting way. Upon his return to LA, someone told him that his master had moved to the area. He began studying with him and told me about it.' In 1969, Sanfield was married at the Zen Centre on Cimarron Street in Los Angeles, with Leonard acting as best man. Never having experienced an actual Buddhist ritual before, Cohen was intrigued by the gentle ambiance of the ceremony as much as anything else.

During the late 1960s Leonard, along with many of his counter-cultural contemporaries, had dabbled in various esoteric religions and quasi-spiritual beliefs. He had been a frequent visitor to the Church of Scientology for a time, before that particular cult failed to live up to its promise, and the idea of Zen Buddhism was not completely unfamiliar or new to him.

Zen had actually been a preoccupation of that previous counterculture, the Beat Generation movement of the 1950s, when writers including Jack Kerouac, Allen Ginsberg and Gary Snyder embraced it enthusiastically. Snyder in particular immersed himself in Zen, his meditative retreat in the California mountains serving as inspiration for Kerouac's book *The Dharma Bums*. Eventually Snyder travelled to Kyoto, Japan, to study Zen, where he led the life of a monk.

At the Sanfield wedding, Cohen met the founder of the Cimarron Street Centre, Kyozan Joshu Sasaki Roshi, a Zen master of the traditional Rinzai school. The pair exchanged few words that day, but Roshi (meaning 'venerable teacher') would become a huge influence in Leonard's life in years to come.

The next time Cohen encountered Roshi was not long after the birth of his son Adam, in the September of 1972. Although the joy of a child should have brought them closer together, Leonard and Suzanne were going through a difficult phase, and he felt the need to escape, although to where or what he had no idea. Cohen since admitted that this had been something of a recurring issue with him over the years:

'I was always escaping; a large part of my life was escaping. Whatever it was, even if the situation looked good, I had to escape, because it didn't look good to me. So it was a selfish life, but it didn't seem so at the time, it seemed a matter of survival. I had to continuingly escape from the situation I was in, because it didn't feel good, so I guess kids and other people close to me suffered because I was always leaving. Not for very long, but I was always trying to get away.'

In this instance, though, he saw a potential way out: Roshi. He had been thinking about the Zen teacher for a while, and one day picked up the phone to Sanfield and asked him to take him to his mentor. Sanfield obliged, and Leonard and Roshi had tea together at the LA Zen Centre, after which the master suggested to Cohen he should visit the Zen monastery at Mount Baldy, forty miles east of Los Angeles in the San Gabriel Mountains.

The Zen Centre at Mount Baldy looked little like a monastery. In fact, it had once been a campsite for Boy Scouts, a collection of crude wooden huts that now served as sleeping accommodation, dining hall and meditation centre. When Leonard drove up there with Sanfield, it was winter and snow was on the ground. It seemed more like a *Stalag* prisoner of war camp from a movie, grim and uninviting, than it did a monastery. Meditation started at three in the morning – the austere rigours of this particular school of Zen were apparent from the start – and Leonard managed to survive his induction for just a week.

Over the next few years, however, Cohen became a frequent visitor to both the LA Zen Centre and the Mount Baldy retreat, forging a bond with Roshi that would last until the master's death in 2014, aged 107. The two would talk for hours, drink sake together (despite his Buddhist vows, Roshi was no teetotaller), and Leonard often drove the Zen master between his two bases.

After Suzanne had finally left him, and moved to southern France with the children, Cohen immersed himself more and more in the Zen lifestyle. He would attend the LA Centre to meditate every day, spend much of his spare time at the monastery, and even became a contributor to a new Buddhist magazine, *Zero*, which Roshi had founded in 1977.

'Religion is my favourite hobby. It's deep and voluptuous. Nothing is comparable to the delight you get from this activity. Apart, obviously, from courting,' he would reflect.

Retreat

It was after the release of *Cohen Live* in June 1994 that Leonard fully committed himself to the way of Zen, when, that September, he upped sticks and made a permanent move to the Mount Baldy retreat. There were several underlying reasons behind this decision. His latest tour, to promote *The Future*, had been perhaps the most physically and mentally exhausting of his career. Cohen had never been able to take his concerts casually, as he himself acknowledged, but on this occasion, due in part to a more intensive touring schedule than usual – his recent successes in America had sent his once indifferent US label into overdrive – he was more stressed than ever. Often, he would finish three or four bottles of wine before performing.

'Religion is my favourite hobby. It's deep and voluptuous. Nothing is comparable to the delight you get from this activity. Apart, obviously, from courting'

Linked closely to this was the end of Cohen's relationship with Rebecca De Mornay. By the time the tour had ended, so had their engagement. Later, Cohen would admit the role he had played in the split. 'She kind of got wise to me. Finally, she saw I was a guy who just couldn't come across, in the sense of being a husband and having children and all the rest.'

With Rebecca no longer a part of his life, and having taken his leave of the music business (shortly before leaving for Mount Baldy, he told his former musical director Roscoe Beck 'I've had it with this music racket'), Leonard had nothing to tie him to LA. What he did have was the motivation to leave for the monastery and that motivation was love – not of a woman, or even of Buddhism, but of his old mentor Roshi.

'Something like this you can only do for love. If Roshi had been a professor of physics at Heidelberg University, I would have learned German and gone to Heidelberg to study physics', he would later explain. 'My old teacher was getting older and I hadn't spent enough time with him, and my kids were grown and I thought it was an appropriate moment to intensify my friendship and my association with the community.'

Yet although by that time he was very familiar with the Centre, having been a regular visitor for over twenty years, at sixty years of age, Cohen was still physically unprepared for the harsh discipline of the Rinzai monastic lifestyle.

Both silent and chanted meditation was the order of the day, from dawn to dusk, plus the various work duties the novices were obliged to fulfil; and with no radio or television, they were genuinely cut off from the outside world. Leonard's main duties were working with Roshi as his personal assistant.

Between acting as chauffeur and cook to Roshi, Leonard still had to observe the rigours of the monastery discipline. This included *sesshins,* the week-long stretches of concentrated study in which the participants were roused at 3am to file across to the dining room for a fifteen-minute tea ceremony before meditation began in earnest.

Sitting on wooden benches, an hour of chanting preceded the first session of *zazen*, of which there were six, with the residents sitting cross-legged in the full lotus position for an hour, monks with wooden sticks ready to prod them should they relax mid-trance. Then came outdoor meditation, which entailed trudging up the mountain in all weathers, before individual *sanzen* instructional sessions with Roshi himself.

The various rituals were repeated throughout a typical day, sometimes until as late as 11pm. And when there were no *sesshins*, manual work and private study was the main order of activity.

The dramatic shift in Cohen's lifestyle, from the height of his musical and commercial success to this most spartan of existences, was hard for many around him to understand. For an urbane, worldly character like Cohen, it seemed an extreme and possibly self-destructive move, especially from a professional point of view.

Some also questioned how he squared a continued devotion to Judaism with his practice of Zen. 'Allen Ginsberg asked me the same question many years ago', he told a journalist in 2009. 'Well, for one thing, in the tradition of Zen that I've practiced, there is no prayerful worship and there is no affirmation of a deity. So theologically there is no challenge to any Jewish belief.'

On 9 August 1996 Leonard was ordained as a Rinzai Zen Buddhist monk, and took the Dharma name of Jikan, meaning 'silence' or 'Silent One'. His ordination ceremony, at which he appeared in full robes and with his head shaved, was attended by his sister Esther and his old friend Steve Sanfield, who had introduced him to the Zen Centre, and Sasaki Roshi, in the first place.

A unique glimpse of Cohen's life in the retreat came in 1997 with the TV documentary *Leonard Cohen: Spring 1996*. Made by the French director Armelle Brusq, it showed Leonard meditating, working in the monastery kitchen, and also featured Roshi as Cohen carried out his duties of assisting him.

Tower of Song

Although to the outsider the Mount Baldy retreat may have had the image of a strict but ultimately benign penal institution, the monks and novices were free to move as they pleased. Leonard's day-to-day presence there was entirely voluntary. As he pointed out more than once, there was no binding agreement – unlike a record contract, or indeed a marriage certificate. And despite his seclusion, which by the fall of 1995 could be counted by the year rather than in months, he did make occasional forays into the outside world.

One such furlough from the monastic life involved a new project dreamed up by his manager, Kelley Lynch (who had taken over the role after the death of Marty Machat back in 1988). With no new album forthcoming, and Leonard showing no inclination to make one, Lynch had come up with the idea of a high-profile tribute album.

Unlike the 1991 tribute release, *I'm Your Fan*, which was basically promulgated by a grass-roots enthusiast (the French rock magazine editor Christian Fevret)

Leonard with his daughter, Lorca, shortly before leaving for the Mount Baldy retreat, May 1991.

and featured cutting-edge 'indie' artists, Lynch's proposal was for a mainstream-appealing set performed by household names. To facilitate the best possible choice of participants, Lynch persuaded Leonard to take a short break from the monastery to help contact some of the artists she hoped to involve.

Recorded in the late summer of 1995, the collection included an array of world-class names including Elton John (singing 'I'm Your Man'), Sting ('Sisters of Mercy'), Bono ('Hallelujah'), Trisha Yearwood ('Coming Back to You'), Tori Amos ('Famous Blue Raincoat') and Willie Nelson with an emotive version of 'Bird on the Wire'.

Tower of Song (taking its name from Cohen's song on *I'm Your Man*, which didn't end up covered on the album) was released in October 1995 to a mixed reception, with one critic describing Elton John's 'I'm Your Man' as a 'karaoke version'. Leonard himself, however, was delighted with the whole enterprise: 'I'm completely knocked out by the project . . . I'd be knocked out by even a much lesser display of enthusiasm for my work, but this happens to be singers of stellar quality. I was very interested

'I was always escaping; a large part of my life was escaping. Whatever it was, even if the situation looked good, I had to escape, because it didn't look good to me. So it was a selfish life, but it didn't seem so at the time, it seemed a matter of survival.'

to hear the various approaches, and I'm very touched by them . . .'

'Except for being written', he told the *New Musical Express*, 'this is the best thing that has happened to these songs. And I am deeply grateful to these eminent artists, who so easily could have done without this project, for their kindness and solidarity.'

But, as he would point out, he didn't get involved in the actual recording of the songs: 'I don't think it's my place, and I don't have any motivation personally to monkey around with that side of things.'

More Best Of…

1997 marked thirty years since Leonard Cohen had signed to Columbia, and so the label, having had no word from him regarding any plans for a new album, decided to commemorate the occasion with a new 'Best Of…' release. The previous *Best Of Leonard Cohen* (or *Greatest Hits*, as it was titled in Europe) had been back in 1975, and although Cohen felt no real need to repeat the exercise, he agreed to take some

time out from his monastic duties to help put it together.

As a sequel to the first collection, the choice of tracks was drawn from Leonard's two most recent studio albums, *I'm Your Man* (1988), and *The Future* (1992), plus three tracks from the 1994 on-tour album, *Cohen Live*. Initially, Cohen had chosen enough material for a double album, but the record company decided to keep it as a single release, adding that it would help sales if there were at least a couple of previously unreleased tracks included.

To that end, Leonard came up with 'Never Any Good', a lively tongue-in-cheek number he'd recorded in Los Angeles for an unfinished album in 1995, in which he gently subverts his own reputation as a ladies' man, comparing himself to a tourist, being able to love and be loved only fleetingly, if at all. With a soul-band horn section, the swinging backing was more akin to the goodtime rhythms of a Texas dancehall than Leonard's typically self-effacing lyrics. The other new item was 'The Great Event'. Running just over a minute, this experimental track featured an electronically synthesised rendition of Leonard's actual voice, sounding eerily female.

Like many a 'greatest hits' compilation, *More Best of Leonard Cohen* sold modestly, not breaking into the charts. The selection of songs, all from relatively recent albums, was probably too 'fresh' for many seasoned fans – except in Poland, it seems, where it hit #4 in the weekly album chart, selling more than 100,000 copies over the next few months.

Moving On

In January 1999, Leonard Cohen decided it was time to make his break with the monastic regime on Mount Baldy. Through the latter part of 1998 he had become increasingly ill at ease with his presence there – not out of any disillusion with Zen philosophy, and certainly with no disrespect to Joshu Sasaki Roshi, his venerable teacher. But he knew it was time to move on.

Initially Leonard had turned his mind to the teachings of a Hindu guru, Ramesh S. Balsekar, whose work he first read while at Mount Baldy. Balsekar was a follower of the Advaita branch of Hindu philosophy, which believed in spiritual liberation through knowledge, with an emphasis on liberating one's soul in this life rather than in a later, after death, existence. Balsekar was definitely a man of this world in comparison to most gurus, with a lifestyle in stark contrast to the strict austerity of the Zen monks. He had studied at the London School of Economics as a young man, and was General Manager of the Bank of India in Bombay (Mumbai) for a decade until his retirement in 1977.

So instead of moving back to Los Angeles and the music business, when Leonard exited the Zen Centre it was to fly to Mumbai in India to sit at the feet of Ramesh in person. He visited the guru every day before returning to LA in the spring, when he would pay a visit to Roshi again. The two doctrines of Buddhism and Hinduism were compatible as far as Leonard was concerned, with his eclectic attitude to religion which also allowed him to continue practicing his Judaism throughout his life. 'I wasn't looking for a religion', he explained in a 2008 interview. 'I already had a perfectly good one. And I certainly wasn't looking for a new series of rituals. But I had a great sense of disorder in my life, of chaos and depression, of distress. And I had no idea where this came from. The prevailing psychoanalytic explanations of the time didn't seem to address the things I felt.' Drawing on strands of thought from a variety of philosophies and religions seemed to go some way in addressing these problems for Cohen.

Another trip to Mumbai ensued later in the year, after which Leonard felt ready to throw himself back into the music milieu full time. He had hooked up with singer-songwriter and producer Sharon Robinson once again, and through the opening year of the new millennium the pair would dedicate themselves to the first Leonard Cohen studio project in almost a decade.

Field Commander

While Leonard and Sharon were working on the new album, studio engineer Leanne Ungar had also trawled through the tapes that Henry Lewy had made of some of the UK dates on the 1979 *Recent Songs* tour. The result, released in February 2001, was *Field Commander Cohen: Tour of 1979*, a live album that presented Leonard Cohen as a concert performer in the best possible light.

The live recordings were culled from four performances in December 1979, three at the Hammersmith Odeon in London, and one from the Dome Theatre in Brighton.

Instrumentally, the band – Passenger from Austin, Texas, plus Raffi Hakopian on violin and John Bilezikjian on oud – were nothing short of sensational. Leonard was in fine voice compared to his previous live album *Live Songs* (1973), and the backing vocals of Jennifer Warnes and Sharon Robinson were what one review called 'especially rich icing on the cake'.

Cohen rated the tour itself as his best ever, and it showed through on every track of the album. *Rolling Stone* called the album 'elaborately, and yet simply, awesome', while AllMusic described it as possessing 'a passionate, aching beauty that's a wonder to behold'.

As evident in previous live albums, Leonard's interpretations of familiar songs varied from tour to tour, and indeed from night to night. This made *Field Commander Cohen* an album full of the surprise and warmth that concert audiences had come to expect when Cohen took to the road. For the legions of fans starved of new releases over the previous few years it was a welcome treat, especially in anticipation of his brand-new studio album, which would arrive in the record stores later in 2001.

14
TEN NEW SONGS

'…You could say that God is speaking to you – or the cosmos, or your lover. It just means, like, forget it. Lean back and be loved by all that is already loving you. It is your effort at love that is preventing you from experiencing it'

All songs written by Leonard Cohen and Sharon Robinson, except where indicated.

1. In My Secret Life
2. A Thousand Kisses Deep
3. That Don't Make It Junk
4. Here It Is
5. Love Itself
6. By the Rivers Dark
7. Alexandra Leaving (based on the poem 'The God Abandons Antony' by Constantine P. Cavafy)
8. You Have Loved Enough
9. Boogie Street
10. The Land of Plenty

Personnel: Leonard Cohen (vocals); Sharon Robinson (vocals, programming, arrangements); Bob Metzger (guitar); David Campbell (string arrangement)

Recorded: Late-1999 – mid-2001, Still Life Studios, Los Angeles; Small Mercies Studio, Los Angeles
Released: 9 October 2001
Label: Columbia
Producer: Sharon Robinson

Cohen in London, 2001.

At home in Los Angeles, August 2001.

After two years of production, 2001 saw the release of *Ten New Songs*, Cohen's collaboration with the singer, songwriter and record producer Sharon Robinson. Robinson had worked as a backing singer for Cohen since the late 1970s and had co-written several of his songs, including 'Everybody Knows' and 'Waiting for the Miracle'.

But Robinson wasn't the only woman in Cohen's life after he 'came down the mountain' from his long seclusion. He had met up again with Anjani Thomas, the Hawaiian-born singer who had been part of the backing team on 1984's *Various Positions* and the subsequent tour, as well as the following albums *I'm Your Man* and *The Future*. Like Leonard, she had been through a failed marriage, sought solace in meditation (in her case following the Maharishi Mahesh Yogi, who had been guru to the Beatles and other rock stars), and ended up alone in LA.

She first renewed her friendship with Cohen shortly after his return from Mount Baldy, played him some songs she had been working on and, before long, the two had struck up a relationship as both lovers and part-time musical collaborators. Anjani had a home in LA, just a short distance from Leonard's duplex – where he now lived with his daughter Lorca – and the couple largely enjoyed autonomous lives, never actually moving in together. 'I like to wake up alone', explained Leonard, 'and she likes to be alone.' Those close to Cohen couldn't help but notice how well this arrangement seemed to suit him. 'I think he had found a kind of inner domestic peace', said Leonard's long-time collaborator, Leanne Ungar, who worked with him again on *Ten New Songs*.

But it was Cohen's renewed partnership with Sharon Robinson that would prove invaluable in the new album's creation, after he had asked her if she would help him out with some of the two hundred-odd songs and poems he had been nurturing since his time at the monastery.

The Cohen Files

Leonard Cohen's output of poems and song lyrics were not all 'under wraps' when he returned from his self-imposed exile, however. From the late 1990s he had been contributing material to the Leonard Cohen Files, a website created by two Finnish fans in 1995. As soon as he discovered the site, while still at Mount Baldy, Leonard began sending new poems and drawings (many of which would end up in his 2006 collection *Book of Longing*), as well as early versions of new songs such as 'A Thousand Kisses Deep'. He continued to contribute to the site throughout the rest of his career, with a section of his online writings, entitled 'The Blackening Pages'.

Still Life and Small Mercies

It was after attending a classical music concert given by Sharon Robinson's son – to whom Leonard was godfather – that he suggested to his ex-backing singer that she work on some new material with him. Rather than struggling with melodies and song structures, as he did more often than not, he began feeding Robinson with lyrics, to which she would create the music.

It was no automatic process, however – unlike the traditional 'words by X and music by Y' relationship of many songwriting partnerships – but a flowing, creative exercise on both their parts. They went through the material bit by bit, Robinson embellishing lyrics with music, Cohen adding the vocals, Robinson remixing the result . . . and so on.

The music was produced electronically, on various computer programmes. In fact, it was Cohen's first album to be recorded entirely digitally, and the first without recourse to a commercial studio in the whole operation. It was quite literally a tale of two studios, and both of them home set-ups. Sharon had converted the three-car garage adjacent to her house into a dedicated recording space, which she called Still Life Studios; Leonard, with help from Sharon and recording engineer Leanne Ungar, had set up his 'Small Mercies' studio in a room above the garage of his duplex.

> 'Canadians are very involved in their country. You know we grow up on the edge of America. We watch America the way that women watch men. You know, very, very carefully. So when there is this continual cultural and political challenge right on the edge of your lives, of course it develops a sense of solidarity.'

Much of the initial preparation for songs came in the form of casual domestic jam sessions, where Cohen would play Robinson an idea, or just recite a lyric. Having an experienced feel for Leonard's vocal style, she would then develop something that seemed appropriate at her own studio, before taking the raw audio on a portable hard drive to Leonard's studio above his garage. There she would give it to Leanne, who transferred the melodies to Leonard's computer so he could add the vocals. Nothing was forced, there was no studio time involved, and no other musicians were present. It was as near to an 'organic' recording process that one could imagine.

Robinson would later explain the collaborative nature of their partnership: 'It took us two years to make that album. Leonard would give me verses that he'd written, for the most part, while he was at Mount Baldy. And I tried to immerse myself in the meaning of the words, so the music would always serve those words. The process is really collaborative. Both of us prefer to do the dirty work in solitude. Then, when we're happy with that, we present it to the other person. He either comes over to my house or I go to where he lives. I usually try to make a rough demo of my idea, in his key, so he can relate to it and he will be able to start singing along if he wants. Then I'll bring that demo to Leonard and play it for him.'

Leonard's manager Kelley Lynch followed the gestation of the new album on an almost day-to-day basis, ever mindful that you couldn't hurry Cohen, as she would explain to a Canadian newspaper in September 2000: 'Right now, he's hard at work on the new one. To tell you the truth, I can't even be sure it will be a 2001 release. You really can't tell with Leonard. He doesn't like deadlines. We're keeping it loose. A number of songs are in various stages of completion; several others – 'My Secret Life', 'Here It Is', 'A Thousand Kisses Deep' – are finished'.

The emerging album, which would be called *Ten New Songs*, was a genuine collaboration in the best sense of the word. Sharon Robinson produced, co-wrote, and co-arranged the recordings as well as singing (and not just backing vocals) on all the tracks. After she had made some demos of the lyrics that Leonard had passed to her, he was so impressed that he insisted Sharon sang duet with him on every track, in some cases taking the lead.

'I would initially sing and play everything, at the time not knowing if we were bringing in other musicians or singers', Robinson would tell Cohen biographer Anthony Reynolds. 'Of course, as it turned out, we didn't, so my voice stayed because Leonard liked what he was hearing'.

The Album

The opening ballad of unrequited love 'In My Secret Life' featured the added contribution of Leanne Ungar's guitarist husband Bob Metzger, and became the first single to be released from the album. A foretaste of the general texture of the album, the raw chill of Cohen's confessional is relieved by the sheer warmth of Robinson's backing vocals. The desolate poetry of 'A Thousand Kisses Deep', with its added string arrangement by David Campbell, dated back to an unfinished collection of songs from the mid-1990s and had first appeared on the Leonard Cohen Files website. There it was set in its original form as a poem, titled 'For

Onstage with Ten New Songs *co-writer and producer Sharon Robinson.*

Those Who Greeted Me'. With some verses re-ordered and others deleted, the song addressed the limits of our desires and ambitions, and how life is not what we intend it to be.

The gently melodic 'That Don't Make It Junk' and the bluesy 'Boogie Street' (with a lead vocal intro by Sharon Robinson) both hinted at an earthy, modern R&B sound, the latter song based on an actual thoroughfare in a red light district of Singapore. 'Here It Is' is another Cohen 'list' song, a catalogue of catharsis, with the potential gloom again lifted by a hypnotic, insistent rhythm. The prevalent device, from a man increasingly conscious of his own ageing and sense of mortality, was to address himself, but in the second person. Even the religious analogies functioned as a plea to the everyman, and through that, to himself.

With a walking bass line reminiscent of an early-Sixties pop song, 'Love Itself' personifies love as an independent entity, which can come and go despite what one wishes. And as with all his albums, Cohen never forgot his biblical Jewish heritage, the stark bleakness of 'By The Rivers Dark' recalling the destruction of the Temple and exile of the Jews.

One song, 'Alexandra Leaving' was not completely original, but an adaptation of a poem – 'The God Abandons Antony', by the Greek poet Constantine P. Cavafy, first published in 1911. In the original, Antony was Mark Antony, the Roman lover of Cleopatra. Antony and his army were besieged in the Egyptian city of Alexandria, and the poem was an emotional farewell to the city, with Antony's protector, the god Dionysus, deserting him. Cohen anthropomorphised Alexandria as a woman called Alexandra, and the song became a ballad of lost love.

In a promotional video for *Ten New Songs*, Leonard offered his own thoughts on 'You Have Loved Enough'. 'You could say that God is speaking to you – or the cosmos, or your lover. It just means, like, forget it. Lean back and be loved by all that is already loving you. It is

your effort at love that is preventing you from experiencing it.'

Closing the album, 'The Land of Plenty' reaffirmed Leonard Cohen's somewhat ambiguous attitude to religion, embracing elements of various faiths while giving unqualified adherence to none.

Despite not doing well sales-wise in the United States, where it only peaked at #143 in the *Billboard* chart, *Ten New Songs* scored well elsewhere. It made the Top 30 at #26 in the UK, climbed to #4 in Canada, #3 in Belgium, Sweden and France, and topped the chart in Denmark, Norway and Poland. The album, which Leonard had dedicated to Roshi, also won four Canadian Juno Awards in 2002: Best Artist, Best Songwriter, Best Pop Album, and Best Video (for 'In My Secret Life', shot by Floria Sigismondi).

The critics, for once, were more enthusiastic about the album than record-buyers in the United States. The *Rolling Stone* review declared that '*Ten New Songs* manages to sustain loss's fragile beauty like never before and might just be the Cohen's most exquisite ode yet to the midnight hour', while *Playboy* concluded: 'He'll never be cheerful, but a Zen-like serenity pervades every song'. And in the UK, *Uncut* magazine – among several others – agreed it was 'worth the wait'.

The Essential

As a result of Cohen's gradual mainstream acceptance and rising in popular support worldwide, in 2002, Columbia decided to put together a comprehensive double-album compilation. Entitled *The Essential Leonard Cohen*, thirty-one chronologically arranged tracks were drawn from all of Cohen's previous albums, with the exception of the Phil Spector-produced *Death of a Ladies' Man*.

The career-spanning collection, which ran to a generous 157 minutes across two CDs, was chosen by Leonard himself, and digitally re-mastered by Cohen and top mastering

'I didn't want to write for pay. I wanted to be paid for what I write.'

engineer Bob Ludwig. All the usual classics that fans would expect were there – 'Suzanne', 'Sisters of Mercy', 'So Long Marianne', 'Bird on the Wire', 'Famous Blue Raincoat', 'Hallelujah', 'Dance Me to the End of Love' – although some reviewers felt the selection was a little top-heavy in favour of his more recent releases from the late-1980s onwards.

However, in spite of this minor quibble, the general consensus was, as *Popmatters* concluded: 'For first-time listeners, this is the absolute best place to start their love affair with Cohen's music; almost every album is represented, and newcomers can decide which full album they'll move onto next.' And *Rolling Stone* was equally effusive in its praise, beginning its review of the album: 'The dark, poetic music of Leonard Cohen should be listed on the table of periodic elements – when you discover it, it suddenly seems as necessary as oxygen.'

Honours and Tributes

Released on 22 October 2002, a year after the critically lauded *Ten New Songs*, *The Essential Leonard Cohen* signaled that, as far as the music world was concerned, Cohen was back, with a double album retrospective to prove it. But more accolades were still to come.

On 17 January 2003 it was announced that Leonard Cohen was to receive Canada's highest civilian honour, being made a Companion of the Order of Canada. He was formally presented with the decoration later in the year, on 24 October, when it was bestowed upon him by the Governor-General, Adrienne Clarkson.

And as part of its Canada Day celebrations, scheduled to take place in the summer of 2003, the Canadian Consulate in New York commissioned a tribute concert to Leonard, to be held in Prospect Park in Brooklyn. The man they hired to organise the show was the promoter Hal Willner, who was long experienced in staging spectacular – and usually highly prestigious – events of this kind.

Willner first cleared the idea with the Cohen management, who said Leonard had no problem with the idea as long as he wasn't expected to take part in any way. So, with a little unofficial help from Cohen with his personal contacts, Willner set about putting together the concert.

First off, on the recommendation of Leonard's back-up singer Julie Christensen, he hired her and Perla Batalla to perform the same duty for the participants of the tribute. Willner took full artistic control, in as much as he not only chose those taking part, but decided what they should sing.

It was an impressive line-up that took the stage on 28 June 2003. The theme of the concert, apart from being a tribute to Leonard Cohen, was 'Celebrate Canada', with a giant maple leaf flag forming a backdrop as the performers made their contributions. The line-up included Rufus and Martha Wainwright, their mother Kate McGarrigle with her sister Anna, Laura Anderson, Nick Cave, Linda Thompson, and the Handsome Family.

The show, titled *Came So Far For Beauty: An Evening Of Songs By Leonard Cohen Under The Stars* was a resounding success, leading a reviewer for the Leonard Cohen Files website to suggest it should be repeated elsewhere: 'Here's hoping that Mr Willner doesn't lose his religion, and that this truly remarkable evening can be approximated again. Thousands more deserve to be transported to the skies as were we lucky ones in Brooklyn Saturday night.' And it would be: over the years, *Came So Far For Beauty* concerts have been staged by Hal Willner at various one-off locations, including Sydney, Australia, the Irish capital Dublin, and Brighton, England.

15

DEAR HEATHER

Personnel: Leonard Cohen (vocals, guitar, Jew's harp); Sharon Robinson (vocals, arrangements); Anjani Thomas (vocals, backing vocals, piano); Bob Sheppard (tenor saxophone); Sarah Kramer (trumpet); Mitch Watkins (guitar); Garth Hudson (accordion); Bill Ginn (piano); Raffi Hakopian (violin); John Bilezikjian (oud); Ron Getman (steel guitar); Stan Sargent (bass); Roscoe Beck (bass); John Crowder (bass) Johnny Friday (drums); Richard Crooks (drums)

Recorded: April-May 1979 A&M Studios, Los Angeles; 9 July 1985, Montreux Jazz Festival, Switzerland; 6 May 1999, 2002–2004, Small Mercies Studio, Los Angeles
Released: 26 October 2004
Label: Columbia
Producer: Leanne Ungar, Sharon Robinson, Anjani Thomas, Ed Sanders, Henry Lewy, Leonard Cohen

All songs written by Leonard Cohen, except where indicated.

1. Go No More A-Roving (words by Lord Byron)
2. Because Of
3. The Letters (Cohen, Sharon Robinson)
4. Undertow
5. Morning Glory
6. On That Day (Cohen, Anjani Thomas)
7. Villanelle for Our Time (words by F.R. Scott)
8. There for You (Cohen, Sharon Robinson)
9. Dear Heather
10. Nightingale (Cohen, Anjani Thomas)
11. To a Teacher
12. The Faith (music based on Quebec folk song, 'Un Canadien errant')
13. Tennessee Waltz (Redd Stewart, Pee Wee King, additional verse by Cohen)

'If I knew where the good songs came from, I would go there more often.'

Leonard's induction at the 2006 Canadian Songwriters Hall of Fame Gala, Toronto.

Released just a fortnight after Leonard's seventieth birthday, *Dear Heather* was originally going to be called *Old Ideas*, on account of the diverse sources of the material. However, in the end, not wanting it to sound like a 'greatest hits' package, Leonard instead decided to name it after one of the songs therein.

The Album

As Leonard would later explain, the album represented a scrapbook of ideas, half-finished works and other odds-and-ends from recent years, although the majority of the recordings were actually put together in his home studio from the summer of 2003 through into 2004. Cohen's primary collaborator there was his girlfriend Anjani Thomas, supported by the technical wizardry and creative input of his long-standing sound engineer, Leanne Ungar.

As Leonard had stressed when recording *Ten New Songs* with Sharon Robinson, his creative partnership with Anjani was kept quite separate – by mutual consent – from any romantic liaisons. This wasn't quite as difficult a scenario as it might sound, given that, at the time, they weren't actually living together. And yet their living situation did nothing to detract from Anjani's creative influence on the album, which was almost equal to Cohen's. She was the inspiration for 'Morning Glory', on which Cohen's part sounded like an understated version of his usual voice against Anjani's multi-tracked vocals.

Initially, Cohen had called on Anjani just to sing a harmony part on 'Undertow', but the end result was the harmony becoming the lead. Things went so well at the recording session that Leonard left Thomas and Ungar to it. After some tweaking at Cohen's insistence, the track was finally cut with Anjani's emotive voice delivering a far more restrained, almost hesitant, lead that worked perfectly for the subject matter of a bereaved, isolated woman.

'Nightingale' was a true labour of love for Anjani. She had composed the music around an old, unused poem of Leonard's, and dedicated the track to a late colleague and friend, the recently deceased R&B and Broadway musical singer Carl Anderson.

Three of the tracks had originated at the *Ten New Songs* sessions – 'The Letters' (a Robinson-Cohen duet), 'There for You', and the opener, 'Go No More A-Roving'. The latter track was, in fact, an adaptation of the famous poem 'So, We'll Go No More A-Roving', by Lord Byron. As with much on the album, Cohen's own delivery was closer to poetry recital than actual singing. Fittingly, he chose to dedicate the track to his old friend and mentor, the Canadian modernist poet Irving Layton.

Similarly, 'Villanelle for Our Time' was also linked to one of Leonard's old associates from the Montreal poetry scene, F.R. Scott. The verses, which Cohen delivered as a jazz-influenced recitation, were actually a poem by Scott. It was recorded shortly after Leonard's return from Mount Baldy, on 6 May 1999. 'To a Teacher', with an evocative sax accompaniment

by Bob Sheppard, was another spoken-word track; this time based on Cohen's own poem from his 1961 collection, *The Spice-Box of Earth*. The song was dedicated to A.M. Klein, a Canadian journalist and poet who had been a leading figure in Canadian-Jewish culture, and a significant source of inspiration for Cohen.

The basic music track for 'The Faith' – an old Quebec folk ballad – was an outtake from the 1979 sessions for *Recent Songs* with new lyrics, re-mixed and with new vocals added. The gospel feel of 'On That Day' served to add to the emotion of the lyrics, inspired by the attacks on New York City on 11 September 2001. Running just over two minutes, the song's bleak, minimalistic language bore witness to the enormity of a subject virtually impossible to address comprehensively. And coming in on the second track of the album, 'Because Of' was a recitation of a new poem, which would appear in Cohen's forthcoming *Book of Longing* in 2006.

Closing the album, the final track of a truly eclectic listing was a live take of the old country stand-by, 'Tennessee Waltz'. Recorded in July 1985 at the Montreux Jazz Festival in Switzerland, Leonard had added an even more brooding final verse. The recording was actually taken from a bootlegged radio tape and cleaned up digitally.

Although it was Leonard Cohen's highest charting album in America since 1969's *Songs from a Room*, *Dear Heather* only managed to reach #131 on the *Billboard 200*. Nevertheless, it hit #5 in Canada, and, as usual, did well around Europe – where it made the Top Ten in six countries, including #1 in both Denmark and Poland. Several critics, the *New York Times* included, thought the production sounded 'homemade', but *Rolling Stone* gave it the thumbs-up, calling Cohen 'Canada's hippest seventy-year-old'.

Kelley Lynch

In October 2004, just as *Dear Heather* was going on sale, a bombshell would hit Leonard Cohen; one that would reverberate through his life and career for the next eight years.

'Before the pesky little problem of losing everything I had, I had the feeling I was treading water – kind of between jobs. A bit at loose ends. When the money problem arose, what bothered me most was that I was spending all my time with lawyers, accountants, forensic accountants… I thought, if God wants to bore me to death I guess I have to accept it.'

Since the death of his previous manager Marty Machat in 1988, Leonard's affairs had been in the hands of Kelley Lynch, who had worked as a secretary and assistant to Machat up until his death. From almost the time she took over, Lynch had access to most of Leonard's personal financial details, and there was no reason for him not to trust her implicitly. As his manager, she had power of attorney over his affairs, and was almost like one of the family. The two were even lovers for a short time.

According to Sylvie Simons' 2012 Cohen biography, a boyfriend of one of Lynch's staff approached Leonard's daughter Lorca, suggesting her father should check his bank accounts as soon as possible. This he did, and was stunned to find $75,000 had gone out of his account to pay a credit card bill for Kelley Lynch. Further investigation revealed that similar withdrawals had been made from his various accounts (including money from his retirement accounts and charitable trust funds) over the years, and he was effectively broke.

Leonard was devastated. He discovered that, as early as 1996, when he was in the Mount Baldy retreat, Lynch had started selling the publishing rights to his songs without his permission, although there was no financial reason to do so at the time.

With the help of Anjani's ex-husband, Robert Kory, who was a music business lawyer, Leonard delved deeper into his misappropriated finances, to find that well over $10 million – possibly as much as $13 million – had gone missing. Further compounding the situation was the fact that the IRS (Inland Revenue Service) were chasing him for tax that should have already been paid, and had been neglected by Lynch.

Having fired Kelley Lynch as soon as the truth about his finances had begun to emerge, Leonard now had to consider his next course of action. He was reluctant to take things to court, with all the time, expense and general stress involved, but Lynch – refusing point blank to consider any redress – gave him no option. So, in

October 2005 Cohen sued Lynch, alleging she had embezzled over $5 million from his retirement fund, leaving only $150,000.

The court ruled in Leonard's favour, ordering Lynch to pay him $9.5 million, but her lawyers claimed she was unreachable. At the time, Cohen's lawyer Scott Edelman said of Lynch: 'She's hard to get in touch with . . . we don't know what she's done with the money'. So began a dispute lasting over six years, with Cohen trying to establish some recompense from Lynch, and his former manager responding with a tirade of abusive phone messages, emails and blogs.

At one stage early in the litigation, Cohen discovered that over thirty boxes of diaries, notebooks, sketches and personal documents had been left in Lynch's office, which she had vacated when the court proceedings began. A court order had to be obtained, to allow the local Sheriff's office to visit Lynch and physically take the items back. The police raided Lynch's home, armed and in riot gear, and over two days recovered what was described as a 'treasure trove' of writings, drawings – including Leonard's drawing of a bird that would decorate the cover of *Book of Longing* – and letters from Bob Dylan, Joni Mitchell, Allen Ginsberg and many others.

Eventually, in 2012, fifty-five-year-old Lynch was sentenced to eighteen months in a California prison, and five years probation, for what the judge called a 'long, unrelenting barrage of harassing behaviour'. The jury was told that Lynch had hounded Cohen with literally thousands of long, abusive voicemails and emails, in which she called him, among other things, a 'sick man', and 'common thief', declaring that he 'needed to be taken down and shot'.

Thanking the judge at the LA County Court, Leonard Cohen was predictably gracious in his language: 'I want to thank the court, in the person of your honour, for the cordial, even-handed and elegant manner in which these proceedings have unfolded. It was a privilege and an education to testify in this courtroom'.

Diversions

The wrangles with Kelley Lynch all but monopolised Leonard's attention through 2005, before it became apparent there was going to be no quick-fix solution to the financial nightmare his former manager had plunged him into. Nevertheless, 2006 presented some intriguing diversions for Cohen, while he considered his longer-term professional plans.

The first of these came with his induction into the Canadian Songwriters Hall of Fame. At the ceremony, which took place at the John Bassett Theatre in Toronto's Metro Convention Centre, Leonard received his induction from the former Governor General of Canada, Adrienne Clarkson. Visibly moved, with tears in his eyes and his hand on his heart, he ended a brief acceptance speech with his oft-repeated remark: 'If I knew where the good songs came from, I would go there more often.'

Cohen was honoured at the ceremony with memorable performances of three of his best-loved songs. Country legend Willie Nelson delivered a stunning version of 'Bird on the Wire', Rufus Wainwright sang a unique 'Everybody Knows', and the Canadian singer-songwriter k.d.lang gave an emotionally charged performance of 'Hallelujah' that had many in the audience reduced to tears.

Pictured in New York City, May 2006.

'I think both of us were working at the top of our form. Collaboration is too formal a term to describe the activity, which was an expression of some kind of deep mutuality – some kind of marriage of purpose.'

Blue Alert

Throughout winter and early spring, Cohen was helping put the finishing touches to an album that would bear his name as producer, but not singer. It was *Blue Alert*, the debut release by his girlfriend Anjani Thomas (billing herself simply as Anjani) in a leading capacity – she had, of course, previously appeared in a backing role for Leonard both on record and in concert.

Anjani was an experienced musician, having trained at the Berklee College of Music in Boston, specializing in piano, guitar and voice. She had performed in jazz clubs around New York, before being picked up by producer John Lissauer to sing back-up vocals for Cohen's 1984 album, *Various Positions*. Now it was time, she felt, to strike out on her own musically, and Leonard was eager to give the project his full support.

In the event, the album was a straightforward collaboration, all the songs credited to Thomas for the music, and Cohen for the lyrics. But unlike Cohen's previous collaboration *Ten New Songs*, with Sharon Robinson, it was not a duet album; this was Anjani singing, with Leonard purely acting as co-writer and producer. One of their songwriting collaborations that had appeared on *Dear Heather*, 'Nightingale', was also on *Blue Alert*, but this time with Anjani very much in the vocal driving seat.

Some of the lyrics had been written years ago by Cohen before being discarded. For instance, the lyrics for 'Never Got to Love You' were derived from verses Cohen had rejected when writing 'Closing Time' for 1992's *The Future*. Another such example was the title track; according to Anjani, it was retrieved by Cohen when he was going through old journals and notebooks to donate to the Toronto University archive.

As far as the musical element was concerned, Anjani was firmly in control. This was first and foremost a jazz album, with her piano playing favourably described as being influenced by, among others, Bill Evans and George Shearing.

'I think both of us were working at the top of our form', Cohen would concur. 'Collaboration is too formal a term to describe the activity, which was an expression of some kind of deep mutuality – some kind of marriage of purpose.' On reflection, Anjani too felt that the project brought out a rare spontaneity in Leonard's approach: 'The fact that he wasn't writing for himself gave him tremendous freedom. He was able to come up with things quickly without labouring too much over it.'

Thomas would later acknowledge that Cohen taught her a lot more about singing than merely contributing the material: 'When singing Leonard's lyrics, my aim is to not over-emote or underreport. Sometimes it's tricky because a vocalist's natural inclination is to milk a great song for all its worth. Leonard has taught me to rein it in, sing less and let the story tell itself. It's the greatest bit of advice anyone has given me about my voice.'

Released in May 2006, *Blue Alert* debuted at #16 in *Billboard*'s Top 200 Jazz Albums. In an interview for *The Music Box* in April 2007, Anjani hoped for more collaborations with Cohen in years to come: 'There are boxes and boxes of stuff in Leonard's closet that I haven't even looked at. I'll just have to continue living this deliciously luxurious life, surrounded by brilliant ideas, great art, and wonderful songs to conceive'.

Book of Longing

Virtually simultaneous with the release of *Blue Alert*, May 2006 also saw the publication of Leonard's first new collection of poetry since *Book of Mercy* in 1984.

Most of the material in *Book of Longing* was created at the monastery in Mount Baldy between 1994 and 1999, and featured previously unpublished poems, alongside a number of drawings and prose pieces. There were also a number of earlier works included, written after 1978's *Death of a Lady's Man*, but omitted from *Book of Mercy*, which only featured spiritual pieces and meditations. Additionally, the book included some of the lyrics to songs from Leonard's most recent albums, *Ten New Songs* and *Dear Heather*.

A landmark spin-off from the 230-page *Book of Longing* came in June 2007, when the modern classical composer Philip Glass premiered his work *Book of Longing: Song Cycle Based on the Poetry and Images of Leonard Cohen* in Toronto. In it, Glass had set twenty-three of the book's poems to music, performed by an ensemble of percussion, strings and keyboard, and sung by four vocalists. There were also passages recorded by Leonard himself.

After the first presentation at the Luminato Arts Festival in Toronto, over the next couple of years the production would travel to major cities in North America, Europe, Australia and New Zealand. A double-CD of the piece was released in December 2007, reaching #17 in the American classical music chart.

In the CD liner notes, Glass described how the project had first evolved: 'Leonard and I first began talking about a poetry and music collaboration more than six years ago. We met at that time in Los Angeles, and he had with him a manuscript that became the basis of the collection of poetry now published as the *Book of Longing* . . . On the spot, I proposed an evening-length work of poetry, music, and image based on this work. Leonard liked my idea, and we agreed to begin . . . For me, this work is both a departure from past work and a fulfillment of an artistic dream.'

16

LIVE IN LONDON

'This is a very unlikely occasion for me. It is not a distinction that I coveted or even dared dream about, so I'm reminded of the prophetic statement of Jon Landau in the early Seventies: I have seen the future of rock and roll and it is not Leonard Cohen.'

All songs written by Leonard Cohen, except where indicated.

Disc 1
1. Dance Me to the End of Love
2. The Future
3. Ain't No Cure for Love
4. Bird on the Wire
5. Everybody Knows (Cohen, Sharon Robinson)
6. In My Secret Life (Cohen, Sharon Robinson)
7. Who by Fire
8. Hey, That's No Way to Say Goodbye
9. Anthem
10. Introduction
11. Tower of Song
12. Suzanne
13. The Gypsy's Wife
Disc 2
1. Boogie Street (Cohen, Sharon Robinson)
2. Hallelujah
3. Democracy
4. I'm Your Man
5. Recitation (Cohen, Neil Larsen)
6. Take This Waltz (Cohen, Federico

Garcia Lorca)
7. So Long, Marianne
8. First We Take Manhattan
9. Sisters of Mercy
10. If It Be Your Will
11. Closing Time
12. I Tried to Leave You
13. Whither Thou Goest (Guy Singer)

Personnel: Leonard Cohen (vocals, guitar, keyboard); Sharon Robinson (vocals); Roscoe Beck (bass, backing vocals); Rafael Bernardo Gayol (drums, percussion); Neil Larsen (keyboards, accordion); Javier Mas (banduria, laud, archilaud, 12-string guitar); Bob Metzger (guitar, pedal steel guitar, backing vocals); Dino Soldo (saxophone, clarinet, harmonica, keyboards, backing vocals); Charley Webb (backing vocals, guitar); Hattie Webb (backing vocals, harp)

Recorded: 17 July 2008, O2 Arena, London
Released: 31 March 2009
Label: Columbia
Producer: Steven Berkowitz, Edward Sanders

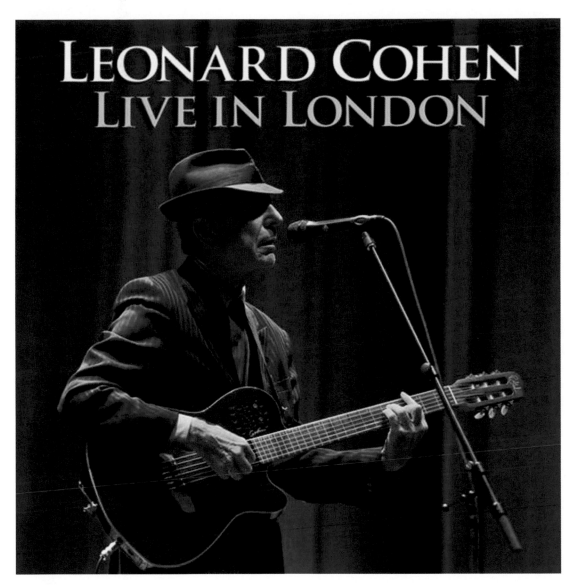

LEONARD COHEN
LIVE IN LONDON

A major incentive in Cohen going back on the road was the financial meltdown that faced him in the aftermath of the Kelley Lynch embezzlement. Appearing on both CD and DVD in 2009, *Live in London* was recorded in July 2008 during a major world tour, and was the first full Leonard Cohen concert to be released in its entirety.

I'm Your Man, The Movie
Following on the heels of *Dear Heather* in 2004, the tribute show *Came So Far For Beauty*

(which had started life back in 2003) became the inspiration for a movie about the life and career of Leonard Cohen entitled *Leonard Cohen: I'm Your Man*. Directed by Lian Lunson, it was based around the version of the tribute that had been staged at the Sydney Opera House in January 2005 involving Nick Cave, Jarvis Cocker, The Handsome Family, Rufus Wainwright, Beth Orton, Martha Wainwright, Linda Thompson, Teddy Thompson, Kate and Anna McGariggle and Cohen's back-up singers, Perla Batalla and Julie Christensen.

The finale of the film also included a

With Anjani Thomas at the LA premiere of the film
Leonard Cohen: I'm Your Man *in 2006.*

performance by Leonard, Anjani Thomas and U2, filmed at the Slipper Room in New York City in May 2005, in which he sang 'Tower of Song' backed by the Irish rock superstars. This performance was later released as the B-side of the U2 single 'Window in the Skies', which went to #1 in the Canadian singles chart.

The movie's live footage was interspersed with a black-and-white filmed interview with Leonard, as he talked through various aspects of his life and work. The film premiered at the Toronto Film Festival in September 2005, followed by a limited release around American art house cinemas. Reviews were generally positive, although it was widely agreed that the live performances were far stronger than the interview footage. As the BBC's David Jones concluded: 'Cohen is clearly a songwriter's songwriter, and the resulting movie brims with an infectious passion for the man's melodies and sardonic wit. Unfortunately, the performances are interspersed with interview footage that is much less captivating.' Nonetheless, the critical consensus was that the film represented 'a winning introduction to the man's work'.

With his own tribute film a success, it was now Cohen's turn to pay homage to the work of others, including some of his most successful contemporaries from the 1960s. In 2007, he recited the lyrics to 'The Sound of Silence', on the album *Tribute to Paul Simon: Take Me to the Mardi Gras*. That same year, he appeared on Herbie Hancock's acclaimed tribute to Joni Mitchell, *River: The Joni Letters*, and performed her song 'The Jungle Line', accompanied by Hancock on piano. Then, in 2008, he contributed a closing dialogue, 'Since You Asked', to the CD collection *Born to the Breed: A Tribute to Judy Collins*.

Blue Alert, The Tour

Early in 2007, Sony – who had acquired Columbia Records in 1988 – decided to re-release Anjani Thomas' album *Blue Alert*, but with the added bonus of a DVD featuring videos of the songs, plus a documentary on the making of the album by Lian Lunson. Although the DVD only initially came with the US and Canadian editions of the release, the company also decided to put together a short tour of European dates for its promotion.

The first three dates, tickets to which were by invite only, were in Warsaw, Oslo and London. Anjani was backed by the trio of Lou Pomanti on keyboard, Rob Piltch on guitar and Scott Alexander on bass. The only other participant was a non-performing one: Leonard himself. Determined that this was to be Anjani's gig, as it was Anjani's album, Cohen restricted his participation to introducing her and then sitting in the audience.

> 'I like the life on the road because it is so regulated and deliberate. Everything funnels down to the concert. You know exactly what to do during the day and you don't have to improvise.'

'I was so happy when she began to put my words to music', he announced at the Warsaw concert. 'So I hope that you will find favor in these songs that we're going to offer you tonight. They are new songs with a new voice, and I'd like to present to you Anjani.' At a London appearance, Anjani invited a reluctant-looking Cohen to join her in a duet, and when the tour hit the 'States, he would turn up occasionally and join her on 'Whither Thou Goest'. As a consequence, as much as he wanted this to be about Anjani, once word got around that Leonard Cohen was likely to make an appearance, the modest *Blue Alert* tour began to sell-out every night.

On the Road Again

With the success of the tribute shows, the spin-off publicity of the *Blue Alert* concerts, the *I'm Your Man* movie, and the worldwide press coverage of his legal battles with Kelley Lynch, Leonard Cohen's profile was certainly higher than would be expected for someone who hadn't released an album for four years.

It was in this context, in the fall of 2007, that he began to think about touring again. As always, he was dubious about the merits of going on the road, especially now, at seventy-three, being well into his biblically prescribed 'threescore years and ten'. But he could see that the financial disaster he was embroiled in wouldn't go away with a legal stroke of the pen, and he needed to earn some big money, fast.

To that end, he hired Robert Kory (Anjani's ex-husband, who had helped him unearth the extent of Lynch's financial mismanagement) to organise things. In January 2008, a world tour was officially announced. In the driving seat for booking the dates was the UK promoter and lifelong Leonard Cohen fan Rob Hallett, who would play an influential role in getting the tour off the ground. 'We discussed the tour and he said, "Well, who wants to see me? What if I'm not good anymore? I haven't picked up a guitar for ten years, it could be a disaster"', Hallett remembered. 'And that was the beginning of our relationship. I said to him, "Look, go in the rehearsal studio, take your time and, if at the end of it, you're not happy with the band or your performance or anything else then all bets are off, it's my bill and I'll see you down the road." Six months later I got a call saying, come down to SIR on Sunset, there was a sofa in front of the stage and Leonard and the band performed for two-and-a-half hours just for me. It was magic.'

But while musicians were being selected, rehearsals honed and concerts booked, yet another honour was laid at Leonard Cohen's feet. 10 March 2008 saw Cohen inducted into the Rock & Roll Hall of Fame. Madonna and John Mellencamp were also inductees that night, but according to *Rolling Stone*, Cohen seemed the most surprised to be there. 'This is a very unlikely occasion for me. It is not a distinction that I coveted or even dared dream about', he was quoted as saying. He then joked, paraphrasing a famous comment about Bruce Springsteen: 'I'm reminded of the prophetic statement of Jon Landau in the early Seventies: I have seen the future of rock and roll and it is *not* Leonard Cohen.'

Cohen's induction was conducted by Lou Reed, who read selections from his lyrics, commenting that 'we are so lucky to be alive at the same time Leonard Cohen is'. As part of the tribute, singer-songwriter Damien Rice performed a version of 'Hallelujah', about which the *Guardian*'s correspondent commented somewhat uncharitably: 'Please let this be as close as Damien Rice ever comes to being inducted into the Hall of Fame'.

The band for the upcoming tour was gradually assembled by Leonard and bass player Roscoe Beck, who was acting as musical director. Apart from Beck, guitarist Bob Metzger and Sharon Robinson, they were mostly newcomers to a Leonard Cohen line-up, either on stage or in the recording studio. In fact, it was Robinson who brought in two new names to share backing vocals with her: the Webb Sisters –Charley (who also played guitar), and Hattie (a harpist) – two singers from England, with whom Sharon had worked with during a recording session in LA.

Canada and Europe

The tour commenced in Canada, at the Fredericton Playhouse, New Brunswick, on 11 May 2008. Leonard had insisted on playing some small Canadian venues to kick things off, and the Playhouse was certainly that: just over 700 seats, which sold out in minutes. From the opening moments of this opening concert, the tour looked in no doubt of being a triumph, as journalist Steve Wilcox would testify: 'He displayed physical vigour and confidence and a certainty about his mission – the audience immediately rose to its feet and began a two-minute ovation. Leonard – who remarked in an interview a few short years ago that he didn't know if he would tour again because he didn't have a sense of there being enough interest in him or his career – looked like he felt justified. There was no longer any question about whether or not to tour.'

Promoter Rob Hallett arranged for eighteen such small concerts in nine cities, before the official start date of 6 June in Toronto. Talking about the mini-dates, Hallett remembered the absurdity of their scale: 'One place . . . advertising a local brass band on Monday, Leonard Cohen Tuesday, and on Wednesday an Elvis impersonator'.

The first leg of the marathon trek, which lasted until 3 August, took in concerts in Canada and Europe. It being summer, several important music festivals were on the itinerary, including three consecutive nights at the Montreal Jazz Festival, the UK's biggest music gathering at Glastonbury, the Montreux Jazz Festival, the Nice Jazz Festival, and the Summer Festival in Lucca, Italy. And it was a gig at London's O2 Arena on 17 July that would form the two-disc *Live in London* album, released in May 2009.

Press reviews of the Grand Tour were almost universally positive, many seeing Cohen's misfortune, forcing him back on the road, as his fans' gain. The UK *Times* was typical: 'Laughing in the face of cosmic absurdity, Leonard Cohen is the Samuel Beckett of pop. His financial misfortunes have been a windfall for the rest of us. On this kind of grand autumnal form, he should tour every year'.

In Dublin, he was the first performer to play an open-air concert at the IMMA grounds, with three gigs on 13 to 15 June. In 2009, his appearances were awarded Ireland's Meteor Music Award as the best international performance of the year.

At Glastonbury, he occupied the main Pyramid Stage, and his performance was hailed by many as the high spot of the festival; as the sun went down, his rendering of 'Hallelujah' had the crowd of 100,000 on their feet for a rapturous reception. Glastonbury organizer Michael Eavis went further, saying that for him, it was one of the all-time high points in nearly forty years of running the event.

At many appearances, Cohen was treated with the kind of adulation usually meted out by teenage girls to the latest pop idols. A review of his set at the Montreux Jazz Festival likened his reception to that for a religious icon, pointing out that in this case the star was in his seventies, and most of the audience far from their teenage years. 'Leonard Cohen had a packed Auditorium of overcome fans

Leonard's appearance at the 2008 Glastonbury Festival was considered by many the highlight of the three-day event.

completely spellbound last night. He is unique, a kind of mythical figure. His voice, of course, but also his style and his too rare appearances make him seem a living god. But a human god, whom one can approach and almost touch. The audience was partly seated, well-behaved, mostly of mature age.'

Europe East and West

There were further dates across Europe on the second phase of the tour, taking in more than a dozen countries between late September and the end of November, among them the former Soviet bloc territories of Romania, the Czech Republic and Poland. In Warsaw, Leonard would draw attention to the fact that the previous time he had played there, the country was still under a strict Communist regime, with a fledgling democracy movement flexing its muscles. Now, things were very different.

'Thank you so much friends . . . I was having a drink with my old teacher, he's one-hundred-and-two now. He was about ninety-seven at the time, and I poured him a drink, and he clicked my glass and he said "Excuse me for not dying" . . . I kind of feel the same way.'

The fall tour, which had begun in the Romanian capital Bucharest on 21 September 2008, wound up in Manchester, England, on the last day of November. During that time, more ecstatic crowds greeted Leonard Cohen and his entourage wherever they appeared, from the northern climes of Helsinki, Finland, to Milan in Italy. In London, they played two nights at the O2 Arena, where they had triumphed back in July, followed by another two at the Royal Albert Hall. And in Paris, the venue was the legendary Olympia, where Leonard appeared for three consecutive nights during the final week of the trip.

The Pacific

After a break for the holiday period, through later January and early February, the Pacific section of the tour took in a dozen dates in Australia and New Zealand. The first port of call was the New Zealand capital of Wellington. The morning after the concert, the *Dominion Post* reviewer summed up his reaction very briefly: 'It is hard work having to put this concert in to words so I'll just say something I have never said in a review before and will never say again: this was the best show I have ever seen.'

After playing Auckland, New Zealand, the tour moved to Australia, and the Rochford Wines venue in the Yarra Valley, for a 'Day on the Green' concert. The Valley was at the heart of one of Australia's major wine-producing regions, and two weeks after Leonard's appearance was struck by a devastating series of bushfires, in which 173 people lost their lives. Known as the

'Black Saturday' bushfires, the disaster occurred on 7 February 2009, when Leonard was winding up his Australian dates with another winery concert in Swan Valley, and the second of two concerts in Melbourne. Hearing about the tragedy, he immediately donated $200,000 to the Victoria Bushfire Appeal.

Before launching the next portion of the tour, which would cover North America from the beginning of April, on 19 February 2009 Leonard Cohen played his first American gig in fifteen years. Showcased as a special performance, it was at the Beacon Theatre in New York City, with little publicity and tickets limited only to the press and fans who had been alerted via fan websites. The three-hour show was a triumph, and a foretaste of the American trek, which was to commence on 1 April. The day before this latest leg was due to begin saw the release of the first new Cohen album to hit the shops since 2004's *Dear Heather*, the in-concert recording, *Live in London*.

The Album

Recorded at London's dome-like 20,000 seater O2 Arena, during the first leg of the still-continuing tour marathon the previous summer, *Live in London* was released as both a DVD and a two-disc CD set. Throughout the two and a half-hour performance, Cohen regaled the crowd with good-humoured banter between the songs. One such break was featured on the CD as a separate 'Introduction' track: 'Thank you so much friends . . . I was having a drink with my old teacher, he's one-hundred-

Greeting the crowd at the International Festival at Benicassim, Spain, July 2008.

and-two now. He was about ninety-seven at the time, and I poured him a drink, and he clicked my glass and he said "Excuse me for not dying" . . . I kind of feel the same way.'

Starting with a richly-layered version of 'Dance Me to the End of Love', the whole gamut of Leonard's repertoire was covered in the twenty-five songs, from the classics of his 1967 debut album 'Hey, That's No Way to Say Goodbye', 'Suzanne', 'So Long, Marianne' and 'Sisters of Mercy', to 2001's 'In My Secret Life' and 'Boogie Street', the latter as a stirring duet with co-author Sharon Robinson.

The nine-piece backing ensemble – as meticulously rehearsed, as one writer put it,

'as a military operation' – were in fine form, giving the support necessary for full-bodied numbers like 'Democracy', while never getting in the way of the subtler offerings. The album garnered good reviews, going on to be long-listed for Canada's coveted Polaris Music Prize. The critical consensus was that this late-period Cohen was characterised by a maturity of voice and instrumentation, the sign of a singer satisfied with the interpretations of his now universally-familiar songs.

17

LIVE AT THE ISLE OF WIGHT 1970

> '**May you be surrounded by friends and family, and if this is not your lot may the blessings find you in your solitude.**'

All songs written by Leonard Cohen, except where indicated.

1. Introduction
2. Bird On The Wire
3. Intro to 'So Long, Marianne'
4. So Long, Marianne
5. Intro: 'Let's renew ourselves now . . .'
6. You Know Who I Am
7. Intro to Poems
8. Lady Midnight
9. They Locked Up a Man (poem) / A Person Who Eats Meat / Intro
10. One Of Us Cannot Be Wrong
11. The Stranger Song
12. Tonight Will Be Fine
13. Hey, That's No Way to Say Goodbye
14. Diamonds In The Mine
15. Suzanne
16. Sing Another Song, Boys
17. The Partisan (Hy Zaret / Anna Marly)
18. Famous Blue Raincoat
19. Seems So Long Ago, Nancy

Personnel: Leonard Cohen (vocals, guitar); Bob Johnston (organ, piano, guitar); Elkin 'Bubba' Fowler (bass, banjo); Charlie Daniels (fiddle); Ron Cornelius (guitar); Corlynn Hanney (backing vocals); Susan Musmanno (backing vocals)

Recorded: 31 August 1970, Isle of Wight Festival, Afton Down, Isle of Wight, UK
Released: 20 October 2009
Label: Columbia
Producer: Steven Berkowitz

To the untrained eye, Leonard Cohen's decision to release the recording of his 1970 Isle of Wight Festival set might have seemed strange. After all, by 2009 Cohen had spent over four decades overcoming stage fright and honing his act to become the captivating performing artist his fans so admired. But the riveting acoustic set delivered by a tired and dishevelled young Leonard – who had to be woken up just moments before his performance at four o'clock in the morning – firmly grabbed the attention of the 600,000-strong crowd then, and continued to resonate on the CD and DVD release nearly forty years later. But before the album came out, Leonard still had to fulfil the next stage of his 2008–2009 tour, which began in the United States on 1 April 2009.

North America

Although Cohen was now receiving serious recognition in America, the tour dates were mostly in small venues more suited to up-and-coming young artists than a seventy-four-year-old who already had fifteen album releases under his belt. Nevertheless, Leonard was booked to appear at the high-profile Coachella Valley Music and Arts Festival in Indio California, in the Colorado Desert. His performance on 17 April was in front of one of the largest crowds in the ten-year history of the event, and his performance of 'Hallelujah' was widely accepted to have been the highlight of the festival.

In a similarly breathtaking performance, Cohen would play the last date of the April–June stretch of the tour at the spectacular Red Rocks Amphitheatre near Denver, Colorado. The dramatic red sandstone stage on which Leonard would perform had been carved by nature over thousands of years to create an acoustically perfect structure, and provided the ideal backdrop to an emotionally-charged set.

A review of the Red Rocks show in the *Denver Post* concluded: 'After bringing as much of his tour crew as possible on stage for a final goodbye (after "I've Tried to Leave You"), he left with a final statement that seemed like a benediction. "May you be surrounded by friends and family, and if this is not your lot may the blessings find you in your solitude." In that regard, his concert was a blessing.'

Europe

For the next portion of Leonard's summer itinerary, he and the band travelled back to Europe. Beginning in Cologne, Germany on 1 July, it would be a huge forty-show trek that visited thirty-six cities in seventeen countries. Alongside familiar places like Germany, the UK and Spain, where a warm welcome was virtually inevitable, the gig sheet also took him to Turkey, Hungary, Monaco and Serbia, where he had never played before.

Many of the venues Cohen would perform at were sports arenas and summer music festivals. The show at the O2 Arena in Dublin won Leonard the second Meteor Music Award in a row for Best International Performance of the Year, while the most stunning open-air event took place amid the awe-inspiring architecture of the Piazza San Marco in Venice.

On 18 September Leonard was on stage in the Spanish city of Valencia when, halfway through singing his fourth number, 'Bird on the Wire', he collapsed. As band members carried him backstage, shock reverberated through the audience. Multi-instrumentalist Javier Mas addressed the crowd in Spanish, explaining that Cohen was now conscious and on his way to hospital, the show had to be cancelled, and that their money would be refunded. It turned out to be a nasty case of food poisoning. But by the next tour date three days later, Leonard would be able to retake the stage for a sensational three-hour performance in Barcelona. It was a memorable way to celebrate his seventy-fifth birthday.

Israel

One more date would round off this 'European'

> 'This is not about forgiving and forgetting, this is not about laying down one's arms in a time of war, this is not even about peace, although, God willing, it could be a beginning. This is about a response to human grief.'

leg of the tour, in Israel on 24 September, at the Ramat Gan Stadium near Tel Aviv. Billed as 'A Concert for Reconciliation, Tolerance and Peace', the proceeds from the 47,000 tickets were to go to a charitable fund in partnership with Amnesty International to help families of both Israeli and Palestinian veterans of the long-running conflict.

But controversy surrounded the concert, which was at odds with the numerous groups campaigning for an all-out boycott of Israel. Seemingly under pressure from all sides, Amnesty withdrew its support for the concert. But Leonard was determined that the show go ahead. While the main boycott lobby claimed that Cohen was 'intent on whitewashing Israel's colonial apartheid regime by performing in Israel', he threw his weight behind the charity Bereaved Families for Peace, who became the recipients of the nearly $2 million raised.

'It was a while ago that I first heard of the work of the Bereaved Families for Peace', Cohen said during an emotional announcement from the stage. 'That there was this coalition of Palestinian and Israeli families who had lost so much in the conflict and whose depth of suffering had compelled them to reach across

*Rehearsing for the Coachella Music Festival in Indio,
California, April 2009.*

the border into the houses of the enemy. Into the houses of those, to locate them who had suffered as much as they had, and then to stand with them in aching confraternity, a witness to an understanding that is beyond peace and that is beyond confrontation. So, this is not about forgiving and forgetting, this is not about laying down one's arms in a time of war, this is not even about peace, although, God willing, it could be a beginning. This is about a response to human grief.'

'He literally danced off the stage before each of three encores', enthused one UK review of the Tel Aviv show, 'one of which charmed the enraptured crowd to their feet in an excited singalong, thousands waving their green glow sticks in time to "So Long Marianne". He and his gravelly bass baritone voice were at peak form, from a gloriously funky "I'm Your Man" to the dark and haunting "Famous Blue Raincoat" and, of course, "Hallelujah" (which served as a reminder that none of the many cover versions are as good)'.

The sixth and final stretch of the epic world tour got underway on 17 October in Fort Lauderdale, Florida. Consisting of just fifteen concerts in the US, the tour soon wound up in San Jose, California on 13 November. The 2009 dates alone were reported to have earned nearly $10 million, with Cohen being cited by *Billboard* magazine as #39 on their list of 'Music's Top Forty Money Makers'. Altogether, the eighteen-month series of concerts had grossed in excess of $50 million, meaning at last that Leonard could put his financial worries behind him.

With the tour over, Cohen had a few months to himself – entirely to himself, for he was once again a single man. Why he and Anjani chose to end their relationship can only be speculated; perhaps it was the result of two years of living largely separate lives while Cohen was on the road, or possibly that the age gap between a

In San Jose, California on November 13, 2009, with Bob Metzger on guitar.

fifty and a seventy-five-year-old simply seemed more daunting than the forty and sixty-five that the two were when their relationship began. Regardless of the reasoning behind the split, Anjani – just like many of Cohen's former lovers – would remain his close friend. They would also continue to collaborate with one another, with each having material that the other had contributed to appear on their respective next studio albums.

During this period, there was also a flurry of activity on the record front. Columbia had decided to re-release Leonard's first three studio albums – *Songs of Leonard Cohen* (1967), *Songs from a Room* (1969) and *Songs of Love and Hate* (1971) – along with the two compilations: *The Best of Leonard Cohen* and *The Essential Leonard Cohen*.

Cohen wasn't best pleased with what he felt was the cavalier way the company handled the re-releases. Without seeking Leonard's approval, the executives at Columbia had chosen to supplement the albums with previously unheard 'bonus tracks'. *Songs of Leonard Cohen* now had 'Store Room' and 'Blessed Is The Memory', *Songs from a Room* featured early versions of 'Bird On The Wire' (called 'Like a Bird') and 'You Know Who I Am' (then named 'Nothing To One'), and *Songs of Love and Hate* had an early outtake of 'Dress Rehearsal Rag'. Cohen felt that these additions ruined the original balance of the albums, and made it clear that it shouldn't happen again.

Not long after the upset, on 20 October, the record company also made the decision to release the second Leonard Cohen live album to appear in less than seven months: *Live at the Isle of Wight*.

The Album

With conditions far from ideal for the recording of a live album, the mood at the 1970 Isle of Wight Festival had been growing increasingly fractious in the hours leading up to Leonard Cohen's appearance. The weather had been

'It's a very tricky occasion, being honoured. In one sense, it feels like an obituary and you don't really feel that about yourself.'

suitably dismal, and battles with the local council over the festival's location had led to serious issues with sound quality. And, earlier in the evening on Sunday 30 August, the audience had been getting restless over the wall that had been erected to keep non-paying fans out. At one point, a riotous section of the crowd had even dared to make their dissatisfaction known by setting fire to the stage during Jimi Hendrix's two-hour performance.

Joan Baez had the daunting task of following the Hendrix set, which she handled with professional aplomb: 'I'm not getting £30,000, or whatever, for this one and I'm not living on some luxury yacht. Leonard Cohen and I are staying in a nice little hotel around here, with breakfast at a quarter to nine.' The switch from scorching electric blues to acoustic folk music certainly helped to calm things down. After Baez had left the stage, Leonard was summoned from the trailer where, by this time, he had fallen asleep.

Kris Kristofferson, who earlier that evening had faced jeering (and some bottle-throwing) from the crowd, recalled the situation on the *Live at the Isle of Wight 1970* DVD: 'I think it was about four o'clock in the morning they went in and woke him up in his trailer and he took a long time to get out to the stage. Everybody had been sittin' there in the filth, in their own squalor – half a million people there – for five days. And Leonard finally came out of his trailer and he was wearing his pyjamas . . . I never have known why they didn't just hoot him off the stage like they did with a lot of people, especially me! I can only think that he was such an honest performer and didn't scramble after anybody's attention. He took his time getting' out there, he took his time tunin' up and he wasn't intimidated by a half million people who'd been very ugly.'

With a khaki safari jacket over his nightwear protecting him from the rain, Cohen finally took the stage. As he slowly tuned his guitar, Leonard began by telling a childhood story of going to the circus with his father. He didn't much like circuses, he confessed, but always remembered the moment when a man would ask everyone in the audience to light a match – which he now asked the crowd to do. As the vast multitude became illuminated, Cohen gently began singing 'Bird on the Wire' and the audience was captivated. As Kristofferson recalled: 'He did the damnedest thing you ever saw – he charmed the Beast. A lone sorrowful voice did what some of the best rockers in the world had tried for three days and failed.'

Kristofferson, Baez and Judy Collins stood at the side of the stage, awestruck by Leonard's performance and its effect on the crowd. Cohen's record producer Bob Johnson, who couldn't take his usual place in the band on stage because the crowd had earlier trashed the keyboards, later concluded, 'It was magical, from the first moment to the last. I've never seen anything like it. He was just remarkable.'

As a full transcript of the performance, the album gave an insight into the

Leonard Cohen of almost four decades earlier. He described the origins of some of the songs, telling the audience that 'One of Us Cannot Be Wrong' was written in the Chelsea Hotel while he was 'pursuing a blond lady that I met in a Nazi poster'. Similarly, he dedicated the track 'Seems So Long Ago, Nancy' to a woman who committed suicide in 1961.

Most of the songs performed that night, and captured on the CD, were from Cohen's first two albums, *Songs of Leonard Cohen* and *Songs from a Room*. There were three numbers in the set – 'Diamonds in the Mine', 'Famous Blue Raincoat' and 'Sing Another Song, Boys' – that would appear on *Songs of Love and Hate*. Although this release harked back to one of his earliest performances, Cohen's musical career was far from over. He would soon make his return to the touring circuit to gather material for his next live album, *Songs from the Road*.

18
SONGS FROM THE ROAD

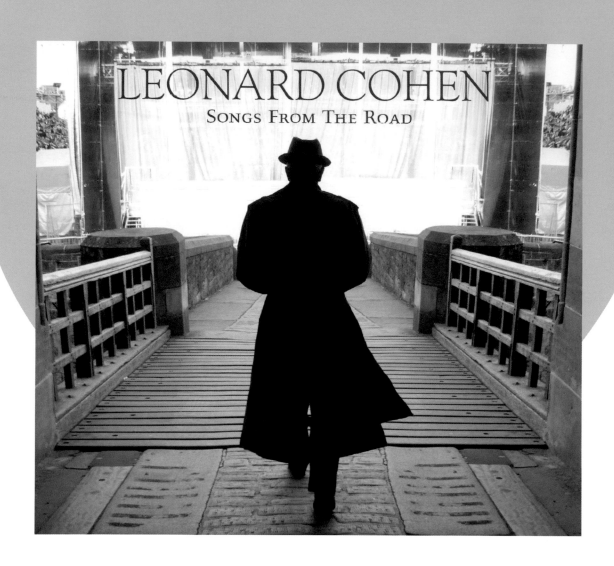

'I never thought I'd get a Grammy Award,
in fact, I was always touched by the modesty
of their interest as to my work.'

All songs written by Leonard Cohen, except where indicated.

1. Lover, Lover, Lover
2. Bird on the Wire
3. Chelsea Hotel
4. Heart with No Companion
5. That Don't Make It Junk (Cohen, Sharon Robinson)
6. Waiting for the Miracle (Cohen, Sharon Robinson)
7. Avalanche
8. Suzanne
9. The Partisan (Hy Zarat, Anna Marly)
10. Famous Blue Raincoat
11. Hallelujah
12. Closing Time

Personnel: Leonard Cohen (vocals, guitar, keyboard); Roscoe Beck (bass, double bass, backing vocals); Rafael Bernardo Gayol (drums, percussion); Neil Larsen (keyboards); Javier Mas (banduria, laud, archilaud, twelve-string guitar); Bob Metzger (guitar, pedal steel guitar, backing vocals); Dino Soldo (saxophone, clarinet, harmonica, keyboards, backing vocals); Charley Webb (backing vocals, guitar); Hattie Webb (backing vocals, harp)

Recorded: 10 October 2008, Hartwall Areena, Helsinki, Finland; 12 October 2008, Scandinavium, Gothenburg, Sweden; 2 November 2008, König Pilsener Arena, Oberhausen, Germany; 6 November 2008, Clyde Auditorium, Glasgow, UK; 13 November 2008, The O2 Arena, London, UK; 17 November 2008, Royal Albert Hall, London, UK; 30 November 2008, Manchester Evening News Arena, Manchester, UK; 17 April 2009, Coachella Music Festival, Indio, California, USA; 24 May 2009, John Labatt Centre, London, Ontario, Canada; 24 September 2009, Ramat Gan Stadium, Tel Aviv, Israel; 13 November 2009, HP Pavilion, San Jose, California, USA

Released: 14 September 2010
Label: Columbia / Legacy
Producer: Edward Sanders, Richard Alcock, Steven Berkowitz

By the time of the release of his third live album, which would feature a selection of crowd favourites from his previous tour, Cohen was already back on the road again. This time, he would be performing a fifty-six date tour across the globe. Kicking off in Croatia, it spanned Western Europe, Eastern Europe and Russia, followed by dates in New Zealand, Canada and the United States. Once a reclusive cult hero, Leonard Cohen was now vying with Bob Dylan in the 'never-ending tour' stakes. His lifestyle had become that of an on-the-road rock star, a far cry from the monastic Zen retreat of the previous decade.

Before Cohen's 2010 tour was due to begin in March in the French city of Caen, it was awards season. As a mark of recognition for his extensive contribution to the music industry, he would receive the Lifetime Achievement Special Merit Award from the National Academy of Recording Arts & Sciences. The very next evening, Cohen was invited to attend the fifty-second annual Grammys ceremony at the Wilshire Ebell Theatre in LA, where he was presented with the prestigious Lifetime Achievement Award. 'I never thought I'd get a Grammy Award', Leonard would joke in his acceptance speech. 'In fact, I was always touched by the modesty of their interest as to my work.' Although reluctant to admit it in so many words, Cohen was touched by the industry's acknowledgment of his life's work, and delivered a heartfelt recitation of the lyrics to 'Tower of Song' in response.

Just a few days later, Cohen suffered a compression injury to his lower back while doing a Pilates exercise. A statement from AEG Worldwide, his promoters, announced that the early dates on his upcoming itinerary would have to be rescheduled as Leonard underwent a four to six month regime of physical therapy. His manager Robert Kory added for the press: 'Doctors have confirmed that Mr Cohen is otherwise in terrific shape, thanks to years of exercise and careful diet, and simply needs appropriate time to recover from the lower back injury'.

By June, Leonard was in New York to be presented with yet another accolade. This time, he was to be awarded with one of the greatest honours in the music business: induction into the Songwriters Hall of Fame. Before Cohen made his acceptance speech, Judy Collins performed 'Suzanne', telling the audience how the number had triggered her interest in Cohen's work all those years ago, and propelled his initial career as a consequence. Then, as she had at the Canadian Songwriters Hall of Fame four years earlier, k.d. lang performed 'Hallelujah'. Her version of the song had since become the stuff of legend, after a sensational performance at the opening of the Winter Olympics in Vancouver, British Columbia.

Smartly dressed as always, Leonard accepted the honour in a black suit and his trademark fedora, thanking everyone and adding that k.d.lang and Judy Collins 'brought my songs to life more than I ever could . . . a sublime experience for me'. He went on to recite a single verse of 'Hallelujah', tipped his hat, and left the stage.

Croatia

With the first dozen of the original European dates postponed until the early fall, the tour finally started on 25 July at the Zagreb Arena, in Zagreb, Croatia. The Balkan state was in the grip of Cohen mania, with sixteen of Leonard's albums entering the Croatian Top Forty in the week of his performance.

Leonard Cohen's literary work would also find favour in Croatia. Following his July performance, there would be a translation of his *Book of Mercy*, the publication of two Cohen biographies, a selection of his poems in the literary magazine *Quorum*, and a translation of the book about his writing by the Canadian academic Linda Hutcheon. At the end of the year, in the national newspaper *Vjesnik*, a poll of dozens of intellectuals and writers voted the show as one of the five most important cultural events in the country that year. It was the only non-native event cited.

Trans-Europe

From Croatia, the Cohen caravan continued across Europe, visiting Austria, Ireland and Scandinavia in quick succession. Performing in Ireland in late July, Leonard played at Lissadel House, an historic country manor in County Sligo, his ninth Irish concert in two years. Not long after, on 12 August, Cohen would play the 200th concert of the tour at the Scandinavium in Gothenburg, Sweden. As if in celebration, the show lasted a marathon four hours.

Picturesque outdoor locations were often the order of the day, and provided the perfect backing to Cohen's stirring performances. Leonard would host concerts in front of the imposingly beautiful medieval abbey at St Peter's Square in Ghent,

Leonard live at the Waldbuehne, Berlin, August 2010.

Belgium, beside the idyllic Florentine Basilica di Santa Croce described by one concertgoer as 'an open-air temple', and inside the ancient Roman quarry of Romersteinbruch St Margarethen in Burgenland, Austria.

From 15 September, the rescheduled dates from earlier in the year were slotted in, beginning in Caen, France. Leonard Cohen's third successive live album had been released the previous day, and would feature recordings from the 2008 and 2009 legs of the 'grand tour'.

The Album

It would be fair to say that Cohen's audience was initially hostile to the promise of yet another live album. To many fans, it felt as though the idea was just a recording company-driven stopgap to compensate for a six year absence of studio material – a last scrape of the barrel of unissued concert recordings. But, although *Songs from the Road* shared the same concert line-up as the recording from *Live in London*, released eighteen months earlier, it provided a completely different listening experience. Rather than just offering up the recording from a single gig – as he had done with his previous two live albums – Leonard had cherry-picked the crowd favourites from the last leg of the tour, by which point he and his band had been giving their slickest, most commanding performances.

From the opening track 'Lover, Lover, Lover', recorded at the emotional Tel Aviv concert in November 2009, it was clear that this selection was a genuine reflection of Leonard Cohen's evolution as a live performer. This was a Leonard Cohen who, in stark contrast to earlier in his career, was genuinely happy and confident on stage. Settled by months on the road, Cohen and his band had fallen into a highly rehearsed routine that, by its laid-back nature, allowed for all the players to express themselves.

On stage in Hanging Rock, Victoria, Australia, November 20, 2010.

'My writing process is like a bear stumbling into a beehive or a honey cache: I'm stumbling right into it and getting stuck, and it's delicious and it's horrible and I'm in it and it's not very graceful and it's very awkward and it's very painful and yet there's something inevitable about it.'

And it was a routine that freed Leonard. He had been singing some of these songs for decades, often with a genuine sense of trepidation as to how they would sound on a particular occasion. Now there was a confidence in his voice that could only have come from the honing of arrangements on an almost nightly basis.

Even on the classic favourites, there was much that was unfamiliar to fans. The November 2008 recording of 'Bird on a Wire' included the addition of a new verse, whilst 'Suzanne' – both recorded at dates in the UK – had its verses completely re-ordered. The album also featured some less-familiar numbers such as 'Heart with No Companion' (from a concert at Oberhausen in Germany) and 'That Don't Make it Junk', recorded at London's O2 Arena. And the only non-original song on the collection 'The Partisan', was represented by a chilling version of the French Resistance song delivered at a concert in Helsinki, Finland.

A high point of any live performance by

'Thanks for inviting us to this sacred place. It's a great honour. I promise we'll give you everything we've got tonight.'

Leonard Cohen, 'Hallelujah' was recorded at the Coachella Festival in California in April 2009 to thunderous applause. 'Waiting for the Miracle', co-written with Sharon Robinson, was a particularly touching inclusion to the album. The track had also been recorded in California, this time at the HP Pavilion in San Jose, a performance that marked the end of Leonard's 2009 tour.

Overall, the album was a stunning confirmation of Leonard Cohen development as a live performer, a point articulated in a BBC review at the time. 'His songs have always been ones of experience, and on some of his earlier recordings especially he didn't sound like he'd grown into them. But the performances here of 'Chelsea Hotel' and 'Lover, Lover, Lover', delivered with an old man's gravitas and Cohen's luxuriantly weather-beaten voice, make it clear just how wise before their time they were.'

The album's evocative cover picture was taken by Leonard's former lover, the French photographer Dominique Issermann. The pair had remained close friends, and she would often photograph Cohen when the opportunity presented itself. She had captured the image of his dramatically silhouetted figure at Edinburgh Castle in Scotland on 16 July 2008, where Cohen would play a concert later that same day.

Although the album – and the complementary DVD released at the same time – was initially greeted with a mixed reaction by the critics, it has since been lauded as an essential in any serious collection of Leonard Cohen's work. 'Despite my initial reservations', wrote the reviewer for *No Depression* magazine. 'I can't recommend this set enough. Of all the "Cohen product" on the market, *Songs from the Road* is certainly the souvenir most worthy of purchase, and for those unfamiliar with his music, it might just be enough to make understand what all the fuss has been about'.

Baltic States and Eastern Europe

As *Songs from the Road* hit the shops in early September, the touring continued with nine dates in France and Germany, followed by five appearances in Central and Eastern Europe, including a concert in Moscow's imposing State Kremlin Palace. A modern building incongruously situated within the historic Kremlin complex, the Palace had been opened in the early 1960s as a modern venue for Communist Party meetings. A very different audience would greet Leonard Cohen half a century later. The Russian concertgoers were well aware of Cohen's repertoire, and the reception to his October concert elicited not one but two encores. The first would feature the much-loved 'So Long, Marianne' and 'First We Taken Manhattan', followed by a second starring the haunting 'Closing Time'.

After a second concert in Poland, the tour moved down to the Baltic state of Slovenia, where Leonard played at the newly-opened Arena Stožice in the capital Ljubljana. During his appearance, Cohen was presented with the Croatian Porin music award for the Best Foreign Live Video Programme, which he won for his *Live in London* DVD. The next evening, 13 October, Leonard played his final date in the European tour, at the Sibamac Arena in Bratislava, Slovakia.

Finale

After a short break, the tour resumed a fortnight later with two nights in Auckland, New Zealand, followed by two in the capital Wellington, and one in Christchurch. Then it was a three-hour flight over the Tasman Sea to Brisbane for the first of nine Australian concerts. The itinerary would be a momentous one. Leonard was to be given the privilege to be the first musician ever to conduct an open-air performance at the spectacular Hanging Rock heritage site in Victoria. Cohen was, as always, modestly grateful: 'Thanks for inviting us to this sacred place. It's a great honour. I promise we'll give you everything we've got tonight.'

With less than a week to recuperate, the ensemble was on the final stretch of a journey that had lasted, in all, for over two years. Leonard's home country of Canada came first, with two dates in British Columbia: Victoria and Vancouver. Both were greeted with what can only be described as adulation, verging on worship. The *Victoria Times Colonist* reported that Cohen received 'an automatic standing ovation at what was clearly the Church of Leonard', whilst the *Vancouver Sun* would call the show 'nothing short of a religious experience'. Finally, it was down the west coast to California to perform in Oakland and Oregon for a show in Portland, before ending up with two nights in the unlikeliest of venues – the Colosseum at Caesar's Palace, in America's glitz capital: Las Vegas. Why the gambling paradise was chosen as a finale for the two-and-a-half year trek wasn't clear, but Leonard's faithful fans made sure it worked. The very last concert was performed on 11 December, the 246th show on the seventy-six-year-old's biggest odyssey yet.

19
OLD IDEAS

'The thing I liked about this award was that I'm sharing it with Chuck Berry. "Roll over Beethoven and tell Tchaikovsky the news" – I'd like to write a line like that.'

All songs written by Leonard Cohen, except where indicated.

1. Going Home (Cohen, Patrick Leonard)
2. Amen
3. Show Me the Place (Cohen, Patrick Leonard)
4. Darkness
5. Anyhow (Cohen, Patrick Leonard)
6. Crazy to Love You (Cohen, Anjani Thomas)
7. Come Healing (Cohen, Patrick Leonard)
8. Banjo
9. Lullaby
10. Different Sides

Personnel: Leonard Cohen (vocals, programming, guitar); Patrick Leonard (programming); Ed Sanders (vocals, guitar); Sharon Robinson (vocals, synth bass); Neil Larsen (Hammond B3, piano, synth bass, percussion, cornet); Robert Korda (violin); Bela Santeli (violin); Jordan Charnofsky (guitar); Chris Wabich (drums); Charley Webb (vocals); Hattie Webb (vocals); Dana Glover (vocals); Jennifer Warnes (backing vocals)

Recorded: October 2007 – August 2011, Small Mercies studio, Los Angeles
Released: 31 January 2012
Label: Columbia
Producer: Edward Sanders, Patrick Leonard

Recorded at his home in Los Angeles as his first studio album in eight years, *Old Ideas* would prove to be Leonard Cohen's most popular record yet. At long last, it would bring him the kind of mainstream US success many would kill for, including a #3 spot in the *Billboard* album chart, just the forty-four years after the launch of his debut album. Cohen's now seemingly universal popularity was reflected all the way around the globe, with the album topping charts in no fewer than eleven countries worldwide.

With touring over – at least for the moment – the opening months of 2011 saw Leonard back at home, working on the album he had been developing on-and-off for the last four years. Many of the songs had already been recorded, after a fashion, on the home-based equipment that now served as his regular studio. Some were still in the writing stage, as they had been since way before the 2008 trek kicked off. And others – like 'Crazy to Love You', which had been co-written with Anjani Thomas for her album *Blue Alert* – were new versions of already developed material.

Prizes and Poems

By April, Cohen would become the recipient of another eminent award. The Glenn Gould Prize, granted in the memory of the sensationally gifted Canadian pianist, was only awarded to those judged to have made a unique lifetime contribution to the arts that had 'enriched the human condition'. In winning the award, Leonard Cohen would join the ranks of other highly-esteemed musicians including the prolific jazz pianist Oscar Peterson and the Academy Award-winning conductor André Previn. Rather than accepting the fantastically large prize winnings, Leonard donated the C$50,000 to the Canada Council for the Arts, which had triggered his musical journey all those years ago by sponsoring his very first trip to the island of Hydra.

The week before, Cohen's work had been

recognised further through the publication of a dedicated volume of the popular *Everyman's Library Pocket Poets* series. The book was a collection of over 130 of Leonard Cohen's poems and song lyrics, hand-selected by the editor, Robert Faggen, from all Leonard's Cohen's publications, including *Stranger Music* and *Book of Longing*. Cohen's fans would also be delighted to discover that the tome featured six previously unreleased song lyrics.

Another prestigious international honour would come Leonard's way not long after when in October he won the Prince Asturias Award for Literature. The much sought-after annual prize had previously been won by other such eminent creatives as film director Woody Allen, pianist Daniel Barenboim and children's author J.K. Rowling. The jury that presented Cohen with the €50,000 reward in the city of Oviedo in northern Spain declared that his work had 'influenced three generations around the world', creating 'imagery in which poetry and music are melded into an unchanging worth'. Leonard, who had always felt a deep artistic connection to the homeland of his hero Federica Garcia Lorca, was profoundly grateful for the honour and pledged in his speech to 'thank the soil and the soul of this land that has given me so much'.

A different kind of acknowledgement of Cohen's work altogether appeared in the mid-January 2012 edition of *The New Yorker* magazine. By way of a trailer for Leonard's new album *Old Ideas*, which would feature the song, it published the lyrics for the song 'Going Home' in full. Cohen's fans wouldn't have to wait long for the teaser to become tangible: the album would be released in full by the end of the month.

The Album

It would have been reasonable to expect that Leonard, now seventy-six-years-old, would have seized the opportunity to – at the very least – take it easy, if not retire altogether. After all, his extended world tour was now complete,

and his perilous financial situation had been more than rectified. But Cohen had never been the type to do what was expected of him. Invigorated by the support and recognition his songwriting was receiving, Leonard returned to the studio to work on what would become his twelfth studio album. Cohen's recording process seemed to have acquired a new lease of life, and – in record time for the notoriously slow-going musician – the album was finished within the year.

Cohen called the album *Old Ideas*, the name he had originally intended for his previous studio release *Dear Heather*, before he was advised that fans might have thought it was a greatest hits compilation. Most of the album was recorded at Leonard's own Small Mercies studio at his house in Los Angeles, with technical assistance from Sharon Robinson and his regular engineer Leanne Ungar. *Old Ideas* had all the hallmarks of a classic Leonard Cohen album. Punctuated with dramatic religious imagery, the lyrics explored the familiar Cohen territories of love, sex, mortality and depression to a melodious bluesy sound evocative of his earliest work.

Much of the album was co-produced with Patrick Leonard, a songwriter and producer renowned for his extensive work with Madonna, who Cohen had met through his singer-songwriter son, Adam. Having worked as a roadie before the 1990 car accident that left him bedridden for over a year, Adam had enthusiastically thrown himself into the music scene, moving to Los Angeles in 1996 and forming a band that signed with his father's label, Columbia, in 1997. He had two albums out under his own name, and one with his band Low Millions, *Ex-Girlfriends,* which had been produced by Patrick Leonard back in 2004.

'I think he's a seminal figure in modern American music, very brilliant', Leonard Cohen said of the producer. 'I was listening to some of his solo piano work, too. I bumped into him with Adam several times, and somehow we got

At 'A Tribute to Leonard Cohen' concert in Gijon, Spain, October 2011.

Leonard launches his album, Old Ideas, *in Paris,*
January 2012.

'A tour is being booked. I haven't signed up for it yet.
I have two minds. I don't like to do a small tour, so
whether I'm going to sign up for another couple of
years . . . is that really where I want to be? Touring
is like taking the first step on a walk to China.'

together and these four songs we did together came very quickly.' The pair co-wrote four tracks – most notably the powerful opener 'Going Home' – including 'Show Me the Place', 'Anyhow' and 'Come Healing'.

The one other writing collaboration was with Anjani Thomas. 'Crazy to Love You' had already appeared on her Cohen-produced 2006 album *Blue Alert*, and 'Darkness' and 'Lullaby', had been tried-and-tested on the recent concert tours before Leonard put them down in the studio. The studio sound itself, which many listeners picked up on right away, marked a noticeable shift back to guitar on Cohen's part after the heavy use of synthesisers on his other 'recent' albums.

Though the album could certainly be described as a maudlin reflection on mortality, it was clear that Cohen's increasing age hadn't dampened his razor-sharp wit. When asked by a journalist to analyse the album at a promotional party in New York's East Village, Leonard responded: 'It's probably not a good idea to do an autopsy on a living thing'. But reviews of the album were almost universally good. The *New York Times* reported '*Old Ideas* is an autumnal album, musing on memories and final reckonings, but it also has a gleam in its eye'. In the UK, *The Guardian* was similarly impressed, advising listeners not to 'take everything he says as gospel, even if it's frequently dressed up as such'.

A BBC review simply called it 'A quite brilliant release from an unmissable artist', and *Rolling Stone* concluded 'as time has gone on, Cohen has shorn the ornament from his language to move from the personal to the universal'. *Rolling Stone* went on to list *Old Ideas* at #13 in its Top Albums of 2012, and also cited 'Going Home' as its twentieth 'best song' of the year.

The album would quickly become Leonard Cohen's most successful release ever. By June, the release had charted at #1 in Canada and had been listed among the nominees for the 2012 Polaris Music Prize. As well as reaching an unprecedented #3 on the American *Billboard* chart, it had topped the chart in eleven countries worldwide, and hit the #2 spot in Australia, Denmark, Sweden and the UK.

Europe 2012

Immediately prior to the album's release, Leonard went on a short promotional tour, turning down one-to-one interviews and instead staging press conferences in London, Paris and New York. The London event was moderated by the singer Jarvis Cocker, best known for his hits in the 1990s with the Britpop band Pulp. Cocker asked Cohen how he felt about receiving the prize for Song Lyrics of Literary Excellence from the American literary association PEN, a joint award shared with rock 'n' roll icon Chuck Berry. Leonard's reply was succinct and to the point: 'The thing I liked about this award was that I'm sharing it with Chuck Berry. "Roll over Beethoven and tell Tchaikovsky the news" – I'd like to write a line like that'.

In March 2012, Cohen's promotional office announced an eighteen-date European tour in support of *Old Ideas*. The tour began with five dates in a familiar venue, the ancient St Peter's Square in the Belgian city of Ghent. And, as before, the band was due to have more or less the same line-up as the 2008-2010 touring outfit, with the only new addition being Moldovan violinist, Alexandru Bublitchi. Now dubbed the Unified Heart Touring Band, the ensemble would perform a similar concert structure to Leonard's last European appearances, with the extensive main set divided into two portions by a brief intermission.

Reporting the announcement of the tour, *Rolling Stone* quoted Leonard as being ambivalent about the prospect just months before the first concert date: 'A tour is being booked. I haven't signed up for it yet. I have two minds. I don't like to do a small tour, so whether I'm going to sign up for another couple of years . . . is that really where I want to be? Touring is like taking the first step on a walk to China'.

As on his previous outing across Europe, Leonard played some spectacular venues, including the Arena di Verona in Italy, an ancient Roman amphitheatre in Piazza Bra that had become famous worldwide for its magnificent staging of large-scale opera performances.

His UK dates had originally been scheduled for the Hop Farm Festival in rural Kent, only to be changed last minute to the huge Wembley Arena in London, presumably on account of the bigger capacity. Reviewing the show, the *Sunday Times* reported: 'The revelation of this concert wasn't so much the music, beautifully performed as it was by a lightly amplified band who never put a foot wrong, but the persona of the man himself. Age hasn't so much mellowed Cohen, as made him much, much funnier'.

In Ireland, four Dublin concerts were staged at the striking Irish Museum of Modern Art, a complete contrast to the Copenhagen venue, the lavish renaissance Rosenborg Castle, dating from 1606.

As befitting a tour named after an album, eight of the ten tracks from *Old Ideas* were featured in the European shows. Other than 'Darkness', which had been performed on the 2010 tour as 'The Darkness', this would be the first time ever that the majority of the songs would be heard on stage. 'Lullaby' and 'Show Me the Place' would be the only two songs from the album that remained unplayed at this stage of the tour.

At the concerts, there would be two, three or even four encores, often with the performance finally coming to an end only when the venue demanded it. And for a closer, Leonard sometimes chose an emotion-filled rendering of the early soul classic 'Save The Last Dance for Me', first made popular by the Drifters in 1960, over fifty years earlier.

This first leg of what would be a sixteen-month world tour ended on 7 October in Lisbon, Portugal, at the Pavilhao Atlantico. Every single concert had been a sell-out. Cohen was drawing his biggest audiences yet: the five nights in Ghent had attracted a staggering 40,000 ticket holders, and his four Dublin performances alone grossed an incredible four-and-a-half million dollars. The man whose retirement fund had been whisked away from him, just a few short years ago, was now very comfortably well-off indeed.

Leonard Cohen was now a record-breaking success on the world stage. Some observers found this popularity a little surprising in non-English-speaking countries, given that Cohen's material was so driven by its lyrical content. It was an issue addressed to his musical director, Roscoe Beck, on the first night of the tour in Belgium. 'The lyrics, the words are really more important than the music', Beck conceded. 'But one never knows, because you're performing for an audience and you don't really know what's going to touch the heart of the person in the audience. Mostly the lyrics are in English and maybe the person in the audience doesn't even speak English. They may have heard some translations of some of the lyrics, but many of the lyrics may not be understood. It may then be the music that speaks to them. So one never knows.'

'Tonight, and especially tonight, we're going to give you everything we've got'

North America

After just three weeks respite, the juggernaut that was the Leonard Cohen touring ensemble trundled into Austin, Texas on 31 October for the start of the first American section of the tour. The set lists had been tweaked slightly – most likely at the behest of a band already two months into a world tour – to include the hauntingly beautiful 'Show Me the Place' on most nights. This would leave 'Lullaby' as the only song from the new album yet to be performed live. Other songs featured that had not appeared on the European leg of the tour were crowd-pleasers 'Joan of Arc' and 'Chelsea Hotel #2'. Leonard would also deliver a homage to 'La Manic', a hit by Quebec singer Georges Dor in 1966, when visiting the two French-Canadian cities of the tour, Montreal and Quebec City.

Reviewing the December concert in Kingston, Ontario, at the K-Rock Centre, *The Journal* of Queens University noted the age group of many of the fans: 'The most noticeable quality of the concert was the respect the audience gave Cohen on what is supposed to be his last ever tour. There was an elderly couple close to me who would give a standing ovation after every song with huge smiles on their faces, proving that Cohen has earned his status as a music legend with a solid fan base that have stayed with him through the years'.

Two highlights of the 2012 set were not actually sung by Cohen, but apportioned to his female co-vocalists after a short introduction from Leonard. 'Coming Back to You' from *Various Positions* was delivered in an acoustic version by the Webb sisters, Charley and Hattie, accompanying themselves on harp and guitar respectively. And 'Alexandra Leaving' was presented as a showcase for Sharon Robinson at every show.

As Craig Jones, reviewing the London Wembley date, reported on the website eGigs, 'Ordinarily, when a singer of Cohen's magnitude stands aside to let others take centre stage, you would expect a rush to the bar. However, with the Webb sisters performing the beautiful 'Coming Back to You' and long-term collaborator Sharon Robinson taking lead vocals for a glorious and heartbreaking version of 'Alexandra Leaving', you would be able to hear a pin drop, such are the captivating renditions of both songs.'

Altogether, Leonard visited eighteen Canadian cities on the *Old Ideas* tour and twenty in the United States, from Seattle, Washington in the north west to Tampa, Florida in the south east. Again, Cohen and his ensemble would be rewarded with substantial box office takings. One New York performance alone, at Madison Square Garden on 18 December, would gross the considerable sum of a million-and-a-half dollars.

The Madison Square Garden date was one of two nights in New York City, the second being two days later at the vast Barclays Center in Brooklyn. This would bring the first leg of the North American tour to an end as the promise of 2013 beckoned.

A three-month break ensued for Leonard Cohen, his band and the road crew, before they took to the North American road again at the beginning of March with two dates at the Paramount Theatre in Oakland, California. Cohen and his entourage would perform at an eccentric variety of venues, from the bizarrely-named Save-On-Foods Memorial Centre, a vast ice hockey arena in Victoria, British Columbia, to the art deco splendour of New York's Radio City Music Hall.

On 26 April, the penultimate date Leonard would play in North America, the country music singer and songwriter George Jones passed away as Cohen was playing in Winnipeg. During Leonard's final show two days later in Regina, Saskatchewan, he would include a touching tribute to one of Jones' biggest hits, 'Choices'. The song remained part of the set list for several of Leonard's future concerts, to honour the loss of an influential country star.

Europe 2013

The second European stretch of the *Old Ideas* tour began in Paris on 18 June at the Palais Omnisports de Paris-Bercy sports arena. Cohen would revisit many of the larger cities from the earlier European itinerary: Berlin, Dublin, Paris, London. There, appearances by Leonard Cohen were now guaranteed to be instant sell-outs. However, keen not to deprive fans in more remote locations, Leonard would also play venues in Croatia, the Czech Republic, Slovenia and Poland that he hadn't played before.

Although by this stage in the tour, Cohen had spent over ten months on the road, his relentless energy and enthusiasm showed no signs of disappearing. Night after night, his audiences would be continually wowed by the veteran performer's stamina. A review from the *Financial Times* seemed to capture the essence of the appearances: 'Leonard Cohen's powers of seduction are undimmed. Once they gave him the reputation of a ladies' man. Now, almost seventy-eight, he deploys his gallantry for a different purpose – to sweep audiences off their feet.'

In Switzerland, by the shore of Lake Geneva, Cohen opened the annual Montreux Jazz Festival with two shows on 4 and 5 July. He had appeared at the festival on several previous occasions – in 1976, 1985 and 2008 – but this was to the most appreciative crowd yet. Leonard's performances would later be fondly recalled by the festival's organisers: 'Kneeling on the stage of the Auditorium Stravinski, he is singing "Hallelujah". Two nights, two generous three-plus-hour concerts to open the festival in 2013: the public reverberated with a single voice to Cohen's deep, majestic mantras'.

Oceania

The European portion of the tour would draw to a close on 20 September in a fittingly magnificent venue, the 17,000 seater Ziggo Dome in Amsterdam. After this, the huge Cohen juggernaut would come to a halt – but only briefly. Leonard Cohen and his ensemble had still to prepare themselves for the final leg of an epic journey that would terminate in Australasia. Starting on 13 November with a show in Perth, twelve Australian dates – including the iconic Sydney Opera House on 2 December – would be soon followed by four shows in New Zealand's three major cities: Christchurch, Wellington and Auckland.

Unbeknownst at the time, the closing date of the tour on 21 December at the Vector Arena in Auckland would carry a particular poignancy. The end of a marathon trek that had seen Cohen spend sixteen months on and off the

August 12, 2012 at St Peter's Square in Ghent, Belgium, with Rafael Gayol on drums.

road, all those watching seemed to sense that this would be the final tour that the seventy-nine-year-old would ever conduct on such a grand scale. But the event carried a far greater significance. This would be Leonard Cohen's last ever in-concert appearance.

Opening the first set with a prophetic speech, Leonard announced to the crowd: 'Tonight, and especially tonight, we're going to give you *everything* we've got'. He alone seemed aware of just how pressing it was that he deliver his most breathtaking performance ever. As if trying to draw out the experience for as long as possible, he and the band would end the concert with four 'exit' songs: 'If It Be Your Will', 'Closing Time', 'I Tried to Leave You', and his cover of the Drifters' 'Save the Last Dance for Me'. Then he bade farewell to a rapturous crowd at the end of the night with the words 'Drive carefully home and don't catch a cold. May you be surrounded by friends and family all the days of your life . . . or god bless you in your solitude.'

20
POPULAR PROBLEMS

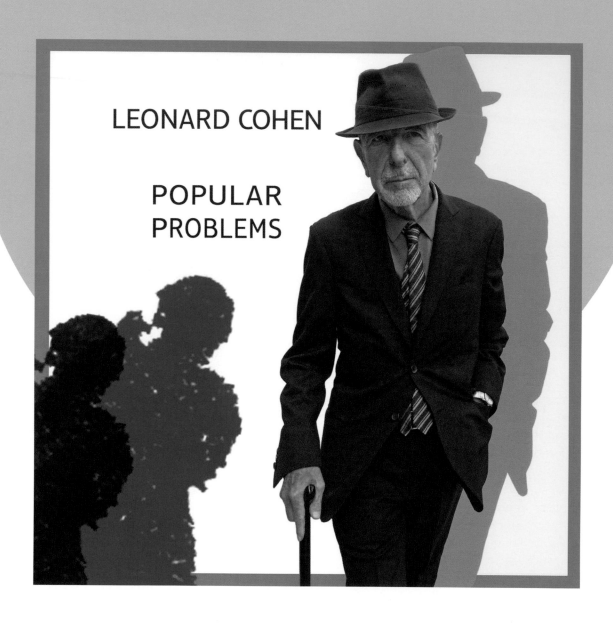

'Usually, I take a long, long time – partly because of an addiction to perfection, partly just sheer laziness.'

All songs written by Leonard Cohen and Patrick Leonard, except where indicated.

1. Slow
2. Almost Like the Blues
3. Samson in New Orleans
4. A Street (Cohen, Anjani Thomas)
5. Did I Ever Love You
6. My Oh My
7. Nevermind
8. Born in Chains (Cohen)
9. You Got Me Singing

Personnel: Leonard Cohen (vocals); Patrick Leonard (keyboards); Joe Ayoub (bass); Brian MacLeod (drums); Alexandru Bublitchi (violin); James Harrah (guitar); Charlean Carmon (backing vocals); Dana Glover (backing vocals); Donna De Lory (backing vocals)

Recorded: 2013–2014, Small Mercies studio, Los Angeles
Released: 22 September 2014
Label: Columbia
Producer: Patrick Leonard

In the wake of the critically acclaimed *Old Ideas*, and the hugely successful world tour that followed it, Leonard Cohen's thirteenth studio collection *Popular Problems* was yet another triumph, released just a day after his eightieth birthday.

Including breaks between tours, Leonard had been on the road for nearly five years by the time the *Old Ideas* concerts came to an end, finishing halfway round the planet in New Zealand. It was time to rest and, now into his eightieth year, Cohen had no plans for another taxing journey from city to city, country to country.

He was, however, in no mood to hang up his boots entirely, and through the early months of 2014 Leonard worked on his next album. As with *Old Ideas*, most of the basic laying down of tracks would be done in Cohen's Los Angeles home studio, Small Mercies. And for the new project, he again worked in collaboration with Patrick Leonard, who had co-produced the previous album. The pair had by now established a comfortable working dynamic. 'It was a very agreeable collaboration because of an absence of ego and an abundance of musical ideas on Patrick's part', Cohen would explain. 'I would have a rhythm in mind and a position. I had the function of the veto. Most of the musical ideas were Patrick's, with a bit of modification. Whether there were horns or violin, all of those things were decided mutually.'

The sheer speed with which the album was produced was a new experience for Cohen fans. It was as if things had to be done, while there was still time to do them. When the album was actually released in September 2014, Leonard was already talking about another to follow. There was a definite sense of being conscious of mortality from the outset.

There had been another reminder of human transience in July, when Cohen's teacher and Zen mentor from the Mount Baldy monastery, Joshu Sasaki Roshi, died in Los Angeles at the age of 107. Although his life as a spiritual master had been tainted of late with well-founded

'He [Sasaki Roshi] became part of my life, and a deep friend in the real sense of friendship. He was someone who really cared – or didn't care, I'm not quite sure which one it was – about who I was, and therefore who I was began to wither.'

allegations of sexual misconduct – even into his later years as a centenarian – Roshi, as Leonard usually referred to him, had been a huge and calming influence. 'He became part of my life, and a deep friend in the real sense of friendship', Leonard would say of his mentor. 'He was someone who really cared – or didn't care, I'm not quite sure which one it was – about who I was, and therefore who I was began to wither'.

The Album

Seven out of the nine songs on *Popular Problems* were co-written with Patrick Leonard, whose previous track record of five albums with Madonna, plus projects with the likes of Elton John and Rod Stewart, might have seemed at odds with the requirements of the self-effacing singer-songwriter. Nevertheless, the seasoned producer brought an urgency to the arrangements that matched the late-in-life rejuvenation of Cohen's music. 'Some of them came together with shockingly alarming speed', Leonard would reveal. 'Usually, I take a long, long time – partly because of an addiction to perfection, partly just sheer laziness.'

With 'Slow' as a bluesy, relaxed opener, it was clear from the start that this was an affirmation of the confidence that had permeated *Old Ideas*. The band added voices layer by layer, with percussion, horns and backing vocals gradually establishing a solid depth of feeling that would characterise the rest of the album. It was a musical self-assurance, sharpened over the recent months and years of playing almost nightly with regular musicians and singers, bolstering the idea that old age was no impediment.

As the title implies, 'Almost Like the Blues' was based on a regular twelve-bar blues, but with lyrics far removed from traditional sentiment, drawing attention to the horrors of the world by way of reference to the Holocaust while satirically drawing a parallel with more personal problems – torture and killing are equated with bad reviews.

Gospel music, too, was there in the fusion – to particular effect on 'Samson in New Orleans', which used the catalyst of the devastation caused by Hurricane Katrina to address wider issues of cultural and racial divides in modern America. And 'Born in Chains', which Leonard had debuted on stage four years previously, also drew on Gospel, both in its musical roots and subject matter, which referenced

September 2013, and a farewell wave after a concert in Rotterdam, Holland.

'In my family, we have a very charitable approach to birthdays – we ignore them.'

Judaism, Christianity and Cohen's practice of Zen Buddhism. Leonard had performed the song in various forms over the years, referring to it as 'Taken Out of Egypt' on previous occasions.

One of the two compositions that didn't involve Patrick Leonard in its authorship, 'A Street', was a collaboration with Anjani Thomas. With its oblique references to the 9/11 attacks on New York City, it draws a parallel between a military battle and a fractious love affair. The song had already appeared in print in *Book of Longing*, in a 2009 edition of *New Yorker* magazine, and in the Everyman's Library collection of Cohen's *Poems and Songs* as 'Party's Over'.

The popular problems of the album's title were indeed 'popular' (though not desired) in their worldwide universality. The focus of Leonard's exploration ranged from civil war (as an analogy for individual relationships in 'A Street'), to the plight of Israel's old enemies – the displaced Palestinian community – acerbically addressed in 'Nevermind', replete with a touch of Arabic singing ('Salaam', Arabic for 'peace'). The song had been published twice before: once as a poem on the Leonard Cohen Files website, and again in *Book of Longing*. The album track, 'Popular Problems', would go on to be used under the opening credits for the second series of hit HBO TV series *True Detective* in 2015.

On 'You Got Me Singing', accompanied only by acoustic guitar and country-flavoured fiddle, Leonard closed the album with a lively ray of optimism shining through the world's traumas, a personal message that he intended to be around for a while yet.

Thumbs-Up

Released on 22 September 2014, just a day after Leonard Cohen's eightieth birthday, *Popular Problems* was greeted with an almost unanimous thumbs-up by the critics and public. In the UK, the *Telegraph* writer Neil McCormick said Cohen had 'created a masterpiece . . . a smoky, late-night concoction delivered with a deceptively light touch that masks deep seriousness', while its broadsheet rival *The Guardian* stated 'An artist who ten years ago could make finishing an album seem like a tough call now makes it sound effortless'.

Allan Jones, in *Uncut* magazine, drew a picture of Cohen 'stirred to something approaching urgency by the sight of a burning world, the camcorder atrocities, the marauding armies, to which he responds with grim vigour and much great writing'. And the *New Musical Express* concluded a short but glowing review: 'As intimate, beautiful and witty as ever, there's an impassioned life in Leonard that's missing from many artists a quarter of his age'.

On the other side of the Atlantic, the *Boston Globe* declared 'There's no giddy youth optimism here; instead, it's all hard-earned truths and uncomfortable conclusions from folk poet Leonard Cohen', and the *New York Daily News* called it 'one of his most musically rich and varied works'.

Sales-wise, *Popular Problems* was another hit worldwide, topping the album charts in ten countries including Canada, where it sold 20,000 copies in the first week. It made the Top Ten in another twelve countries, including the #5 spot in the UK, and the Top Twenty in the United States where it peaked at #15 on the *Billboard* 200, #1 in Folk Albums and #4 on Top Rock Albums.

At a listening event and press conference prior to the album's release, Cohen described the coincidence of his eightieth birthday and the album's release date as 'a happy accident', adding: 'In my family, we have a very charitable approach to birthdays – we ignore them'. His only plan to begin his ninth decade, he said, was to start smoking, asking the crowd of reporters: 'But quite seriously, does anyone know where you can buy a Turkish or Greek cigarette? I'm looking forward to that first smoke. I've been thinking about that for thirty years.'

21
LIVE IN DUBLIN

'If these are the crumbs of compassion that
you offer to the elderly, I am grateful'.

LEONARD COHEN
LIVE in DUBLIN

RECORDED LIVE in CONCERT
at the O2 DUBLIN, SEPTEMBER 12TH, 2013

All songs written by Leonard Cohen, except where indicated.

Disc 1
1. Dance Me to the End of Love
2. The Future
3. Bird on the Wire
4. Everybody Knows (Cohen, Sharon Robinson)
5. Who By Fire
6. The Gypsy's Wife
7. The Darkness
8. Amen
9. Come Healing (Cohen, Patrick Leonard)
10. Lover, Lover, Lover
11. Anthem

Disc 2
1. Tower of Song
2. Suzanne
3. Chelsea Hotel #2
4. Waiting for the Miracle (Cohen, Sharon Robinson)
5. The Partisan (Cohen, Anna Marley, Emmanuel D'astier De La Vigerie, Hy Zaret)
6. In My Secret Life (Cohen, Sharon Robinson)
7. Alexandra Leaving (Cohen, Sharon Robinson)
8. I'm Your Man
9. Recitation (Cohen, Neil Larsen)
10. Hallelujah

11. Take This Waltz (Cohen, Federico Garcia Lorca)

Disc 3
1. So Long, Marianne
2. Going Home (Cohen, Patrick Leonard)
3. First We Take Manhattan
4. Famous Blue Raincoat
5. If It Be Your Will
6. Closing Time
7. I Tried to Leave You
8. Save the Last Dance for Me (Doc Pomus, Mort Shuman)

Personnel: Leonard Cohen (vocals, guitar, keyboard); Roscoe Beck (bass, backing vocals); Rafael Bernardo Gayol (drums, percussion); Neil Larsen (keyboards, accordian); Javier Mas (banduria, laud, twelve-string guitar); Mitch Watkins (guitar, backing vocals; Alexandru Bublitchi (violin); Sharon Robinson (backing vocals); Charley Webb (backing vocals, guitar, clarinet); Hattie Webb (backing vocals, harp)

Recorded: 12 September 2013, O2 Arena, Dublin
Released: 2 December 2014
Label: Columbia
Producer: Edward Sanders

Leonard Cohen's fourth live album in five years, *Live in Dublin* might have seemed like overkill following the 2009 releases of *Live in London* and *Live at the Isle of Wight 1970*, and the issuing of *Songs from the Road* the year after. But as a record of a complete concert appearance – in the same format as *Live in London* – during Leonard's more recent tour dates, the album stood as further evidence of Cohen's revitalised stage presence in the later years of his life.

Live in Dublin was released in December 2014, just a couple of months after *Popular Problems* and Leonard's eightieth birthday. The possibility of Leonard Cohen going out on the road ever again was looking increasingly unlikely. His physical condition had begun to deteriorate and slow him down, although he was yet to be in a totally debilitating situation. A record release representing his most recent live tour was therefore more than just a collector's item: it was an essential record of the final stage in the evolution of his classic material. And for those new to the vast Cohen oeuvre, it was a perfect career-spanning introduction to his music.

Track By Track, Disc 1

From the lilting opening of the anthemic 'Dance Me to the End of Love', it was clear this was Cohen in prime form. His voice may have been weathered, but it oozed authority and was accompanied fittingly by Alexandru Bublitchi's exceptional violin, which gleaned Leonard's first spoken credit of the evening.

It was apocalypse right now with the bleak imagery of 'The Future' echoing across the vast O2 Arena, before a seven-minute organ-backed version of the waltz-time classic 'Bird on the Wire'. With Leonard's recently deepened delivery reminiscent of a Johnny Cash country ballad, guitarist Mitch Watkins elicited the verbal cue this time, with Neil Larsen on the Hammond organ also name-checked.

The first co-written number of the night was 'Everybody Knows', the desolate lyrics of the 1988 collaboration with Sharon Robinson as grim as ever, allowing the leader to acknowledge Robinson as his backing vocalist alongside the two Webb sisters, Charley and Hattie. An extended flamenco-tinged guitar intro, courtesy of Javier Mas, drew the audience into the portentous 'Who By Fire', based on an ancient Hebrew prayer. And 'The Gypsy's Wife', from 1979's *Recent Songs* and written after his separation from his long-time partner Suzanne, prolonged the Mediterranean feel of the previous number.

The blues-drenched 'Darkness' proved an atmospheric outing for the instrumentalists, with Leonard's lyric of dangerous love as sinister as when it first appeared on *Old Ideas* at the beginning of 2012. Another song from *Old Ideas*, 'Amen' was also heard for the first time in the context of a live recording.

The voices of the female back-up singers delivered a spine-tingling introduction to the redemptive 'Come Healing', an evangelical affirmation of faith without mention of a particular creed or creator. 'Lover, Lover, Lover', which Leonard had debuted when visiting Israeli troops in the 1973 Yom Kippur War, was delivered with an infectiously repetitive Latin American beat. And the first disc of the set closed with Cohen reciting the lyrics to the chorus of 'Anthem', to thunderous applause, before he broke into the song proper. It heralded the first interval in the concert, with Leonard introducing the entire ensemble before exiting the Dublin stage.

Track by Track, Disc 2

'Thanks for staying, and not going home', Cohen announced when he returned after the break before launching into a feather-light version of 'Tower of Song', interrupting the self-effacing lyrics with the mid-song invocation: 'If these are the crumbs of compassion that you offer to the elderly, I am grateful'.

Two chords on his acoustic guitar were all that was needed to prompt the crowd into instant recognition of 'Suzanne', Leonard's voice now stronger as he worked

'This is the most challenging activity that humans get into, which is love. You know, we have the sense that we cannot live without love, that life has very little meaning without it.'

Performing at the 02, Dublin on September 11, 2013.

his way through one of the best-known items in the Cohen canon. This was classic music, and the crowd knew it.

The autobiographical 'Chelsea Hotel #2', another standard in the Cohen repertoire, was an essential inclusion at a 'best of' gig like this. As was the third co-composition of the evening ('Come Healing' was the second, written with Patrick Leonard), 'Waiting for the Miracle', another collaboration with Sharon Robinson. Arguably resonant in the Irish capital for a number of historic reasons, 'The Partisan' brought a waft of gentle patriotism to the proceedings with its folk tale of the French Resistance during World War II.

Two more co-writes with Robinson followed. Firstly there was what one reviewer called a 'smouldering' performance of 'In My Secret Life', followed by Sharon Robinson's riveting solo delivery of 'Alexandra Leaving'. There were audible yelps of delight as Cohen slid gently into the catalogue of supplication in 'I'm Your Man', with particular lines drawing spontaneous applause from the audience. And 'Recitation', an extended version of 'A Thousand Kisses Deep' with an eerie, barely audible organ accompaniment from Neil Larsen, illustrated the stark power of Cohen's delivery in reading, rather than singing, his poetry.

'Hallelujah', undoubtedly Cohen's most famous song, sounded as fresh as yesterday in the hands of the master – and, it has to be added, his instrumental and vocal back-up. The second disc – and Leonard's second set – came to a close with the ever-pleasurable swing time of 'Take This Waltz', inspired by the poetry of Federico Garcia Lorca, and first heard on the Lorca tribute album *Poet in New York* in 1986.

Track by Track, Disc 3
Another Cohen classic and all-time crowd pleaser, 'So Long Marianne', opened the third disc of the collection, which was the first of no fewer than eight songs in an elongated encore. Against a loping, dance-hall treatment from the band and vocalists, Cohen sounded like he could have sung all night.

Next came the humorously audacious 'Going Home', co-written with Patrick Leonard. In a self-deprecating account of someone addressing Leonard, the half-spoken and half-sung lyrics were delivered almost as comedic one-liners. The 'someone' in question, making the comments to Cohen, could be seen as a godlike figure passing judgement on him, or his alter-ego, looking critically at himself. Calling the song 'a piece of self-indulgent introspective writing that doesn't deserve to see the light of day', Cohen had been reluctant to develop the number (which opened 2012's *Old Ideas*) until being prodded by Patrick Leonard, who was convinced it could be a really worthwhile collaboration. Its raucous reception by the Dublin fans certainly vindicated this decision.

Unison hand-clapping from the crowd heralded the funky-bass intro to 'First We Take Manhattan'; the song sounded even more sinister sounding in live delivery, the jaunty voices of the girls contrasting with the menacing message of the actual lyrics. 'Famous Blue Raincoat', which was first heard on 1971's *Songs of Love and Hate*, had long been a favourite of Cohen's live shows, and was appropriately greeted as such by the Dublin crowd.

The two voices of the Webb sisters, accompanying themselves on harp and guitar with Neil Larsen on the keyboards, took the vocals for an evocative version of 'If It Be Your Will', introduced by a recitation by Leonard of the first eight lines of the song. The up-tempo 'Closing Time', with its pictures of whirling dancers and more personal, bitter-sweet memories, had an ecstatic audience, clapping in time to the incessant rhythm, never wanting this particular dance to end.

'I Tried To Leave You', running to nearly eight minutes, gave the instrumentalists – as well as Sharon Robinson, and the Webb sisters – plenty of opportunity for individual solo breaks. It would be the penultimate song of the evening, and the last Cohen composition performed that night. The final offering to the Dublin audience was Leonard's poignant interpretation of the old Drifters' classic, 'Save The Last Dance For Me', with the crowd joining in on the choruses, doubtless many with a tear in the eye.

'Act the way you'd like to be and soon you'll be the way you act.'

Worth the Price

The album received almost unanimously positive reviews, with many critics acknowledging that this might be the definitive record of late-period Cohen in concert.

In the Canadian monthly music magazine *Exclaim!* Mackenzie Herd wrote: 'Leonard Cohen has always been to some more of a poet than a musician, but it's hard to deny that even in his golden years, his booming voice still carries a weight that has not waned.'

For *Rolling Stone*, Andy Greene felt it was 'well worth the price to hear backup singer Sharon Robinson's exquisite take on "Alexandra Leaving", Cohen's hilariously self-referential "Going Home" and a finale where he covers "Save the Last Dance for Me".'

And on the website *The Line of Best Fit*, Luke Cartledge wrote: 'Its true value lies in its function as a worthy addition to the latter-day Cohen canon, as a reminder that he is still an active, relevant artist and performer, rather than a self-aggrandising nostalgia act. But then, when has anyone ever come close to levelling such an accusation at the world's coolest eighty-year-old?'

Indeed, as Cohen was coming up to his eightieth birthday, the album served as startling evidence that there seemed no limits to his stamina, or to his ability to constantly adapt his music to changing circumstances. The chemistry of the touring ensemble had adapted to fluctuations in personnel, and with over five years on the road, the interplay between Cohen and his backing vocalists was more finely tuned than ever. In many ways, his advanced years had only served to improve Cohen as a performer. As more than one reviewer rightfully concluded, the triple disc set was well worth the price, and the next best thing to the actual live experience.

The box set didn't show as well in the album charts as his single-disc releases had, for obvious reasons, only making it to the Top Fifty best-sellers in Austria, Belgium, Holland, Hungary and Switzerland. But over the months and years, *Live in Dublin* would prove to be a valued record of Leonard Cohen's concert zenith, in what had become the final stages of his career as a performing artist.

22

CAN'T FORGET: A SOUVENIR OF THE GRAND TOUR

'The big change is the proximity to death, I am a tidy kind of guy. I like to tie up the strings if I can. If I can't, also, that's okay. But my natural thrust is to finish things that I've begun.'

All songs written by Leonard Cohen, except where indicated.

1. Field Commander Cohen
2. I Can't Forget
3. Light as the Breeze
4. La Manic (eorges Dor)
5. Night Comes On
6. Never Gave Nobody Trouble
7. Joan of Arc
8. Got a Little Secret
9. Choices (Mike Curtis, Bill Yates)
10. Stages

Personnel: Leonard Cohen (vocals, guitar, keyboard); Roscoe Beck (bass, double bass, backing vocals); Rafael Bernardo Gayol (drums, percussion); Neil Larsen (Hammond B3, keyboards); Javier Mas (banduria, laud, twelve-string guitar); Mitch Watkins (guitar, backing vocals; Alexandru Bublitchi (violin); Sharon Robinson (backing vocals); Charley Webb (backing vocals, guitar); Hattie Webb (backing vocals, harp)

Recorded: 25 August 2012, Rosenborg Castle, Copenhagen, Denmark; 6 September 2012, Warsteiner Hockey Park, Monchengladbach, Germany; 11 September 2012, Irish Museum of Modern Art, Dublin, Ireland; 3 November 2012, IstBank Center, Denver, Colorado, USA; 2 December 2012, Colisée Pepsi, Quebec City, Canada; 14 July 2013, O2 World, Hamburg, Germany; 17 August 2013, The King's Garden, Odense, Denmark; 2 December 2013, Sydney Opera House, Sydney, Australia; 14 December CBS Canterbury Arena, Christchurch, New Zealand; 21 December 2013, Vector Arena, Auckland, New Zealand

Released: 12 May 2015
Label: Columbia
Producer: Mark Vreeken, Edward Sanders

Released just five months after *Live in Dublin*, Leonard Cohen's penultimate album, *Can't Forget: A Souvenir of the Grand Tour*, was a collection of live recordings and sound checks from the 2012–2013 *Old Ideas* marathon tour. Despite its 'for collectors only' angle, it managed to appear in the album charts in nine territories worldwide. This second album from the tour appeared at a time when Cohen had begun to suffer from various cancer-related physical problems, which had started to affect his mobility.

The Album

Rather in the spirit of Bob Dylan's ongoing 'Bootleg Series' that began in 1991, this was a collection of live performances and sound checks recorded on the road. The tracks gave listeners a rare insight into Cohen's exacting rehearsal process, the in-depth 'concerts before the concert' that few fans had ever got to hear before.

The album opened with a sound check of 'Field Commander Cohen', first heard in a studio take on 1974's *New Skin For The Old Ceremony*. A number of reviewers felt that this rehearsal version, with some impressive guitar accompaniment by Javier Mas and the vocal back-up of Sharon Robinson and the Webb Sisters, was actually better than the original.

'I Can't Forget', with a spoken farewell from Leonard (thanking the audience for turning up, despite the rain), was recorded towards the end of a concert at the Rosenborg Castle in Copenhagen, Denmark. And the ambling 'Light as a Breeze' was likewise recorded at the actual performance, at the Irish Museum of Modern Art in Dublin, and highlighted by an evocative violin break by Alexandru Bublitchi.

A number that Leonard usually reserved for French Canadian audiences followed: 'La Manic', originally by the Quebec singer Georges Dor, recorded in Quebec City in December 2012. This would be the first time that any fans, outside of those attending the Canadian concerts where he performed it, would have heard Cohen's version of the song.

The fourth of the five recordings from the live concert performances was 'Night Comes On', recorded in September 2012 at a hockey stadium in Monchengladbach, Germany. Apart from the final track, the rest of the album comprised sound checks, including a new Cohen composition, the twelve-bar blues 'Never Gave Nobody Trouble', with a fine guitar solo from Mitch Watkins.

The only venue represented twice on the album was the Colisée Pepsi in Canada's Quebec City, where 'Joan of Arc' was recorded during the warm-up behind closed doors. Hattie Webb took the lead female vocal, before being joined by her sister Charley. Even listening today, it's hard to believe that such perfection was achieved in just a preliminary run-through.

'I think the term poet is a very exalted term, and should be applied to a man at the end of his work. When he looks back over the body of his work, and he's written poetry, then let the verdict be that he is a poet.'

The other previously unheard Cohen composition was 'Got a Little Secret', all the more poignant for its recording at his last-ever concert appearance, on 21 December 2013 in Auckland, New Zealand. And the only other cover on the album was the atmospheric country ballad 'Choices', written by Mike Curtis and Bill Yates, and most successfully recorded by George Jones in 1999. Like 'La Manic', Leonard Cohen's cover never got to be recorded in the studio.

The closing track 'Stages' consisted of some humourous introductory banter from Leonard, recorded at a concert at the Sydney Opera House in Australia, followed by the first two verses of 'Tower of Song' from a sound check at the O2 World venue in Hamburg, Germany. It ends with a fade-out which, one suspects, was before the rehearsal of the song had actually finished. One review described it as 'leaving one slightly unfulfilled. Maybe that was the intention. Always keep 'em wanting more. And we do Len, we do.'

When the album was released in May 2015, it was greeted as yet another essential piece of aural documentation of Leonard Cohen's music that was, as the reviewer for *Rolling Stone* put it, 'a fascinating glimpse into his creative process'. In *Mojo* magazine, Sylvie Simmons gave more insight into Leonard's unique pre-concert rehearsals: 'Cohen's sound checks, as lengthy as the shows, where he'd experiment with old songs and try out new ones, were celebrated by insiders.'

The *Financial Times* concluded that 'for all his much-vaunted depressiveness, Cohen's outlook is essentially comic, a beacon of light amid the darkness.' And the *New York Daily News* applauded the backing musicians, who had often played second fiddle (no pun intended) to Cohen's lyrics in the past: 'Because of their wry erudition, Cohen's words have long stolen attention from his music. How sweet that, at this late stage, the waltzes get the last word.'

Cohen on stage at Sportpaleis, Ahoy, Rotterdam, Netherlands, November 3, 2008.

The AllMusic website, however, still felt it was Leonard's, and only Leonard's, album: 'Good as his bandmates are, on *Can't Forget'*, Cohen is the star, and he's as strong, as witty, and as willing to lay himself emotionally bare as ever; it's anyone's guess how much longer he intends to keep going, but there's nothing here to suggest he needs or wants to quit now.'

Decline

Unfortunately, although he had no intention of quitting as such, since the release of *Popular Problems* in September 2014, Leonard Cohen's health had been in serious decline. He had been battling cancer since the end of his touring in December 2013, and other health problems included multiple fractures of the spine, which increasingly restricted his mobility.

Nevertheless, he carried on working, thinking about his next album and other projects. In 2015, he moved into the second floor of his daughter Lorca's home in the Mid-Wilshire area of Los Angeles. And although he was no longer able to do much travelling, it meant he saw his son, daughter and grandchildren (Adam's son Cassius, and Lorca's children, Viva and Lyon), more often.

By mid-2015, when the *Can't Forget* collection had appeared, Leonard was working from a large blue medical chair, to ease the discomfort of the compression fractures in his back. His hands were starting to be a problem, so he was playing less guitar and turning to the synthesizer more often, as he continued to write and create music in the makeshift home studio that son Adam had set up for him. Using medical marijuana to alleviate the pain, he persevered on new songs and poems.

Leonard was thinking about a new book of poetry, in which the poems were annotated on the side of the page with various interpretations. He was also planning an album of his songs recorded with string arrangements, and another dedicated to new compositions inspired by old rhythm and blues music.

Central to this creative activity was his next album, which Adam would co-produce, with Leonard increasingly conscious that time was not on his side. 'The big change is the proximity to death', he said in an interview in the *New Yorker* on the release of the album in 2016. 'I am a tidy kind of guy. I like to tie up the strings if I can. If I can't, also, that's okay. But my natural thrust is to finish things that I've begun.'

'He felt the window getting narrower', Cohen's frequent collaborator and producer Patrick Leonard recalled. 'He wanted to use the time as productively as he could to finish the work that he was so good at and so devoted to.'

The album, *You Want It Darker*, would be released on 21 October 2016, by which time Leonard seemed resigned to the reality of his impending death: 'I've got some work to do. Take care of business. I am ready to die. I hope it's not too uncomfortable. That's about it for me.'

The 'Old Ideas' tour at the König-Pilsener Arena in Oberhausen, Germany, June 2013.

23
YOU WANT IT DARKER

'I said I was ready to die recently, and I think I was exaggerating. I've always been into self-dramatisation. I intend to live forever.'

LEONARD COHEN

YOU WANT IT DARKER

All songs written by Leonard Cohen, except where indicated.

1. You Want It Darker (Cohen, Patrick Leonard)
2. Treaty
3. On the Level (Cohen, Sharon Robinson)
4. Leaving the Table
5. If I Didn't Have Your Love (Cohen, Patrick Leonard)
6. Travelling Light (Cohen, Adam Cohen, Patrick Leonard)
7. It Seemed the Better Way (Cohen, Patrick Leonard)
8. Steer Your Way
9. String Reprise / Treaty

Personnel: Leonard Cohen (vocals); Bill Bottrell (guitar, pedal steel guitar); Michael Chaves (keyboards, bass guitar, drum programming); Adam Cohen (classical guitar); Patrick Leonard (keyboards, organ, piano, bass synthesiser, bass guitar, percussion, drum programming); Sean Hurley (bass); Brian Macleod (drums); Rob Humphreys (drums); Michael Hassler (viola); Luanne Holmzy (violin); Zac Rae (guitar, classical guitar, mandolin, keyboards, Mellotron, celesta, piano, Wurlitzer, floor tom, octophone); David Davidson (violin); Etienne Gara (violin); Yoshika Masuda (cello); Tom Hemby (bouzouki); Athena Andreadis (backing vocals); Dana Glover (backing vocals); Alison Krauss (backing vocals); Cantor Gideon Y. Zelermyer (solo vocal); Shaar Hashomayim Synagogue Choir (voices)

Recorded: April 2015 – July 2016
Released: 21 October 2016
Label: Columbia
Producer: Leonard Cohen, Adam Cohen, Patrick Leonard

Due to his physical difficulties, Leonard Cohen recorded what would be his final album 'confined to barracks' in the living room of his Los Angeles home – which was a second-floor apartment in his daughter Lorca's house – working in close conjunction with his son Adam. Released just two weeks before Cohen's death, it received widespread acclaim and became a posthumous tribute to his memory.

Recording

Leonard began work on the album around the time *Can't Forget'* was released, in the spring of 2015. Initially Cohen collaborated with Patrick Leonard, but when the producer had to quit the project due to personal problems, Adam Cohen took over as his father's right-hand man. Adam converted Cohen's living quarters into an improvised recording studio, fixing an old Neumann U87 microphone to the dining table and setting up computers, mixing boards and speakers.

It was Adam who brought in the orthopaedic medical chair, specifically designed to accommodate someone with mobility problems who would have to spend hours on end in it. As he told *Rolling Stone*, 'You can sleep in it, eat in it and practically stand in it.' Running a ProTools audio digital workstation on his laptop, Leonard could record and mix everything he needed before adding his vocals on top. Some songs Leonard dictated into his phone, others he kept on a notepad in his pocket.

A team of session players were on stand-by in a Los Angeles studio, where they worked on the material that Cohen provided, via directions given to Adam: 'I spoke to him at length, got his instructions before every session. Then I faithfully tried to serve what I understood his vision to be in the studio. He also had final say and veto power.' Leonard was as meticulous as ever, with two or three songs not actually making it onto the album. Adam was perhaps in a better position than anyone to gauge when the final results would be what his father wanted.

When the album came out, on 21 October 2016, Leonard was quick to acknowledge the support his children had provided on the project. 'My son and my daughter have both been an incredibly sustaining force, especially through this recent bad patch, so I've been blessed and grateful for their company . . . Adam is a great singer/songwriter in his own right. To have his own microscopic attention to my work is really a great privilege.'

Marianne

While he was still putting the finishing touches to the new album, Leonard learned in July via an e-mail from Jan Christian Mollestad, a close friend of his ex-lover and lifelong friend Marianne Ihlen – the inspiration for 'So Long, Marianne' – that Marianne was dying of cancer in Norway. When he'd last heard from Marianne, she had said she was selling her beach house to make sure Axel (her son by her first husband, Axel Jensen, who she had left for Cohen in 1960) was taken care of. At no point had she mentioned her illness. It now seemed she only had days left to live.

Leonard wrote to her as soon as he got the message, in a letter that appeared to anticipate his own death: 'Well Marianne, it's come to this time when we are really so old and our bodies are falling apart and I think I will follow you very soon. Know that I am so close behind you that if you stretch out your hand, I think you can reach mine . . .' concluding 'Now, I just want to wish you a very good journey. Goodbye old friend. Endless love, see you down the road.'

A couple of days later, Leonard received an emotional e-mail from Norway. 'Marianne slept slowly out of this life yesterday evening. Totally at ease, surrounded by close friends. Your letter came when she still could talk and laugh in full consciousness. When we read it aloud, she smiled as only Marianne can. She lifted her hand, when you said you were right behind, close enough to reach her.' It ended with a poignant message: 'We kissed her head and whispered your everlasting words.

So long, Marianne . . .'

The Album

The new album opened with something of a surprise, a full male voice choir intoning a hymn-like backing to the title track. It was in fact the full Shaar Hashomayim Synagogue Choir, from Leonard's family place of worship in Montreal. What the Columbia press release called 'an unflinching exploration of the religious mind', the intimations of religious ambiguity were enhanced by the voice of the Montreal cantor, Gideon Y. Zelermyer.

Most of the songs on the album were of recent origin, emanating from Cohen's hospitalised workroom, although the second track, 'Treaty', dated back at least a decade. Again, it constituted an old man's confessional, with synthesised strings and backing voices emphasising the melancholy of the words.

The whole album, in one way or another, made it clear that Leonard was

YOU WANT IT DARKER

very aware of his own mortality, making good sometimes fractured relationships, even coming to terms with God . . . in his own way, of course. In the waltz-time 'Leaving The Table', for instance, the sense of an impending farewell could hardly be more explicit; he is leaving the table and out of the game.

The album closed with a heartfelt reprise of 'Treaty', this time as a string treatment. The album was finished with a final vocal verse that ended the collection – and, as it transpired, Leonard's lifetime body of work – with a hope for a repairing of broken relationships.

A week ahead of the album's release, Cohen and Columbia Records set up a promotional listening session followed by a thirty-minute Q&A. But before the assembled journalists got on to the subject of the album itself, or Leonard's future plans, there was inevitable reference to a lengthy interview in the *New Yorker* magazine, in which the singer appeared to anticipate his impending death.

The event's host, Chris Douridas, asked Cohen directly how he was feeling. Proving to be just as sharp as ever, Leonard replied: 'I said I was ready to die recently, and I think I was exaggerating. I've always been into self-dramatisation. I intend to live forever.'

Another subject raised as a result of the *New Yorker* piece was that of Bob Dylan, who had heaped praise on Cohen at length to the article's author, David Remnick: 'When people talk about Leonard, they fail to mention his melodies, which to me, along with his lyrics, are his greatest genius.' When asked whether he preferred Cohen's later work, Dylan had the perfect response. 'I like all of Leonard's songs, early or late.'

Cohen was asked what he thought of Dylan's effusive complements, replying 'It was very generous and very kind.' Asked to go into further detail, he declined, shifting the subject to a related topic: 'I won't comment on what he said, but I will comment on his receiving the Nobel Prize, which to me is like pinning a medal on Mount Everest for being the highest mountain.'

The album was well received by critics and public alike. *Rolling Stone* reported that Cohen was in 'slightly better health' than during the making of the record, ending the review with a word from Adam Cohen: 'They say that life is a beautiful play with a terrible third act. If that's the case, it must not apply to Leonard Cohen. Right now, at the end of his career, perhaps at the end of his life, he's at the summit of his powers.'

The online music magazine *Pitchfork* called it 'a pristine, piously crafted last testament, the informed conclusion of a lifetime of inquiry', while the *Guardian*'s Alexis Petridis, giving it a five-star rating, said: 'Throughout, he sounds wise and honest, and – despite the occasional lyrical protestations of weariness – full of life.'

'My son and my daughter have both been an incredibly sustaining force, especially through this recent bad patch, so I've been blessed and grateful for their company.'

Record Collector magazine concluded 'It's as strong a collection as any of his in recent times', the *Telegraph* called it 'a bleak masterpiece for hard times from pop's longest-serving poet', and *Uncut* prophetically stated that 'it's become a cliché to treat every latter-day Cohen album like a potential swansong but it's hard to imagine a richer, finer or more satisfying finale than this.'

The End

Just three weeks after the release of *You Want It Darker* came the announcement that Leonard Cohen had passed away overnight, after a fall in his Los Angeles home. His manager Robert Kory broke the news to a reeling world: 'Leonard Cohen died during his sleep following a fall in the middle of the night on 7 November. The death was sudden, unexpected and peaceful.' It was three days before the news was made public, on the day of his funeral on 10 November 2016. The burial took place in Leonard's home city of Montreal, at the Shaar Hashomayim Cemetery on the slopes of Mount Royal, with the words of Kaddish, the Jewish prayer of memory – 'Magnified, sanctified be Thy holy name' –recited at the graveside. As Adam Cohen would describe on Facebook: 'My sister and I just buried my father in Montreal. With only immediate family and a few lifelong friends present, he was lowered into the ground in an unadorned pine box, next to his mother and father. Exactly as he'd asked. Thank you for your kind messages, for the outpouring of sympathy and for your love of my father.'

Whether *You Want It Darker*, which was suddenly a posthumous hit, would have experienced the same levels of commercial and critical success had Cohen survived his fall is open to conjecture. So short was the period between its release and Leonard's death, the impact of the latter was immediate. Regardless, it was an instant hit in Canada, where its chart debut was at #1. The album held the top position for three consecutive weeks, selling over 100,000 copies by the end of the year.

In the United States, the album peaked in the *Billboard* chart at #7, being only Cohen's second to reach the American Top Ten. It topped the charts in no fewer than thirteen countries worldwide, as well as making the Top Five in Australia, France, Germany, Hungary, Spain, Switzerland and the UK. In all *You Want It Darker* earned gold records in nine countries, and platinum in three – including two platinum discs in Poland.

It went on to be cited as one of the year's best albums by various magazines, including *Rolling Stone*, *Mojo* and the online *Pitchfork*. At the Canadian Juno Awards in 2017, it was cited as Album of the Year, with Cohen being posthumously named Artist of the Year.

Tribute

As soon as the news of Leonard's death broke, people of all ages and walks of life paid tribute to his memory. Almost immediately, on the streets of Montreal, fans held a musical vigil outside the house he had bought in the 1970s, the three-storey duplex in Rue Vallières, in the borough of Plateau-Mont-Royal. Within hours of the announcement, the steps of the building were covered with wreaths, candles and

Cohen salutes one of his largest ever concert audiences at Glastonbury, June 29, 2008.

'Well Marianne, it's come to this time when we are really so old and our bodies are falling apart and I think I will follow you very soon.'

written messages, as fans gathered in the Parc du Portugal opposite to sing some of Cohen's best-loved songs – including, of course, emotional renditions of 'Hallelujah'.

Similar impromptu shrines also appeared outside his old house on the island of Hydra in Greece, and the Chelsea Hotel in New York City, which Cohen had lived in for several periods in his life and memorialised in one of his most celebrated songs.

The media reaction to Leonard Cohen's passing was as instantaneous and wholehearted as that of the fans. BBC News called him 'one of the most enigmatic poets and songwriters of his generation', while the *New York Times* described him as 'an unlikely and reluctant pop star, if in fact he ever was one', adding that 'he was thirty-three when his first record was released in 1967 . . . he maintained a private, sometime ascetic image at odds with the Dionysian excesses associated with rock.'

The UK *Guardian* newspaper similarly drew attention to Cohen's maturity in a world seemingly dominated by youth: 'Leonard Cohen was always the grown-up in the room. He was young once, of course, but the world never saw much of the modestly successful poet and novelist from Montreal. He was already thirty-three – ancient by '60s standards – when he gazed out from the sepia-tinted, photo-booth snapshot on the cover of 1967's *Songs of Leonard Cohen* with his shirt, tie and smart side-parting.'

Individual tributes appeared from all over the world, including from those close to Leonard. In the Canadian national paper *Globe and Mail*, Adam Cohen confirmed the loss of his father, and acknowledged the tremendous legacy left behind. 'My father passed away peacefully at his home in Los Angeles with the knowledge that he had completed what he felt was one of his greatest records. He was writing up until his last moments with his unique brand of humour.' In the same edition, Cohen's close friend and manager Robert Kory also paid tribute: 'I was blessed to call him a friend, and for me to serve that bold artistic spirit first hand, was a privilege and great gift. He leaves behind a legacy of work that will bring insight, inspiration and healing for generations to come.'

The co-producer and co-writer on Leonard's final three albums, Patrick Leonard, recalled how Cohen was working and creating until the end: 'There's five or six songs that were ready to be finished. There's another record that could have happened. It sounds crazy, but yes, there was. I think maybe that my biggest value to him was that I could help him get these things finished, so that the poetry got out. Because he wrote every day, all day, and every night, all night.', Producer John Lissaur, who had worked on *New Skin For The Old Ceremony* and *Various Positions*, told BBC Radio 4's *Today* programme: 'He was so consistent in his devotion to the craft and his devotion to recording and performing.'

Fellow artists and other members of the music industry were quick to acknowledge Cohen's legacy. Neil Portnow, chief executive of the Recording Academy – which organises the annual Grammy Awards – described him as 'one of the most revered pop poets, and a musical touchstone for many songwriters . . . His extraordinary talent had a profound impact on countless singers and songwriters, as well as the wider culture.'

Among dozens of singers and songwriters who registered their sorrow at Leonard's death, Elton John remembered the way 'his ability to conjure the vast array of human emotion made him one of the most influential and enduring musicians ever.' Nick Cave described Leonard as 'the greatest songwriter of them all. Utterly unique and impossible to imitate, no matter how hard we tried.' And Leonard's great supporter and friend, k.d.lang, was moved to call him 'an elegant practitioner of the senses. Fully engaged in the realm of desire and yet fully dedicated to the spiritual. The quintessential Renaissance man who will never be matched.'

Artists from other disciplines were also among those paying tribute. Actor Russell Crowe's brief eulogy read 'Dear Leonard Cohen, thanks for the quiet nights, the reflection, the perspective, the wry smiles and the truth.' And the eminent Canadian writer Michael Ondaatje summed up Leonard as 'a hero for our generation and for the next – stepping bravely into new forms, a great writer who then became a great songwriter.'

Several civic and political leaders paid tribute to Cohen, including Israel's Prime Minister Benjamin Netanyahu who described him as 'a great creator' and 'a talented artist.' David Johnston, the Governor General of Canada, said: 'Leonard Cohen's passing is a lost for us all. He was a unique voice and poet of our time, loved around the world.'

The Canadian Prime Minister Justin Trudeau led the multitude of tributes with a fulsome statement that celebrated Cohen's enduring relevance. 'His ability to conjure the vast array of human emotion made him one of the most influential and enduring musicians ever. His style transcended the vagaries of fashion. His music has withstood the test of time.' Trudeau ended the lengthy eulogy with a message addressed directly to the deceased singer: 'Leonard, no other artist's poetry and music felt or sounded quite like yours. We'll miss you.'

Aftermath
In January 2017, just two months after Cohen's death, *From the Shadows* was released on the Zip City label. It was a bootleg recording of a live radio broadcast, made from the legendary Olympia concert hall in Paris in June 1976. While some fans welcomed the release, applauding it for its surprisingly good sound quality, most saw it as simply cashing in on Leonard's death.

Bootlegs notwithstanding, in the aftermath of Cohen's death, there was an inevitable boost in the sales of *You Want It Darker*. Many of the reviews had already raised the question of whether it would be Leonard's final album, as they often had in years before. This time, it was indeed Leonard's parting shot, the final collection of work for which he would be remembered.

DISCOGRAPHY

STUDIO ALBUMS
Songs of Leonard Cohen, December 1967
Songs from a Room, March 1969
Songs of Love and Hate, March 1971
New Skin for the Old Ceremony, August 1974
Death of a Ladies' Man, November 1977
Recent Songs, September 1979
Various Positions, December 1984
I'm Your Man, February 1988
The Future, November 1992
Ten New Songs, October 2001
Dear Heather, October 2004
Old Ideas, January 2012
Popular Problems, September 2014
You Want It Darker, October 2016

LIVE ALBUMS
Live Songs, April 1973
Cohen Live: Leonard Cohen in Concert,
June 1994
Field Commander Cohen: Tour of 1979,
February 2001
Live in London, March 2009
Live at the Isle of Wight 1970, October 2009
Songs from the Road, September 2010
Live in Dublin, December 2014
Can't Forget: A Souvenir of the Grand Tour,
May 2015

COMPILATION ALBUMS
The Best of Leonard Cohen / Greatest Hits,
January 1975
So Long, Marianne, May 1989
More Best of Leonard Cohen, October 1997
The Essential Leonard Cohen, October 2002
The Collection [Box Set], June 2008
Greatest Hits, July 2009
The Complete Studio Albums Collection
[Box Set], October 2011

BOOKS BY LEONARD COHEN
Poetry collections
Let Us Compare Mythologies,
Contact Press (Canada), 1956
The Spice-Box of Earth,
McLelland & Stewart (Canada), 1961
Flowers for Hitler,
McLelland & Stewart (Canada), 1964
Parasites of Heaven,
McLelland & Stewart (Canada), 1966
Selected Poems 1956-1968,
McLelland & Stewart (Canada), 1968
The Energy of Slaves,
McLelland & Stewart (Canada), 1972
Death of a Lady's Man,
McLelland & Stewart (Canada), 1978
Book of Mercy,
McLelland & Stewart (Canada), 1984
Stranger Music: Selected Poems and Songs,
Jonathan Cape (UK), 1993
Book of Longing,
McLelland & Stewart (Canada), 2006
The Lyrics of Leonard Cohen,
Omnibus (UK), 2009
Poems and Songs,
Random House (US), 2011
Fifteen Poems,
Random House (US), 2011 [eBook]
The Flame,
Penguin (UK), 2018

NOVELS
The Favorite Game,
Secker & Warburg (UK), 1963
Beautiful Losers,
Viking (US), 1966

REFERENCES

Ch 1

Christian Fevret, *Les Inrockuptibles* (1991); M. Young, *25 Lessons in Hypnotism: How to Become an Expert Operator*; Leonard Cohen, The Prince of Asturias Awards Speech, 2011; Anthony Reynolds, *Leonard Cohen: A Remarkable Life* (2010); McClelland and Stewart, July 2006; LC interview with BBC, September 20, 1986; Sylvie Simmons, *I'm Your Man* (2012); Kari Hesthamar, Interview with Leonard Cohen, 2005; Kari Hesthamar, Interview with Marianne Ihlen, 2005; Ira B. Nadel, *Various Positions* (1996); Interview, 1961; Robert Weaver, *Toronto Daily Star*, 10 June 1961; Erica Pomerance quoted in Sylvie Simmons, *I'm Your Man* (2012); Leonard Cohen Archive (Thomas Fisher Rare Book Library, University of Toronto), Letter to Jack McClelland, July 1963; Ibid, Letter to Leonard Cohen from McClelland, August 1963; Milton Wilson, *Toronto Quarterly*, July 1965; Frank DiGiacomo. New York Observer, Oct 15, 2001; *The Guardian* online books blog, July 16, 2008; Robert Fulford, the *Toronto Daily Star*, 1966; CBC, 1966; Boston Globe, 1966; *New York Times*, 1969; Tim Footman, *Leonard Cohen: Hallelujah: A New Biography* (2009).

Ch 2

Village Voice, December 28, 1967; Anthony O'Grady, *RAM*, April 1980; LC interview with BBC, September 20, 1986; Judy Collins quoted in Sylvie Simmons, *I'm Your Man* (2012); John Hammond interview with BBC, September 20, 1986; *Uncut* magazine, February 26, 2015.

Ch 3

Melody Maker February 17, 1968; LC to concert audience, 1988; LC to concert audience, 1976; Kari Hesthamar, Interview with Leonard Cohen, 2005; Ibid; Bob Johnston, quoted in Sylvie Simmons, *I'm Your Man* (2012); *Songtalk* magazine, 1993; John McKenna, RTE, Ireland, 1988; Alec Dubro, *Rolling Stone* review, May 17, 1969.

Ch 4

Suzanne Elrod, quoted in *People* magazine, January 14, 1980; Bob Johnston, quoted in Sylvie Simmons, *I'm Your Man* (2012); Ron Cornelius, quoted in Howard Sounes, *Down The Highway: The Life Of Bob Dylan* (2011); *Sounds* magazine, October 1971;

LC talking to *Melody Maker*, 1970; Review, *Melody Maker* September 5, 1970; Robert Sward, December 1984; Liner notes, *The Best of Leonard Cohen* (1975); *New Musical Express*, March 1973; Sylvie Simmons, *I'm Your Man* (2012).

Ch 5

Mike Jahn, *New York Times Special Features Syndication*, 9 June 1973; *Sounds*, Oct 23, 1971; *Melody Maker*, March 1 1975; Jennifer Warnes, talking to Randall Roberts, *LA Times*, November 14, 2016; Billy Walker, *Sounds*, Mar 4, 1972; *New Musical Express*, quoted in Anthony Reynolds, *Leonard Cohen: A Remarkable Life* (2010); Roy Hollingworth, *Melody Maker*, February 24, 1973; Jaan Uhelszki, *Creem*, August 1973.

Ch 6

Grace Lichtenstein, *New York Times* Sept. 8, 1973; Aussie Dave, israellycool.com, November 11, 2016; Judy Maltz, haaretz.com, Nov 11, 2016, Alastair Pirrie, *New Musical Express,* March 10, 1973; Robin Pike, *Zig Zag*, October 1974; *Melody Maker*, March 1 1975; John Lissauer, quoted in Sylvie Simmons, *I'm Your Man* (2012); LC interview with BBC, 1994; LC talking to John McKenna, RTE 1988; Paul Nelson, *Rolling Stone*, 1974; Bob Woffinden, *New Musical Express*, September 21, 1974; Michael Watts, *Melody Maker*, September 28, 1974.

Ch 7

Mick Brown, *Sounds*, July 3, 1976; LC talking to Valerie Pringle for CTV's *W5*, 28 October 1997; Paul Williams, *Crawdaddy!,* Mar 1975; LC quoted in Larry Sloman, *On the Road with Bob Dylan* (1978); Harvey Kubernick, *Melody Maker*, March 6, 1976; Mick Brown, *Sounds*, July 3 1976; Dan Kessel quoted in Sylvie Simmons, *I'm Your Man* (2012); Harvey Kubernick, *LA Phonograph*, January 1978; Adrian Deevoy, *Q* magazine, 1991; LC quoted in Sylvie Simmons, *I'm Your Man* (2012); LC quoted in Anthony Reynolds, *Leonard Cohen: A Remarkable Life* (2010); LC quoted in Alan Light, *The Holy or the Broken*; Sandy Robertson, *Sounds,* November 26 1977; Paul Nelson, *Rolling Stone*, November 1977.

Ch 8

Chris Bohn, *Melody Maker*, January 5, 1980; Suzanne Elrod, quoted in Sylvie Simmons, *I'm Your Man* (2012); John Bilezikjian talking to Anthony Reynolds, *Leonard Cohen: A Remarkable Life* (2010); Debra Rae Cohen, *Rolling Stone*, February 21, 1980; Chris Bohn, *Melody Maker*, January 5, 1980; Sharon Robinson talking to Philippe Sands, *Financial Times*, August 9, 2013; Anthony O'Grady, *RAM*, April 1980; Scott Cohen, *Spin*, August 1985; Robert Sward, December 1984.

Ch 9

Elizabeth Boleman-Herring, *Huffington Post*, 1 September 2012; Dominique Issermann speaking to Claire Guillot, *Le Monde*, 12 November 2016; LC talking to Vicki Gabereau for CBC's *Variety Tonight*, 6 September 1984, transcribed in *Leonard Cohen on Leonard Cohen* edited by Jeff Burger (2014); John Lissauer talking to Anthony Reynolds, *Leonard Cohen: A Remarkable Life,* 2010; LC talking to Paul Zollo, *Songwriters on Songwriting*, 1991; Jason Ankeny, AllMusic.com; Don Shewey, *Rolling Stone*, June 20, 1885; Judith Fitzgerald, *The Globe and Mail*, 2000; Richard Cook, *NME*, February 9, 1985; Mick Brown, *The Guardian*, February 27, 1985; *Santa Cruz Sentinel*, June 23, 1985

Ch 10
Publicity for *Night Magic*, RSL Entertainment Corp. Fildebroc & TF1 France; Lewis Furey, Sylvie Simmons, *I'm Your Man* (2012); Steve Turner, *Q*, April 1988; Len Brown, *New Musical Express*, June 20, 1987; Jennifer Warnes in *Take This Waltz: A Celebration of Leonard Cohen*, 1994; Nigel Williamson, *Uncut*, 1991; LC on stage, London, June 1, 1988; Stephen Holden, *The New York Times*, June 21, 2006; Andy Green, *Rolling Stone*, November 26, 2014; "Morning Becomes Eclectic", KCRW Radio, 1997; LC talking to John Archer, BBC, 1988; Mat Snow, *The Guardian*, February 1988; Richard North, *New Musical Express*, March 5, 1988; David Brown, *Rolling Stone*, February 1988; Prince Charles, ITV interview, 1988.

Ch 11
Adam Cohen, *Kitchener-Waterloo Record,* November 10, 1998; Adam Cohen, *The Guardian*, 2011; Stina Lundberg Dabrowski, Swedish National TV, September 1997; Sylvie Simmons, *I'm Your Man* (2012); Rebecca De Mornay, *Rolling Stone*, 1992; Pico Iyer, *The Buzz Magazine*, 1995; Adrian Deevoy, *Q*, 1991; LC interview with Austrian magazine *Basta*, translated for *Intensity* by Johannes Knapp-Menzl; Anthony Reynolds, *Leonard Cohen: A Remarkable Life* (2010); Paul Zollo, *Songwriters On Songwriting* (2003); Vin Scalsa, *Idiot's Delight*, WXRK FM, June 13, 1993; *Rolling Stone*: January 21, 1993; Christian Wright, *Rolling Stone*, December 1992; Cliff Jones, *Rock CD*, December 1992; Andy Gill, *Q*, January 1993; Sean O'Neal, The AV Club, May 10, 2016; Andy Gill, *The Independent*, May 13, 1993.

Ch 12
Ottawa Citizen, November 1993; *Expresso*, (Portugal) July 9, 1994; *Publishers Weekly*, November 1, 1993; *Toronto Star*; November 1993; LC acceptance speech, Canadian Music Hall of Fame, 1991; *Globe and Mail*, May 28 1969; LC at Governor General's Performing Arts Award ceremony, November 1993, quoted in Sylvie Simmons, *I'm Your Man* (2012); *Time*, 1994; Andy Gill, *Mojo*, August 1994.

Ch 13
Gilles Tordjman, *Les Inrockuptibles*, October 15, 1995; Kari Hesthamar, Interview with Leonard Cohen, 2005; Elena Comelli, *La Nazione*, Florence (Italy), November 25, 1998, translated by Andrea Della Rossa; Pico Iyer,

The Buzz Magazine, April 1995; Sylvie Simmons, *I'm Your Man* (2012); Larry Rohterfeb, *New York Times*, February 24, 2009; Susan Nunziata, *Billboard*, August 5th, 1995; *New Musical Express*, September 1995; Terry Gross, NPR, May 22, 2006; James Hunter, *Rolling Stone*, 2001; Mark Denning, *All Music Guide*, March 2001.

Ch 14
Sarah Hampson, *Shambhala Sun*, November 2007; Frank DiGiacomo, *New York Observer*, February 22, 2002; Sharon Robinson, quoted in Simon Worrall, *The Independent*, June 14, 2008; Kelley Lynch talking to Judith Fitzgerald, *The Globe and Mail*, September 25, 2000; Sharon Robinson talking to Anthony Reynolds, *Leonard Cohen: A Remarkable Life* (2010); *Leonard Cohen's Thoughts 'On You Have Loved Enough'*, LeonardCohen.com; Steven Chean, *Rolling Stone*, October 9, 2001; Pico Iyer, liner notes / CD booklet *The Essential Leonard Cohen* (Sony Music) 2003; Pat Blashill, *Rolling Stone*, 22 October 2002; Dick Straub, The Leonard Cohen Files (leonardcohenfiles.com), 2003; Michael Bonner, *Uncut*, September 17, 2014; Charlie Rose, *Nightwatch*, BBC, 1998.

Ch 15
Michaelangelo Matos, *Rolling Stone*, November 2004; Scott Edelman quoted in *New Musical Express*, March 6, 2006; *The Guardian*, April 20, 2012; Acceptance speech at Canadian Songwriters Hall of Fame induction, February 5, 2006; Neil McCormick, the Telegraph, May 26, 2007; Sylvie Simmons, *I'm Your Man* (2012); Anjani Thomas, talking to Neil McCormick, *The Telegraph*, May 2007; Anjani Thomas talking to Douglas Heselgrave, *The Music Box*, April 2007; Anjani Thomas, anjani-music.com; Philip Glass, CD liner notes *Book of Longing. Song Cycle Based on the Poetry and Images of Leonard Cohen,* December 2007.

Ch 16
David Jones, BBC, November 12 2006; LC on stage in Warsaw, March 31, 2007; Psalm 90, the *Holy Bible*; Rob Hallett talking to Mark Sutherland, *Music Week*, November 22, 2016; *Rolling Stone*, March 11, 2008; Lou Reed, quoted in *Rolling Stone*, March 11. 2008; Seam Michaels, *The Guardian*, March 12, 2008; Steve Wilcox, the Leonard Cohen Files, (leonardcohenfiles.com) May 11, 2008; Rob Hallett, quoted in Sylvie Simmons, *I'm Your Man* (2012); Stephen Dalton, *The Times*, June 2008; Gregoire Nappey, *20 Minutes,* July 2008 (leonardcohenfiles.com); Simon Sweetman, *Dominion Post* (Wellington, New Zealand), January 21, 2009; LC, 'Introduction' from *Live in London*, recorded at the O2 Arena, London, July 27, 2009; Sylvie Simmons, *I'm Your Man* (2012); Sylvie Simmons, *Daily Telegraph*: June 14, 2013.

Ch 17
Steven R. Rosen, *Denver Post*, June 4, 2009; *The Palestinian*

Campaign for the Academic and Cultural Boycott of Israel quoted by Rachelle Kliger, *Jerusalem Post*, July 13, 2009; LC, on stage at Ramat Gan Stadium, Tel Aviv, September 24, 2009; *The Independent*, September 2009; Joan Baez, quoted in Brian Hinton, *Message to Love: The Isle of Wight Festival 1968 – 1969 – 1970* (1995); Kris Kristofferson, *Leonard Cohen Live at the Isle of Wight 1970* DVD, 2009; Kris Kristofferson talking to Ira Nadel, *Various Positions: A Life of Leonard Cohen* (1996); Bob Johnson, quoted in Sylvie Simmons, *I'm Your Man* (2012); LC spoken introduction on *Leonard Cohen Live at the Isle of Wight 1970*, 2009

Ch 18
LC, acceptance speech at Grammy Awards ceremony, January 31, 2010; AEG Worldwide, press statement February 2010; Robert Kory, press statement February 2010; LC, acceptance speech at the Songwriters Hall of Fame induction ceremony, June 17, 2010; Andrew Mueller, *BBC* (bbc.co.uk), 2010; Doug Heselgrave, *No Depression*, (nodepression.com) August 10, 2010; *Victoria Times*, December 2010; *Vancouver Sun*, December 2010; Pico Iyer, *Shambhala Sun*, November/December 1998.

Ch 19
Prince of Asturias Award jury, quoted by BBC, June 2, 2011; Sylvie Simmons, *Mojo*, 2012; *Mojo*, 2013; *New York Times*, January 27, 2012; Jon Pareles, *New York Times*, January 27, 2012; Maddy Costa, *The Guardian*, January 26, 2012; Ian Winwood, BBC review, 2012; Joe Levy, *Rolling Stone*, January 26, 2012; LC to Jarvis Cocker, *The Guardian*, January 19, 2012; *Rolling Stone*, March 26, 2012; *Sunday Times*, September 16, 2012; Roscoe Beck, talking to Francis Mus, *Leonard Cohen Files*, August 16, 2012; Michael Green, *The Journal*, December 17, 2012; Craig Jones, eGigs (egigs.co.uk), September 13, 2012; *Financial Times*, quoted in AEG press release, December 10, 2012; Montreux Jazz Festival website, (montreuxjazzfestival.com), 2016; LC on stage, Vector Arena, Auckland, December 21, 2013, as reported in *Stuff*, December 2013.

Ch 20
LC at press conference, Canada High Commission, London, September 16, 2014; Gavin Edwards, *Rolling Stone*, September 19, 2014; Lian Lunson, *Leonard Cohen: I'm Your Man* (2005); Steve Appleford, *Rolling Stone*, September 11, 2014; Neil MacCormick, *The Telegraph*, September 23, 2014; Alexis Petridis, *The Guardian*, September 18, 2014; Allan Jones, *Uncut*, November 6, 2014; Leonie Cooper, *New Musical Express*, September 2014; Steve Morse, *Boston Globe*, September 29, 2014; Jim Farber, *New York Daily News*, September 19, 2014;

LC as reported by Associated Press, 2014, quoted by Julia Felsenthal, *Vogue*, November 10, 2016; LC at press conference, Canada High Commission, London, September 16, 2014.

Ch 21
The Sun, January 2012; Mackenzie Herd, *Exclaim!* December 2, 2014; Andy Greene, *Rolling Stone*, December 30, 2014; Luke Cartledge, *The Line of Best Fit* (thelineofbestfit.com), December 3, 2014; Jian Ghomeshi, *The Guardian*, 13 July 2009

Ch 22
Jon Dolan, *Rolling Stone*, May 12, 2015; Neil Spencer, *Uncut*, June 1, 2015; Sylvie Simmons, *Mojo*, May 11, 2015; Ludovic Hunter-Tilney, *The Financial Times*, May 8, 2015; Jim Farber, *New York Daily News*, May 8, 2015; Mark Deming, AllMusic website (allmusic.com), May 2015; David Remnick, *The New Yorker*, October 17, 2016; Patrick Leonard, quoted by Ben Sisario, *New York Times*, November 16, 2016;

Ch 23
Adam Cohen, talking to Andy Greene, *Rolling Stone*, November 2, 2016; LC speaking to journalists at Canadian Consulate Los Angeles, October 13, 2016; David Remnick, *The New Yorker*, October 17, 2016; Bob Dylan, talking to David Remnick, *The New Yorker*, October 17, 2016; Adam Cohen, talking to Andy Greene, *Rolling Stone*, November 2, 2016; Stacey Anderson, *Pitchfork*, October 24, 2016; Alexis Petridis, *The Guardian*, October 20 2016; Jamie Atkins, *Record Collector*, November 3, 2016; Neil McCormick, *The Telegraph*, November 11, 2016; Jason Anderson, *Uncut*, November 1, 2016; Robert Kory quoted in *The Guardian*, November 17, 2016; Adam Cohen, Facebook, November 10, 2016; BBC News, November 11, 2016; Larry Rother, *New York Times*, November 10, 2016; Dorian Lynskey, *The Guardian*, November 11, 2016; Adam Cohen, *Globe and Mail*, November 11, 2016; Robert Kory, *Globe and Mail*, November 11, 2016; Patrick Leonard, *Globe and Mail*, November 11, 2016; John Lissauer, interviewed on *Today*, BBC Radio 4, November 11, 2016; Neil Portnow, quoted by BBC News, November 11, 2016; Elton John, quoted by Hannah Ellis-Petersen, *The Guardian*, November 11, 2016; Bette Midler, *Entertainment Weekly*, November 10, 2016; Nick Cave, *Entertainment Weekly*, November 10, 2016; k.d. lang, *Globe and Mail*, November 11, 2016; Russell Crowe, quoted by Hannah Ellis-Petersen, *The Guardian*, November 11, 2016; Michael Ondaatje, *Globe and Mail*, November 11, 2016; Benjamin Netanyahu, quoted by BBC News, November 11, 2016; David Johnston, *Entertainment Weekly*, November 10, 2016; Justin Trudeau, quoted in *The Independent*, November 11, 2016.

A catalogue record for this book is available
from the British Library

ISBN-13: 978-0-85965-519-4

Cover Photo by Roz Kelly/Michael Ochs Archives/Getty Images
Cover and book design by Coco Balderrama
Printed in India by Replika Press PVT Limited

ACKNOWLEDGEMENTS
It is often an impossible task to thank all of the people who helped to
create a book. This is especially true of *Leonard Cohen: An Illustrated
Record.* Many people have lent their voices here but we must first make
a friendly salute to the late Leonard Cohen without whom. . .

To enable us to create such a definite work a team is necessary.
For his help editorially and for going the extra mile, we would like to
thank Cillian Dunn for editing, researching, weeding, transcribing,
annotating, and finally integrating millions of facts and dates. Ellie
Keeling assisted him with much of this; she also helped with picture
research and the gathering of visuals. Coco Balderrama created the
look and cover design.

We would like to give a special thank you to all of the individuals,
newspapers and magazines, book publishers and websites, authors and
journalists, record companies and photographers for their contribution
in helping us to create the text and visuals for this book. A full list
of sources used can be found in the Chapter by Chapter References
section on pages 205-207, but a particular debt is owed to the body
of literature that already exists on Leonard Cohen, which has proved
invaluable in the writing and researching of this book.

Newspapers, magazines, periodicals, TV and radio interviews:
*American Songwriter, AEG Worldwide, BBC, Billboard, The Boston
Globe, Crawdaddy!, Creem, Dominion Post, Entertainment Weekly,
Exclaim!, Expresso, The Financial Times, The Globe and Mail, The
Guardian, The Huffington Post, The Independent, The Jerusalem Post,
The* Journal, *KCRW Radio, Kitchener-Waterloo Record, LA Phonograph,
Le Monde, Melody Maker, Mojo, The Montreal Gazette, The Music Box,
Music Week, The New Musical Express, The New York Daily News, New
York Times, The New Yorker, People, Pitchfork, Pop Matters, Publishers
Weekly, Q, RAM, Record Collector, Rock CD, Rolling Stone, RTE,
Songtalk, Sounds, Stuff, The Sun, The Sunday Times, The Telegraph, The
Times, Uncut, The Vancouver Sun, The Times Colonist, Village Voice,
Vogue, Zig Zag.*

Websites: allmusic.com, anjani-music.com, cohencentric.com,
egigs.co.uk, haaretz.com, israellycool.com, leonardcohen.com,
leonardcohenfiles.com, thelineofbestfit.com, montreuxjazzfestival.
com, nodepression.com.

Books: Jeff Burger, *Leonard Cohen on Leonard Cohen* (2014),
Jim Devlin, *In Every Style of Passion* (1998), Tim Footman, *Leonard
Cohen: Hallelujah: A New Biography* (2009), Brian Hinton, *Message
to Love: The Isle of Weight Festival 1968 – 1969 – 1970* (1995), Harvey
Kubernick, *Leonard Cohen: Everybody Knows* (2015), Liel Liebovitz,
A Broken Hallelujah: Leonard Cohen's Secret Chord (2014), Alan Light,
*The Holy or the Broken: Leonard Cohen, Jeff Buckley, and the Unlikely
Ascent of Hallelujah* (2012), Ira B. Nadel, *Various Positions* (1996),
Michael Ondaatje, *Leonard Cohen* (1970), Anthony Reynolds, *Leonard
Cohen: A Remarkable Life* (2010), Sharon Robinson, *On Tour with
Leonard Cohen* (2014), Sylvie Simmons, *I'm Your Man* (2012), Larry
Sloman, *On the Road with Bob Dylan* (1978), Paul Zollo, *Songwriters
on Songwriting,* (1991).

Ecco Press, and McClelland and Stewart for the covers of:
Let Us Compare Mythologies, Ecco Press, 50th Anniversary edition
(1 Jun. 2007); *Parasites of Heaven*, McClelland and Stewart, Toronto,
1st edition (1966); *The Spice Box of Earth*, McClelland & Stewart,
Toronto, 1st edition (1961); *Beautiful Losers*, McClelland and Stewart,
Toronto, 1st edition (1966); *Flowers For Hitler*, McClelland and
Stewart, Toronto, 1st edition (1964).

Record Companies for the covers of: *Songs of Leonard Cohen*,
Columbia Records/Sony Music Entertainment; *Songs from a Room*,
Columbia Records/Sony Music Entertainment; *Songs of Love and
Hate*, Columbia Records/Sony Music Entertainment; *Live Songs*,
Columbia Records/Sony Music Entertainment; *New Skin for the Old
Ceremony*, Columbia Records/Sony Music Entertainment; *Death of
a Ladies' Man*, Warner Bros. Records Inc; *Recent Songs*, Columbia
Records/Sony Music Entertainment; *Various Positions*, Columbia
Records/Sony Music Entertainment/Passport Records; *I'm Your
Man*, Columbia Records/ Sony Music Entertainment; *The Future*,
Columbia Records/Sony Music Entertainment; *Cohen Live*, Sony
Music Entertainment; *Field Commander Cohen*, Columbia Records/
Sony Music Entertainment; *Ten New Songs*, Columbia Records/
Sony Music Entertainment; *Dear Heather*, Columbia Records/Sony
Music Entertainment; *Live in London*, Columbia Records/Sony Music
Entertainment; *Songs from the Road*, Columbia Records/Legacy
Recordings/Sony Music Entertainment; *Old Ideas*, Columbia Records/
Sony Music Entertainment; *Popular Problems*, Columbia Records/
Sony Music Entertainment; *Live in Dublin*, Columbia Records/Sony
Music Entertainment; *Can't Forget: A Souvenir of the Grand Tour*,
Columbia Records/Sony Music Entertainment; *You Want It Darker*,
Columbia Records/Sony Music Entertainment.

Photographs: Getty Images/Oliver Morris; Getty Images/
Redferns/Rob Verhorst; PA-190166 Woodbridge Company Limited/
Library and Archives Canada/*Montreal Star*/Allan R. Leishman;
Toronto Star via Getty Images/Dick Darrell; Getty Images/The LIFE
Picture Collection/James Burke; Getty Images/Jack Robinson; *Toronto
Star* via Getty Images/Richard Lautens; Getty Images/Michael Ochs
Archives/Roz Kelly; Getty Images/David Gahr; Getty Images/Michael
Ochs Archives; Getty Images/WireImage/ Chris Walter; Getty
Images/1970 K & K Ulf Kruger OHG/Redferns/Gunter Zint; Getty
Images/ Redferns/Tony Russell; Getty Images/GAB Archive/Redferns;
Getty Images/Redferns/Gijsbert Hanekroot; Getty Images/Redferns/
Gus Stewart; Getty Images/Hulton Archive/Michael Putland; Getty
Images/K & K/Redferns/Hans-Jurgen Dibbert; *Toronto Star* via Getty
Images/Reg Innell; Getty Images/The LIFE Images Collection/Ian
Cook; Getty Images/WireImage/Tom Hill; s.e.t./ullstein bild via Getty
Images; action press/ullstein bild via Getty Images; *Toronto Star* via
Getty Images/Ron Bull; Getty Images/Oliver Morris; CBS/ullstein bild
via Getty Images; *Paris Match* via Getty Images/Jean-Claude Deutsch;
Sygma via Getty Images/Eric Préau; Ritter/ullstein bild via Getty
Images; *Toronto Star* via Getty Images/Andrew Stawicki; *Toronto Star*
via Getty Images/Keith Beaty; Getty Images/Redferns/Ebet Roberts;
Getty Images/Redferns/ Eamonn McCabe; Getty Images/Paul Harris;
Corbis via Getty Images/Ann Johansson; Getty Images/FilmMagic/
Gary Miller; Getty Images/WireImage/George Pimentel; *Bloomberg*
via Getty Images/Andrew Harrer; Getty Images/Vince Bucci; Getty
Images/Redferns/Hayley Madden; Getty Images/AFP/Diego Tuson;
Getty Images/Kevin Winter; Getty Images/Tim Mosenfelder; Getty
Images/Frank Hoensch; Getty Images/Redferns/Martin Philbey;
Getty Images/AFP/Javier Soriano; Getty Images/AFP/Joel Saget; Getty
Images/AFP/Nicolas Maeterlinck; Getty Images/AFP/Paul Bergen;
Getty Images/WireImage/Phillip Massey; Brill/ullstein bild via Getty
Images; Getty Images/AFP/Ben Stansall.

It has not always been possible to trace copyright sources and
the publisher would be glad to hear from any such unacknowledged
copyright holders.